for the Soul®

Just for

Chicken Soup for the Soul: Just for Preteens
101 Stories of Inspiration and Support for Tweens
Jack Canfield, Mark Victor Hansen, Amy Newmark

Published by Chicken Soup for the Soul Publishing, LLC   www.chickensoup.com
Copyright © 2011 by Chicken Soup for the Soul Publishing, LLC. All Rights Reserved.
No part of this publication may be reproduced, stored in a retrieval system or transmitted in any form or by any means, electronic, mechanical, photocopying, recording or otherwise, without the written permission of the publisher.

CSS, Chicken Soup for the Soul, and its Logo and Marks are trademarks of Chicken Soup for the Soul Publishing LLC.

The publisher gratefully acknowledges the many publishers and individuals who granted Chicken Soup for the Soul permission to reprint the cited material.

Front cover photo courtesy of iStockphoto.com/JBryson (© Jani Bryson). Front cover, back cover, and interior illustration courtesy of iStockphoto.com./enjoynz (© Jamie Farrant). Back cover photo courtesy of Photos.com. Interior photo courtesy of iStockphoto.com/monkeybusinessimages (© Catherine Yeulet Photos.com).

Cover and Interior Design & Layout by Pneuma Books, LLC
For more info on Pneuma Books, visit www.pneumabooks.com

Distributed to the booktrade by Simon & Schuster. SAN: 200-2442

Publisher's Cataloging-in-Publication Data
(Prepared by The Donohue Group)

Chicken soup for the soul : just for preteens : 101 stories of inspiration and
  support for tweens / [compiled by] Jack Canfield, Mark Victor Hansen, [and]
  Amy Newmark.

    p. ; cm.

  Summary: A collection of 101 true personal stories from older kids and adults about
their preteen years, recalling issues with friends, embarrassing moments, bullies, family, sports, self-confidence, crushes, life lessons, and learning to do the right thing.

  Interest age group: 009-012.
  ISBN: 978-1-935096-73-3

  1. Preteens--Conduct of life--Literary collections. 2. Preteens--Conduct of life--
Anecdotes. I. Canfield, Jack, 1944- II. Hansen, Mark Victor. III. Newmark, Amy. IV.
Title: Just for preteens

PN6071.P67 C483 2011
810.8/02/09283   2011927548

PRINTED IN THE UNITED STATES OF AMERICA
on acid∞free paper
20 19 18 17 16 15 14 13   02 03 04 05 06 07 08 09 10

101 Stories of
Inspiration and Support
for Tweens

Jack Canfield
Mark Victor Hansen
Amy Newmark

Chicken Soup for the Soul Publishing, LLC
Cos Cob, CT

www.chickensoup.com

Contents

❸
~Learning Lessons and Doing What's Right~

❹
~Crushed~

❺
~The Kindness of Others~

❻

~When the Going Gets Tough...~

❼

~Finding Your Passion~

❽
~That Was Embarrassing~

❾
~Family Ties~

❿
~Bullies and Bully Payback~

⑪
~Friendships to Last a Lifetime~

Chicken Soup for the Soul

Introduction

During my preteen years I had a wonderful best friend. She and I had been friends since we were toddlers and we spent hours on the phone every day after school. She was the most popular girl in our whole grade but she was really nice — a NICE popular girl, not a MEAN popular girl.

Everyone copied whatever my friend did. I remember in sixth grade I bought a pair of shoes, in black. My friend loved them and bought them for herself, but in navy blue. By the next week, all the girls in our class were wearing those same shoes, but in navy blue! I remember being disappointed that I had started the trend but that all the girls had bought the shoes in blue instead of black because that was the color my friend chose.

Four decades later, that seems pretty silly and unimportant, but since I still remember it, I guess it was pretty important to my eleven-year-old self. I reconnected with my old friend a few years ago — she had moved 2,000 miles away but I was able to find her through the Internet — and I told her that story and also commented on the fact that she had been the most popular girl in our grade for years. If there was a boy we all had crushes on, that boy would end up liking her; if she bought milk in the cafeteria, the other girls would buy milk too...

Guess what? My friend was shocked. She had no idea that she had been popular and that all the girls had copied everything she did and that the cutest boys liked her. She had actually been just as insecure as all the rest of us! That was a real eye opener for me and I thought that I would pass it along to you.

I think it is safe to say that almost every single preteen kid is insecure about something, whether it is looks, or sports ability, or schoolwork, or friends, or clothing, or just knowing what is cool. Being a preteen can be tough. Your bodies are starting to change and sometimes that is embarrassing and even scary. Your schoolwork is getting harder. Your parents are giving you more responsibilities. Your friends are changing too, and sometimes you end up joining a new group of friends, or switching best friends. Boys and girls start to notice each other and that can be scary and fun and embarrassing at the same time.

The preteen years can be an awkward time but they are lots of fun and exciting too. That's why we have made you this book. Think of it as a guidebook for your preteen years. You'll read stories written by older kids and adults who vividly recall their preteen years—the good and the bad times—and these people share their experiences with you so that you know that you are not alone. Millions of other boys and girls feel the same way as you do, and they are going through the same changes as you too!

We hope you will view this book as a portable support group for preteens, like another friend you can turn to. You might want to encourage your parents to read it also—it will help them to remember their own preteen years and better understand what is going on in your life these days!

Enjoy the book! Our editor Madeline Clapps and I loved making it for you, and we hope you will love reading it.

~Amy Newmark

Chapter
1

Just for
Preteens

Feeling Good About Yourself

Success is liking yourself, liking what you do, and liking how you do it.

~Maya Angelou

Fried Hair

He who trims himself to suit everyone will soon whittle himself away.
~Raymond Hull

There she is, sitting at the lunch table placed precisely in the middle of the cafeteria. Not the tables by the garbage cans, not the square tables, but the circular one exactly in the center. Her friend beside her whispers something into her ear. They both giggle simultaneously. She and her friend look the same. In fact, everyone at this particular lunch table looks the same. They all have blond, perfectly straightened hair. The brunettes have dyed their hair to match the others. Curls are fried straight. Every girl at the table wears a different version of the same, tight T-shirt with "HOLLISTER" written in obnoxious letters across the front. They all wear their jeans skin tight, like Spandex to their legs. Their eyes are rimmed with black eyeliner, taking away their child-like cuteness and replacing it with the I'm-not-a-little-kid-anymore look. This specific girl seems to choose her words carefully as she whispers something back to her friend. She makes sure to match her movements with the people around her. Her eyes tell a different story than her attitude portrays.

I was, in fact, this Hollister-obsessed, fried-haired monster. I cared way too much about what other people thought and way too little about what I thought. Today, I am completely different from how I was back in junior high. How did I make this transformation?

It was an ordinary day at South Junior High. I had my arm linked with one of my friends as we walked down the hall. She was eagerly telling me a story about a girl who "MySpaced" her boyfriend the day before. I went along with it, trash talking the girl. I acted completely engaged, putting in a forced "Oh my God, who does she think she is?" every time she paused, but I was feeling distracted. As I tried to refocus on her story, I heard a piece of someone else's conversation. "Taylor Haglin has cancer," was all I caught. Taylor Haglin, who had barely been at school for the past two weeks, had cancer. My brain started spinning and my feet stuck to the floor.

"Did you hear that?" I choked out.

"What?" she asked, annoyed that I had interrupted her.

"Taylor Haglin has cancer?"

"Oh, that's really sad," she mumbled. We walked in silence for a few paces. "Do you want to go to the mall Friday?" she asked as we came to the end of the hall and split into our different classrooms.

"Um, yeah, I'll text you later," I replied weakly.

As I sat in English that day, my mind spun. And it wasn't a gentle around-the-merry-go-round kind of spin, but an uncontrollable-tornado kind. I couldn't pinpoint any certain feeling, except for extreme annoyance that my friend had just asked me to go to the mall. On any other day, I would have been excited by this question. But today, as my friend walked beside me, she suddenly seemed more like a little mosquito buzzing in my ear. I felt an urge to swat at her the next time she tried talking to me. I cannot describe to you what was happening that day; all I know is that something was changing inside me. I sat through English and the rest of the day trying to act the same way I always did. I went to track practice and did my homework. While going through my normal routine, I couldn't seem to get the tornado to calm down. The storm continued spinning, and Taylor was in the middle of it.

Taylor was not one of my good friends. As a matter of fact, the only sort of connection we had was that our lockers were next to each other. I sometimes told her I liked her shirt. She once asked me if she could use my phone. That was the extent of our relationship. She started showing up at school less and less until she stopped showing up at all. I began searching for her in the halls and then making excuses for when I didn't see her at her locker. I convinced myself she was just staying late after class.

After a few weeks of no Taylor, I finally grasped the reality that the rumor must be true. I stopped making excuses for why she wasn't there. But ever since I had overheard that conversation in the hallway, the way I looked at everything was different. I started to be irritated by the stories and whispers that went around the lunch table. One day I asked myself, "Why am I even hanging around these people?" If I got cancer and died the next day, I wanted to be at complete happiness. I decided that if I wanted to achieve this, I had to be around people who made me completely happy. Sounds kind of obvious, but it's something so many of us overlook.

The girls I hung around with in junior high weren't all terrible. A few of them were genuinely nice, just poorly influenced by some of their friends. I know I wasn't the worst of these girls, but I was just as judgmental and exclusionary as any of them. I knew I needed a change. I started to be more my own person and less like all of them. I stopped pretending to care about all the gossip that went around the lunch table. I stopped going over to girls' houses who I didn't like being around. I started hanging out with people I actually liked. I decided anyone who made me feel bad about myself was not worth a second of my time. At the end of my junior high years, I found myself to be much happier. I wrote down a few sentences on a piece of paper one day and vowed I would always live by these lines:

> *The best advice I can give you, when it really comes down to it, is to simply surround yourself with people you love. You know — those people who never leave your side, who constantly make you feel good about yourself. Those people are worth sticking by. They are the ones worth surrounding yourself with.*

So now, here I am, sitting at the lunch table placed randomly on the left side of the cafeteria. Not the circular lunch table exactly in the center, but the odd rectangular one towards the left. My friend beside me tells a story to the whole table. We all burst out laughing, not caring how loud we are or how ridiculous we look when we're laughing so hard. My friend and I look completely different. In fact, everyone at the table looks different. We all do something different with our hair. Curls are enhanced. Fried hair is a thing of the past. Everyone at the table has her own style. Our jeans are not skin tight, but rather loose fitting. Some of us are wearing skirts, others of us sweatpants. My hair might be a little bit messier and my jeans a little bit looser, but my eyes still hold the same motivation and intensity. They are completely unaware of what my future holds, yet prepared for whatever comes next.

~Claire Illies

2

Chicken Soup for the Soul

Not Just an Ordinary Flower

Always be a first-rate version of yourself,
instead of a second-rate version of somebody else.
~Judy Garland

I could feel the panic stirring in my gut, the tears forming in one big mass at the back of my throat. It was Sunday night, and that meant school was coming. It would arrive first in the form of my blaring alarm that would wake me before the sun crept through my blinds. Then it would take the shape of a garish yellow bus that I could see coming between the houses from across the street—the bus that would carry me into enemy territory.

School itself wasn't my enemy. No, the enemy existed in the crowds of kids who didn't care about me, the teachers with too many students to pay me much attention, the students who left me to play alone on the playground. I would walk through the halls of the school as my "peers" bumped me, passing by in their cliques, and I would be alone.

At the end of the year in health class, we played a game where we taped pieces of paper onto our backs and ran around the room, writing something nice about each person in the class on the paper. When we were done, I looked at what people had said about me: "Nice," "Smart," "Smart," and "Nice." Three that said "Funny" were mixed in with one that said "Cool"—probably from one of the other unpopular kids or the teacher.

For years after, I let that define me. "Hello, I'm the smart, nice wallflower. If only you knew that there was so much more to me" was what I would often think when I met people who would pass me by.

My dad once told me, "What other people do or say about you tells you more about them than yourself." I would repeat that to my friends who came to me for comfort and advice. I hoped it comforted them the way it did me.

The more I quoted my dad's words to myself, the more I realized what he meant. The kids at school might call me ugly, they might ignore me or use me, but their words and their actions did not have to make me into someone I was not. Instead of feeling sorry for myself or being angry at them, I could choose to forgive them and recognize that being mean was their way of making themselves feel better. I learned to pity them, because often when people are bullies or when they are rude or manipulative, it is because of their own insecurities. What they said and did still hurt, but recognizing that they wounded me as a result of their own pain made it easier to take the focus off myself and onto them. Even though loving my enemies was hard, it was the right thing to do.

One time, my dad and I were driving in the car, and I was telling him about my latest school trials. I told him that I felt like no one liked me because they didn't know me. I knew I was quiet, but I also knew that there was a part of me that just wanted to break out of my shell and be the outgoing, fun-loving girl I used to be.

Dad leaned over to me and said, "You remember in Disney's *Aladdin* when Genie turns into a bee and buzzes into Aladdin's ear while he's talking to Jasmine on the balcony? What does he say? 'Just beeee yourself.' Right?"

I smiled and nodded, giggling bashfully. I really wanted to "beeee myself"—I just didn't know how! What was my true identity? Was I a wallflower? Or was I a rose? What made me who I was? Should I really let the bad things that happened at school define me?

My trials at school began a journey for me. Destination? True identity. I always knew that I was more than just a wallflower. While there is certainly nothing wrong with being nice and smart, I know now that I am designed to bloom and be more than just an ordinary flower.

~Stephanie Warner

Chicken Soup
for the Soul

The Girl Who Couldn't

Try and fail, but don't fail to try.
~Stephen Kaggwa

She was just a girl,
A lonely soul of eleven.
She was an average kid,
The fifth sibling among seven.
Neither here nor there,
With no thoughts or friends to call her own,
She was, in the world of raging lions,
A weak and stumbling fawn.

Never on the top,
Nor even in the bottom,
She never stood out,
She was like a fallen leaf in autumn.
Neither eyes nor lips
Ever spoke a word.
Unnoticed and uncared for,
She was lost in the herd.

Not a giggle, not a smile
Escaped her pink lips.
Her tears were wiped by none

But her own tiny fingertips.
Lost and insecure, oh what
She must have gone through every day!
A girl of just eleven
What more can I say?

A child is a believing creature
With a mind as brittle as pure gold
"A loser" and "a failure,"
That's what she was told.
She accepted it always,
With her head held like a broken bow.
And she became the girl who couldn't
Only 'cause they told her so.

~Sneha Pillai

Chicken Soup
for the Soul

Slapshot to Popularity

True popularity is not the popularity which is followed after,
but the popularity which follows after.
~Lord Mansfield

I grew up in a town that was so small, I had almost the same people in my class each year, and all of them knew me as a weird, overweight, unpopular kid. Even when the county redistricted schools, my reputation remained the same.

On the first day of seventh grade, we were all in the gym. Our parents had preordered our physical education uniforms during the summer, and we were picking them up. That was all that was on the agenda. Our gym teachers got creative and set up some hockey equipment for us. There was a ball, two sticks, and a goal on the gym floor. They asked the crowd if any students had ever played ice hockey on a team. I had played floor hockey as a church activity for many years. I loved the sport, but I had no real experience. I kept my hand down.

A boy raised his hand and instantly he became the goalie after he received his P.E. uniform. The teachers explained that they would call names in threes. We were to go down the stairs, try to make a goal, and then get our uniforms. Seventh grader after seventh grader came down as their names were called and tried their best to make a goal, but the goalie blocked each shot with ease. He even complained about a few people high sticking and going inside the boundaries. It was obvious he played frequently.

Finally my name was called. I took my time going down the bleacher steps. I could see myself falling in front of everyone. I took the hockey stick and rolled the ball around. Back and forth, side to side. It felt just like I was in the church fellowship hall. The goalie was yelling at me to finally take the shot. I looked up at him and frowned. I was going to take my time with this shot. Slowly I began to push the ball towards him, moving my stick to control the ball in almost a straight line. My heart began to beat faster. I knew to aim for the corner of the goal, but what if I missed? Up came my stick nearly parallel to the ground. I didn't need to commit a foul to score a goal. I knew the rules too.

"C'mon!" he shouted as I struck the ball with all the energy in my wrists. I knew I had missed, like everyone else. I went to get my uniform. Then I noticed the room was silent. I turned around to look at the goalie. He was on his side, the ball just out of his reach, safely tucked into the back of the net. The ball had gotten past him. I had scored a goal. The crowd of seventh graders didn't get up and cheer until I had my uniform in hand. I sat back down and all eyes were on me.

"I couldn't even see the ball!" said a voice over the murmuring.

"Where did you learn to do that?" said another voice. My face turned red.

"Church," I replied.

After that, if we were playing hockey in gym class, I was never picked last. Even in high school my athletic achievement was known to the upperclassmen. Sadly my talents did not transfer over to field hockey. But it was the one thing I had in middle school, and no one could take it away from me.

~Sarah L.M. Klauda

Chicken Soup for the Soul

View from the Top

Always act like you're wearing an invisible crown.
~Author Unknown

I was so excited to make the cheerleading squad in eighth grade. I was one of the "smart girls" so most of the time I wasn't accepted by the popular crowd. I felt sure that cheerleading was a way to get to know them and maybe even get invited to some of their parties.

Our first few practices were fun, with everyone getting fitted for uniforms and learning the easiest cheers. Most of the time I talked with my best friend since the popular girls still didn't talk to me much.

The cheers got harder and we started to practice flips and turns to go with the cheers, and then we started to build pyramids. The coaches chose me to be on the bottom of the pyramid every time. The girls began to call me "thunder thighs" since I was bigger than most of them.

I hated being on the bottom of the pyramid and longed to be higher up or even on the top for one of the cheers, but that wasn't going to happen. The most popular girl on our squad always got the top position. She was petite and had the most beautiful blond hair. It was so pale that it was almost white. My own hair was sort of this blond/brown color and I thought it would be great to have hair like that.

The day we had all waited for finally came—our uniforms had arrived! I remember getting my skirt and sweater and heading to the girls room to change. Our school colors were red and white and the skirts were split to show both colors when we spun around. I hurried into the uniform and looked at myself in the mirror. I looked horrible.

Oh, I knew I wasn't the thinnest person on the squad, but when I saw how I looked in that short skirt, well, I was really disappointed and even embarrassed. We had to tuck our sweaters in and you could see every line of my sweater through my skirt because it was pretty tight. I smoothed it out as best I could but I still didn't like the way it looked.

I spent as much time as I could in the bathroom because I didn't want anyone to see me. I didn't realize that the girl from the top of our pyramid was also trying on her uniform. She came out of the stall, looked at herself in the mirror and started to cry.

I asked her what was wrong and she said she hated the way she looked. She was so thin her skirt gaped open at the waist. I realized then that the uniforms we both had been so excited to get weren't such a great gift after all.

I tried to cheer her up and said that at least she had really great hair and she surprised me by saying she wished her hair looked more like mine. She said her hair was so light people thought she bleached it and that she'd love to have honey colored hair like mine instead.

We talked a little bit more until the coach came in and asked what was wrong. We showed her our uniform problems and her solution was to have the whole team wear their sweaters outside the skirts.

The next time we formed the pyramid I smiled to myself, knowing that the girl up there on the top that everyone was looking at wished she had my hair. Maybe the view from the bottom wasn't so bad after all.

~Shawn Marie Mann

The Steeple

Whenever you find yourself on the side of the majority,
it is time to pause and reflect.
~Mark Twain

 om and Dad were thrilled to move from Paterson, New Jersey to the green suburbs. "Just think," Mom sighed. "We can grow a garden and breathe fresh air!"

Dad said, "And no more gangs!" In Paterson, my little brother was pushed around by older kids, and the high school I would have gone to had a tough reputation. "In Midland Park you'll have nice friends and be safe."

But I wasn't happy. I knew who to watch out for in Paterson, and my brother soon would too. You became street smart. The suburbs scared me—trees hanging over you, no sidewalks, silent houses that made it feel like people were watching you. I told my dad I didn't want to move.

"Are you nuts? Trust me, it'll be lots safer and friendlier."

I wanted to trust Dad, but I had just turned twelve and knew the difference between sure things and hope.

The suburban junior high was cleaner and newer than my city school, but it was not Disney World. Being a new kid was awful. Everybody stared, and I walked around lost for a week. Teachers mispronounced my name. They tried to be nice by asking where I came from, but when I said, "Paterson," twenty noses wrinkled. Guys bumped me. If I bumped back, a bigger guy bumped me harder. If I didn't bump back, a smaller guy bumped me. The new kid is supposed to be nobody, not there. If I talked to a girl, somebody dumped Jell-O down my neck.

But every new kid gets a chance sooner or later. Mine came outside the Dutch Reformed Church a few blocks from our new house. It had a tall steeple. The first thirty feet were built of cobblestones and the top was made from white wood that tapered up into the blue. Two guys from my class were climbing the cobblestones. No one said anything—not even "What's up"—but I joined them. We squeezed our sneakers into the spaces between the cobblestones and felt for handholds, climbed three or four feet, then jumped down. The rounded rocks stuck out from the mortar at most an inch, so we slipped a lot. Then we climbed sideways and around the corner. They gave me a regular turn so I felt pretty good. Like I was with them, almost.

After twenty minutes the big one said to me, "Let's see how high you can go."

"Yeah," the other said.

I shrugged, climbed up maybe five feet, started slipping, pushed away and jumped. I rolled when I hit the concrete.

"Wuss."

"I bet you can't touch that window," the big guy said. The stone windowsill was at the top of the cobblestones, way up there.

"Yeah, right!" I said. Just bending back to look made me dizzy.

"Hey, we did it."

"Sure you have," I said.

"You saying we didn't?" They stared hard, and I knew what was going down.

I glanced up. The guys made cackling chicken noises and flapped their arms like wings. "Brrrack! Braack! Braack!"

I could hear Dad's voice in my head. "No! Don't be stupid! You'll break your neck! Be smart. Trust me." But I didn't. Dad made me move here, didn't he? If I had to be stupid to make friends, I would do it.

After a deep breath, I climbed fast to get it over with. My foot slipped about two feet up and down I came. The guys smirked. "Real sweet!" So I went slower, feeling for the roughest, most protruding stones, got a good hand grip, then another, wedged a sneaker tight in a crack, then the other a little higher. One stone at a time, steady and slow. Until one guy below me hissed, "Man, he's doing it!"

I looked down. Mistake. I couldn't see their bodies, just their upturned faces, mouths open. I must have been fifteen feet up. I swayed, pressed my face to the stones and shut my eyes. I wanted to melt into the stones. No escape ladder, no rope. I was hanging up there by myself. I glanced up. The stone windowsill didn't seem that far, but my toes were cramping. I reached for a new hold, then another and inched higher. I knew now—knew for sure—those guys had never done this. But I would. They suckered me into it, but I'd do what they only dreamed of.

I inched higher until the sill was maybe six or eight feet away. If I touched it, they'd respect me. They'd know I had guts. They'd want me around. They'd tell everybody I climbed the steeple. There'd be no more Jell-O and bumping in the halls.

As soon as I thought that, I didn't want to do it—not for them. If I could do this on my own, stupid as it was, what did I need them for? Teasing seemed like nothing now. I felt with my feet for cracks below me and inched lower. Descending was more difficult, and when my toes found slick places, the panic rose again. But I kept at it. If you got up, I told myself, there's a way down. You just have to find it. My fingers were killing me. When the ground came closer, I jumped.

The guys came up to me. "You almost did it! You could have got there. Why'd you stop?"

They were excited, and I had the respect I had wanted. But it didn't feel good. I shrugged and said, "Why don't you show me how you did it?"

"Aw well..." They made empty sputtering noises, and I walked away. I had done something stupid that I would never do again, but I realized it had nothing to do with moving to a new school. Nobody pushed me up there. It was about me deciding if I would do whatever people wanted so they'd be my friends. I didn't need them that much.

~Garrett Bauman

Basketball Star

I've got a theory that if you give 100 percent all of the time,
somehow things will work out in the end.
~Larry Bird

Two seconds were left on the clock, we were down by one point, and I was at the free throw line. If I made the first shot, I would take a second shot. If we lost, we were out. It was the playoffs. Elimination style.

I started playing basketball for a recreational league in the sixth grade, and from the beginning, I had to play hard. I am not a natural athlete, but I liked basketball. I practiced outside for hours and hours, days and days and my shot had become very good. I spent part of my summers at basketball camp, in spite of the Florida heat. More importantly, I hustled. I came out and played as hard as I possibly could, every game.

I was finally able to make the team in eighth grade, and had even worked my way up to being a starter. I was known as the unofficial rebounder of the team. I would run, jump and grab the rebounds. And I could shoot with very good accuracy. I could not run as fast or jump as high or dribble the ball as well as my naturally athletic teammates, but that never bothered me. We all have our gifts, but through hard work and dedication, I could do anything I wanted to do.

So this was my moment. I had the ball in my hand, all eyes on me. I was a good free throw shooter. I'd practiced a thousand times.

But on that day, on that shot, I missed.

I immediately jumped up for the rebound.

Someone from the other team got it though, and the game was over. The season was over. We were out.

After the game, all the players and parents met outside for water. Coach thanked everyone for a great season. He mentioned a few people who he thought had a good game.

Then he said, "Mallory, where's Mallory?"

He found me and pointed to me.

"Outstanding," he said. And everyone in the room applauded.

I learned that day that there isn't such a thing as "your moment" in this life. Who you are does not come down to one success or one failure. What you do—and how hard you work every single day—that does matter. And it is remembered.

~Mallory Albeck

Being Twelve

You cannot dream yourself into a character;
you must hammer and forge yourself one.
~James A. Froude

What's my name, who am I?
Why don't I feel I belong?
Why are there pimples on my face?
Why are my legs so long?

Why are the boys still shorter than me,
And why am I so tall?
When will I understand these things?
Maybe sometime next Fall?

My little brother thinks I'm great,
Big sister thinks I'm small.
She says my worries in life are dumb,
That they don't matter at all.

The boy I have a crush on,
He looked my way today!
I almost said hello to him,
But my brain got in the way!

Mom says that I'll grow out of this.
Dad tells me to be strong.
I'm not a kid, but I'm not a teen,
Why does this feel so wrong?

There's the girl who is so pretty,
She's the leader of the pack.
There's the nerd who solves equations,
And his friend, the quarterback.

I wish I could be just like them,
With something of my own,
Something I'd be good at,
Besides talking on the phone.

They say, "Someday you'll miss it,"
They say, "Being twelve is fun."
So I guess I'll just enjoy it,
'Cause at thirteen, I'll be done!

~Kimberly Winget

My Own Label

If you doubt yourself,
then indeed you stand on shaky ground.
~Henrik Ibsen

It seemed to me that I had two different identities when I was in fifth grade. Outside of school, I was a reasonably happy kid who enjoyed spending time with her friends, reading about ancient Egypt, and listening to rock music. When I was in class, however, I turned into a very different Denise, one who was on guard all the time—one who wanted nothing more than to get through the day without being teased.

To my classmates I was weird, because I wasn't just like them. They focused on that which was most obvious—that I didn't wear the same name brand designer clothes that they did. In my class, where everyone worked overtime at being fashionable, this was no light offense. The class photo was a parade of designer labels—expensive shoes and sweaters with conspicuous logos, shirts with embroidered marks, and jeans with glittery patches and buttons. Even their hair accessories had little designer tags.

Designer clothes were beyond my family's reach. My mother was a single parent, and she worked long hours to support our small household. In the currencies of love and attention, I was rich beyond all imagination. I was adored, supported and cared for. The only currency my classmates dealt in was fashion, though, and there, I was poor. There just wasn't any justification for spending the entire clothing budget on one silly shirt or pair of jeans that happened to have a label the cool kids liked.

I never knew if my classmates would torment me in class, but on the bus I could count on it. My trips to and from school were the horrific, painful bookends to stressful days. Sometimes my classmates insulted me to my face; at other times, I merely heard the snickers behind me. One girl made a point of running down the aisle every morning to see what I was wearing, and then returned to her friends to laugh about it. I shrank into myself and stared out the window.

I was the smallest girl in my class. One of my classmates' mothers noticed, and offered me a denim skirt that her daughter had outgrown. I wore it happily, thrilled to have a cool item of clothing for once. When I outgrew the skirt, my mother bought me a new one of my own, albeit one without a label. When my classmate saw it, she hooted. "Oh, that's not my skirt, is it? Where did you get this one, Denise?" she sneered. "The poorhouse?" My classmates giggled, and I slunk away, my eyes locked on the ground. I stopped wearing the skirt.

After fifth grade ended, over the summer, I spent a month at day camp, where I found kids who liked me for who I was, not for the clothes I wore. Many of them came from wealthy families, and I spotted plenty of designer shoes, high fashion swimsuits and T-shirts that cost three figures. Unlike the kids at school, though, my fellow campers didn't mind my no-name wardrobe. They simply accepted me as a friend. We spent our days splashing around in the pool, riding horses, and making bracelets. We had a fashion show and I was encouraged to participate. And I did. My weekends were filled with fun with my best friend in the neighborhood, who would have liked me even if I'd shown up at her house in a potato sack dress.

With the love and support of my friends, I started to remember something I'd forgotten: there was nothing wrong with me. Nothing at all. It wasn't my fault that my classmates had targeted me. They were only one small, cruel group of people, and there was no reason to pay any attention to them at all.

It took a while for the message to sink in, though. When sixth grade started, my classmates resumed their bullying. For the first few months of school, I was desperately unhappy. The warm glow of friendship I had fostered over the summer was dimmed by the open hostility and insults I faced every day in class.

Finally, I begged my mother for a fashion shirt. I liked the garment for its design, but more than that, I thought that it would be an antidote for the bullying. I knew that my classmates were so shallow that they only looked at my wardrobe. I didn't want to impress them or be friends with them. If I dressed just like them, though, maybe they'd run out of reasons to bother me.

The shirt did not appear for my eleventh birthday in November. Wishes do come true, though, even if they take time, and somehow, on Christmas morning, there was a very special green and white box waiting under the tree for me.

When I went back to school after the holiday recess, I proudly wore my new shirt. For once, nobody mocked me when I boarded the bus. Instead, they stared. The girls in my class were so upset that they actually held a meeting in the library to talk about it. I tried not to laugh as I saw them clustered around a table, whispering and looking furtively in my direction. One of them ran up to me, grabbed me by the shoulder, and yanked at my collar to look at the tag. Her breath caught, and I realized that she hadn't expected the shirt to be authentic.

On the bus that afternoon, one of my classmates told me that she liked my outfit. I smiled and nodded. I'd finally met their approval... and yet, I knew that I didn't even want it. What they thought, or didn't think, about me was irrelevant. I was the exact same person they had tormented before the holidays. Moreover, I wasn't wearing my shirt to impress them; I was wearing it because I liked it. The only label that mattered to me was my own—how I "labeled" myself. It was something they would never comprehend.

After that day, my classmates still bothered me, but I stopped listening. Their taunts weren't worth even a moment of my time. Instead of getting upset, I was bored by their remarks.

In the spring, the denim skirt that my classmate had mocked made a reappearance. I wore it proudly to both the school dance festival and to my sixth-grade graduation ceremony.

There would be no diploma for positive thinking, no award for finally learning to ignore cruel words. There never would be. The one person I had to learn to impress was myself, and I'd done it.

~Denise Reich

Just for

Preteens

New Faces and New Places

Life can only be understood backward, but it must be lived forward.

~Soren Kierkegaard

Chicken Soup
for the Soul

A New Best Friend

There are big ships and small ships. But the best ship of all is friendship.
~Author Unknown

Lisa and I squeezed each other as tears rolled down our cheeks. She pulled away and looked into my swollen eyes. "I want you to stay. You're my best friend."

I frowned and reached for her hands. "You're my best friend too, and I don't want to leave either. But I don't have any say."

"You're moving so far away. What if I never see you again?"

"Mom promised we can call each other and have sleepovers."

Although I was only moving ten miles away, to us it felt more like a million. I couldn't imagine life without her. She was the jelly to my peanut butter. We were always together. I knew all of her secrets and she knew mine. We doubled our joys with combined laughter, and cut sorrows in half with our tears.

I didn't want to go to a different school, and I was afraid of being the new kid. With only one six-week period left of my fifth grade year, I couldn't understand why I had to change schools, but my parents insisted. I had been going to my school for five years and knew everyone there. Now, I would have to start all over with making friends.

Life was so unfair. Why did my parents have to be so mean? Why did we have to move? Even though I loved the new house, I resented having to change schools and leave my friends behind.

"You'll like your new school," Mom said. "You'll make friends."

I didn't believe her. I curled up like a kitten on the couch and cried. "All the kids there already have best friends. I'll be a stranger to them." I buried my face in the sofa and sobbed. "I'll never have another best friend."

Mom sat down next to me and stroked my back. "Of course you will, sweetheart." Her efforts to help didn't fill my emptiness.

The entire family made piles and packed boxes over the next couple of weeks. I put my broken Lite-Brite and cracked Etch A Sketch in the trash pile with some outfits I didn't like and wanted to get rid of without Mom knowing. I didn't really play with my Barbie dolls anymore, but I put them and all their accessories in the keep pile anyway—along with my books and Lucky, my special teddy bear.

Moving day arrived. I felt important when I got to make big decisions, like where to put furniture, which drawer the silverware should be in, and what color the bathroom would be.

I jumped with joy when Mom suggested Lisa sleep over on our first night in the new home. That night we stayed up way past our bedtime talking, giggling, and eating Cheetos. We even made some prank calls and played with the Barbies—for old time's sake. We had such fun together that it made saying goodbye the next day even harder.

The night before my first day of school, I couldn't sleep. My mind wandered to my first day at my old school as a first grader. I had gone to kindergarten in Oklahoma before we moved to Texas, and although I missed my friends when we moved, the worst part was the teasing I endured. As a six-year-old, I couldn't understand why the kids had to be so mean. No one knew how much it hurt when I was called "freckle face" and "carrot top." They didn't understand how rejected and lonely I felt when they wouldn't let me play with them and when they knocked books out of my arms and laughed.

Although I did have a few special people in my life—my sister and two brothers and a girl that lived across the street—they each had other friends they played with more than me. Their friendship did diminish some of my misery from the teasing, but it didn't keep a girl from attacking me as I walked home from school one day. She hit me several times, and the only reason she stopped was because a kind adult drove by and yelled at her. She shook her fist at me and snapped, "I'll finish with you later."

Relief washed over me as she ran away, but pain and humiliation made me cry the rest of the way home.

The teasing finally died down after third grade. A few kids still made fun of me, but most of them quit. After two years of hating school and despising myself, I found enjoyment in having friends. I was even invited to do fun things, like roller skating and birthday parties. Then I met Lisa, and everything was better with a best friend. And now, I was losing her.

I lay in bed and soaked my pillow with my tears. What if I'm teased again? What if no one likes me? I didn't expect to find another friend like Lisa, but what if I didn't make any friends at all?

Monday morning, I tried on four different outfits and redid my hair three times. My mom had to force me to eat. I trembled as the principal walked me down the hall, wondering how long it would be before I was teased or beat up. When she opened the door to my new classroom, everyone looked at me. Heat rose in my cheeks and my eyes widened as I tried to hide behind the principal. My stomach tumbled and churned, and I thought I was going to throw up on my favorite shoes.

"Okay everyone," the teacher said. "This is Leigh Ann, and she will be joining our class for the rest of the school year." She looked at me and smiled, then pointed to an empty seat in the last row. "You can sit there."

I tried to disappear into the wall as I made my way to the back of the class, but everyone watched me. I looked around trying to decide who was nice and who was mean. As I did, several kids smiled at me.

As the day went on, I felt accepted. No one teased me or called me names. In fact, a few even seemed interested in getting to know me better.

By the end of the school year, I had made several friends. Although none of them considered me their best friend, I had found more happiness than I expected.

When I returned to school for my sixth grade year, I met another new student, Jennifer. She and her family had moved to Texas from New York over the summer, and we had an instant bond—I was born in New York. We talked and hung out and had fun together.

A couple of weeks later, she invited me to spend the night. When she introduced me to her parents, she said, "Mom and Dad, this is Leigh Ann—my best friend." She looked at me and smiled.

I smiled in return and a warm sensation flooded my heart. She was right. I had a new best friend.

~Leigh Ann Bryant

11

Chicken Soup
for the Soul

New Girl in School

Whoever gossips to you will gossip about you.
~Spanish Proverb

The new girl joined our fifth grade class in February. Her name was Kiki, short for Jacqueline, pronounced the French way. It wasn't only her name that had French flair.

Everything about her was different — the way she wore her hair, her shoes. She couldn't change the school uniform, yet Kiki wore hers with more flair — her uniform shorter and more tightly fitted.

All the boys had crushes on her. They'd stare at her as she walked into class, make excuses to walk by her desk or talk louder when she was nearby. All the girls wanted to be her best friend. So I was thrilled when Kiki singled me out from the others.

For weeks, we'd spend recess together, whispering and giggling about the other girls in the class. That one was too fat. That one was too thin. Another one had a big nose. A fourth one had stringy hair. No one was safe from Kiki's sharp tongue, except me.

Every so often, I'd feel a little pang of unease. After all, I had been friends with some of these girls before I met Kiki. But compared to her, my old friends were dull and boring.

Two weeks before her birthday, Kiki handed out beautiful invitations to a select group of girls, including me, for a Saturday luncheon at her house. Her mother was going to cook real French food.

I wanted to look my best so I persuaded my mother to buy me

a new outfit for the party. When I tried it on, I felt very sophisticated, as if a little of Kiki's fashion flair had rubbed off on me.

I spent hours trying to find her the perfect present. Books, puzzles or a stuffed animal seemed too childish for her. I finally decided on a silver necklace. It cost my entire savings—two months' allowance—but I wanted to be sure she'd like my gift.

I couldn't wait for the party.

The day before the party, Kiki and I got into an argument. I don't even remember what it was about. But Kiki's face turned red, she put her hands on her hips, and narrowed her eyes. She stared at me for a moment. Then she said, "I don't want you to come to my party."

I was crushed. I spent that Saturday in my bedroom, gazing at my new outfit and feeling sorry for myself. At noon, when I ate a peanut butter and jelly sandwich, I wondered what marvelous French food the other girls were eating. As I read a book, I wondered what kind of games they were playing.

As the day wore on, another thought occurred to me. Since Kiki had said so many mean things about other girls, was she now saying mean things about me? I rushed to my bedroom mirror. My nose wasn't big, but maybe she thought it was too small. My hair wasn't stringy but maybe it was too curly. And while I was neither the fattest girl in the class, nor the skinniest, I definitely fell on the heavier side. Was Kiki telling the other girls it was a good thing I wasn't there because I'd probably eat too much birthday cake and get even fatter? Would she have even liked my new clothes?

On Monday, when Kiki saw me in the school playground, her first words were, "Why didn't you come to my party?"

"Because you told me not to," I said.

She shrugged. "Oh that. I didn't mean it." Then she waved her hand as if it were nothing. "Too bad you missed it. It was a really good party. I got lots and lots of gifts. You can bring me my gift tomorrow."

I stood there for a minute, not quite believing what I'd heard. The school bell rang and Kiki walked toward the front door. I began to follow her and then stopped.

I decided I would bring her gift to school tomorrow. However, instead of giving it to Kiki, I'd wear it around my neck.

That recess, instead of gossiping with her, I joined another group of girls in a game of tag.

Within a day, Kiki had a new best friend. Every so often, they'd look over at me and giggle. That hurt. At first, I would automatically pat my hair or smooth my shirt over my hips. But as I renewed my friendship with my former friends, I stopped caring as much about what Kiki said about me.

Over the next few months, Kiki had many new best friends. Some lasted a couple of days, some lasted a couple of weeks. But one by one, they were tossed aside when they disagreed with her or she tired of them. One by one they learned the same lesson I had learned. By the end of the school year, when she moved away for good, few people were sad to see her go. But I had learned that friends are supposed to make you feel good about yourself.

~Harriet Cooper

12

Chicken Soup for the Soul

This Too Shall Pass

If you can find a path with no obstacles, it probably doesn't lead anywhere.
~Frank A. Clark

By the time I was in middle school, my family had already relocated enough times that I had been in three different elementary schools. Yet, I found myself again being told that we were moving, this time to Ohio. This was to be my second middle school. My dad's company often promoted and transferred employees. I now understand that the relocations were not cruelty... they were just the way he supported a family with five children.

We moved to Ohio over the summer and the neighborhood that we moved into was just beginning development. There were few houses and even fewer kids my age. I had no friends, but I made lots of money babysitting.

I dreaded starting the school year at yet another new school and knowing no one. I anticipated what was coming. I had bright red hair, freckles, enormous glasses, and, even worse, I was obese. It was not going to be easy for me. I had already heard the nickname "Big Red" often enough. In addition, I wasn't very gregarious and making friends did not come easily to me.

Getting on the school bus that first day, I felt all eyes looking at me. I could hear the whispers of, "Who's that?" and, "Where did she come from?" and even, "She's huge!" Obviously the kids on my bus route had known each other over the years and I was a newcomer—a stranger. I spent that initial bus ride in silence.

The following day was even worse. A couple of the boys on the bus decided that it would be funny to tie a shoelace across the aisle, connected to the bottom of the bus seats. As anticipated, I did not notice the shoelace and tumbled face first, dropping everything I was carrying. As I frantically and embarrassingly gathered up my supplies and belongings, I could hear the laughter. Then I began hearing the comments. "Wow! Did you feel the whole bus shake when she fell?" "That felt like an earthquake!" I managed to avoid any eye contact and found a seat. I looked out the bus window and held back the tears that were welling up in my eyes.

It was then that I pretty much sunk into myself. I began walking everywhere. I would walk through the yet undeveloped woods behind our house to my favorite spot. It was a thick vine that had attached itself to the trees like a swing. I would sit in silence on that vine swing with my thoughts, rhythmically gliding back and forth. I would imagine that I was thin and pretty with a multitude of friends.

I would walk to a church about two miles down the road where there was an outdoor area set up with tree stump seats and an enormous cross. I would sit on my tree stump and chat silently with God. I would ask God to help me be thin and pretty with a multitude of friends.

I began missing the afternoon school bus intentionally and I would walk the two or three miles home from school, dodging traffic or jumping into yards since there were no sidewalks.

And I started losing weight.

Not only did I start losing weight, I became more content with myself with each pound that I lost. And, as I became content with myself, I began making friends.

Unbelievably, one of my newfound friends was actually a very popular cheerleader. She suddenly noticed that I was much thinner and she said, "Wow! You look great! How did you lose so much weight?"

She also struggled with her weight and we began walking together. She was not nearly as large as I had been but was not the stereotypical "perfect" cheerleader either. She lived in the neighborhood adjoining my own so we would each walk to the middle and walk together from there. This became a nearly daily activity with chatter and laughter along the way — a far cry from the lonely walks that I had taken so often. My new popular friend also demonstrated to me that I didn't have to be perfect. I just had to be me, and be happy with myself.

Whenever I am struggling with any of life's issues, I always remember the proverb, "This too shall pass." It certainly was hard during that first year in Ohio to comprehend that I would ever have anything but misery for the rest of my life, but that misery did indeed pass. While I absolutely would not want to relive that time of loneliness, sadness and embarrassment, I am proud of the fact that I made it through and emerged a better person because of it.

~Lil Blosfield

Hang In There

*You have to leave the city of your comfort
and go into the wilderness of your intuition.
What you'll discover will be wonderful.
What you'll discover is yourself.*

~Alan Alda

In my nine years of life, I had some brief nights away from home at my girlfriends' sleepovers, but I had never been subjected to the snores of total strangers. I was infected with excitement as I read about all of the sports and activities I would encounter at Camp Rippowam in upstate New York on the flyer distributed at school. I never dreamed my parents could afford to send me to this heaven in the woods or that I was grown-up enough to spend two weeks in a log cabin with unfamiliar peers. In any case, there I was, my world vanishing in backward motion as I rode in the third seat of our white station wagon. I had ample time during the two-hour ride from Connecticut to change my mind but, as the baby of the family, I felt the need to show my parents my strength and maturity.

Upon our arrival, we were given a complete tour of the camp, which was as picturesque as the brochure had portrayed. Following some juice and home-baked goodies, my father gave the director, Dan, his overly firm handshake, kissed me goodbye and assured me of his return in one week.

My first week at camp proved my strength and maturity a

delusion. Thank goodness the blond, snooty cabin queens I shared sleeping space with could not see the tears I shed each night. I had developed a severe case of homesickness within the first two days that would not even subside during the archery classes I enjoyed so much.

Each morning I awoke, cringing with fear that was accompanied by the screeching melodies of native birds and the aroma of wet, dewy pine needles. I survived the required morning sessions, but during daily "free time" between 3:00 p.m. and 5:00 p.m., while the other girls ran down to the lake to learn water skiing and ogle the camp counselor who taught it, I would return to the cabin to be alone with my sorrow. I began to count the minutes until my parents would return.

When my parents arrived for the mid-session visit, I pleaded with them to take me home. I explained to them how sad I was and how I was unable to make any friends. They did not say yes or no, only strolled with me over to the pavilion to get the attention of Dan, who was speaking with other parents. While Dan was putting his arm around my shoulder and drawing me near, my parents told him how I was feeling. Dan and my father offered a compromise. They asked if I could "hang in there" for just three more days. If, after these three days, I felt the same sadness, then Dad would come and retrieve me. They convinced me with their confident and encouraging words. I trusted my father and wanted him to be proud of me. I truly wanted to be mature enough to follow this through.

At the end of each two-week session, the campers performed a recital of *Pocahontas* for the parents when they came to pick up their children. The preparation for this event was a part of the daily curriculum. Some of the campers would audition for roles in the play while others would offer their artistic abilities creating stage props. I cowardly volunteered for the stage crew.

It was no surprise when the most popular camper, Christy, was awarded the role of Pocahontas. Her ever-perfect golden tresses held together with butterfly barrettes and her child-star charisma was irresistible to nearly everyone at the camp—except me. I was more than certain she had been chosen because of her status rather than her talent. It was on day one of the three-day agreement, as I was miserably slapping green paint on a prop tree while the actors rehearsed, that Rachael came over to me and whispered in my ear, "I think you should be Pocahontas."

From then on, Rachael and I no longer whispered our childish opinions of Christy, who we both agreed, did not possess the smarts or talent to carry out her title role. Every day at lunch, Rachael and I would giggle loudly about our award-winning versions of Christy's Pocahontas lines, which we knew by heart. Tall, lanky Rachael, with her messy, long, red hair and broken sneaker laces, would turn out to be the best friend I ever had.

It was on the night of the performance, with fifteen minutes until curtain, that I realized an entire week had passed and my camp session was almost over. Backstage, in the scurry to accomplish last-minute improvements with the other prop artists, I overheard Christy crying to Dan about how sick she was and how she could not perform. Oh, I couldn't wait to tell Rachael about this latest tidbit! But as I searched for her, Dan found me. In as close to a whisper as he could muster, he asked, "How quickly can you get into costume and be Pocahontas?" With little thought and a great deal of excitement, I jumped at the opportunity and blurted out, "About ten minutes."

I felt my insecurities disappear as I recited each line perfectly. I could see my own shining performance reflected in the faces of my father, mother and Rachael in the front row. I can still smell the aroma of the bouquet given to me by Dan at the end of my performance and whenever it is necessary, I can still hear my father's voice on that night saying, "Aren't you glad you hung in there?"

~Sandy Bull

Chicken Soup for the Soul

Content with What I Have

The foolish man seeks happiness in the distance;
the wise grows it under his feet.
~James Oppenheim

My grandma hugged me tight. "I wish you didn't have to go," she said, and tears fell down her wrinkled cheeks. I didn't understand why we had to leave our hometown, our country, my friends and the grandma I loved so much.

But my parents had decided that Bolivia would not be the place for us. The United States would give us more opportunities to go to school, build a career when we grew up and live better lives.

"You'll see," my mom said. "The United States has so many things to do that are exciting and fun, some of which you've never even seen or done before."

Two months after my twelfth birthday, the day to board the plane came. I snuck some of my favorite things under the clothes Mom had packed in one of the two huge suitcases, but she found them.

"No, this can't go," she said. "There's a weight limit for our luggage."

So I had to leave the things I liked so much, including my favorite magazines with the characters I'd grown to love.

A lump formed in my throat as my mom, my brother and I rode

in the old taxicab, passing through the narrow dirt streets as we left our neighborhood. Mom must have seen my sad face because she patted my leg. "It'll be okay. Remember, Dad is waiting for us."

Dad had left Bolivia a few months prior. During his time in the United States, he'd managed to get a job, an apartment and a small car. After all those months of separation, we finally would be together.

I turned to my left and looked out the window. A couple of neighborhood kids played on the familiar playground. The rope holding the wooden swing was frayed and the seat had some splinters on the side. The slide was rusted underneath and dull from the sun beating on it. Weeds grew everywhere, and spots with dirt had rocks protruding here and there.

Although it wasn't pretty, it was the place where my friends and I played ball and dared each other to climb the monkey bars. But now, all of this was staying behind and I was heading to a strange and unknown place.

I managed to sleep for a time during the eight-hour plane ride that was sometimes bumpy and loud. They served us food wrapped in plastic—something I'd never seen before.

When we got to Miami, we entered the huge airport. People rushed everywhere. We stood in long lines while loudspeakers called out stuff in a language I couldn't understand. No one spoke Spanish besides Mom, my brother and me. We finally got to the counter, and the officials behind it were taller than any men I'd ever seen. When Mom placed papers on the counter, none of them smiled as they stamped our passports. And their blue eyes had such a serious look.

As we walked among crowds of people looking for the exit, we came to a set of stairs. A strange and bizarre set of stairs—they moved! Mom told me to place my hand on the black banister while putting my foot on the first step at the same time.

I froze. I'd never seen steps that moved. I waited for them to stop, but when they didn't, I grabbed tight to the banister and stepped on with trembling legs.

Once on the next floor, we found the glass doors marked "Exit." And then, a few feet before we reached them, they opened on their own! That was the scary part. How did those doors know we were coming?

Then we saw Dad at a distance. He waved and my brother and I ran to give him hugs.

As we drove through the streets of the new city, I gazed out the window at the scenery that was so different than in Bolivia. Streets were clean and wide, with white lines marking the lanes of traffic. But unlike the crowded sidewalks back home, the streets had a ghost-like appearance. The sidewalks were completely empty.

"Remember, we're in the greatest country in the world," Dad said as he drove the small car. "See how that police officer stopped to check our registration?" He glanced at me and my brother in the back seat. "That's efficiency we never saw in Bolivia." Some time later, with the aid of a dictionary, he learned that what the officer had given him was a speeding ticket.

Weeks went by, and attending school while we spoke no English was a nightmare. At the time, there was no "English as a Second Language" program, so we went to school unable to understand the teacher or students.

My parents didn't understand English either. Days passed before we learned that Mom was serving us cat food. She saw the picture of a fish on the can and thought it was tuna.

One Saturday afternoon, we went to Sears and Mom bought me the gym shorts indicated on a note I brought from school. Although she used a dictionary to figure out what it said, she purchased the wrong thing anyway. When all the girls in sixth grade took off their uniform skirts on the first day of gym class, they had navy blue shorts on. And me? I wore old-lady underwear.

The United States was nothing like they'd told me. Everything we encountered was kind of scary. And the adjustment was difficult. I missed home and my friends more than ever.

I had no friends until one day when a nice girl took me by the hand and offered me a chair beside her at the lunch table. She became my friend. Slowly, I learned some words in English, then some sentences, and pretty soon, I was able to communicate with her and the other girls.

More months went by, and I could laugh at their jokes. I could tell them about my country and teach them some games I knew. Before long, we even played some of them at recess.

One day, on the way home, we stopped at a park and I saw the same things I'd left in Bolivia. But here, they were new. The ground had nice green grass. The swing had chains rather than frayed ropes. Just for fun, my friends and I raced to the water fountain and they later invited me to their homes to watch TV.

Years later, Grandma visited us from Bolivia. I showed her some parts of my new life—the music and songs I'd learned, the books in English I read and the certificate showing I'd made the honor roll.

She placed her folded lace handkerchief on the table beside her, cupped my face in her hands, and looked into my eyes. "I missed you so much," she said, "but I'm so proud of you."

I learned that when I moved from Bolivia, I didn't leave things behind; I'd just exchanged them for better ones. And the experiences in both countries taught me to be happy where I live and to be content with what I have.

~Janet Perez Eckles

A Hair-Raising Experience

The hair is the richest ornament of women.
~Martin Luther

When Dad died of a heart attack, we moved to another town where I'd be attending a new middle school. Still feeling the loss from Daddy's death and overwhelmingly nervous about making new friends, I was eager to make a good impression. Mom took me on a shopping spree, purchasing the latest fashions.

I begged to get my hair cut and styled before the first day of class. Seated in the stylist's chair, I kept my eyes squeezed shut in hopeful anticipation of it turning out just like the picture I'd clipped from a teen magazine.

"All finished," the hair stylist exclaimed proudly.

I opened my eyes, staring in horror at the reflection looking back at me. My hair didn't look like the photo in the magazine at all. I'd never worn a style so short in my entire life. I looked like my little brother!

That night it took an entire box of tissues to wipe away the tears and heartache. What was I going to do? I just couldn't attend school the following week looking like a boy. I fell asleep enveloped in one of Daddy's soft flannel shirts.

Inspiration dawned like the morning sun when I woke up.

I'd remembered seeing an old wig in one of Mom's dresser drawers. It was a long shoulder length extension, the same shade of chestnut brown as my own hair. I spent the morning locked in my bedroom pinning the fake head of hair into place.

"Not bad..." I smiled, turning my head from side to side for inspection. Granted, my bangs were a little different shade of brown, but at least the short haircut was hidden from view.

I hunted Mom down, eager to see her reaction.

She tactfully remained silent, biting her lower lip. Finally, she spoke.

"There's nothing as beautiful as your own hair, sweetie. But it's your decision."

The following weeks were nerve-wracking as I juggled school-work, making new friendships and dealing with the loss of a father. I wore the extension every time I left the house. I didn't think anyone had really noticed my fake hair, but I didn't speak to many people yet either.

One evening as I sat in front of the vanity mirror in my room, I noticed a little bare spot on the top of my head where I'd been pinning the hair into place. I heard Mom's voice behind me.

"You better give your scalp a break from that wig, sweetie."

"It's okay, Mom. My hair's still way too short."

Mom slowly shook her head, placing a neatly folded stack of clean laundry on the bed.

"Suit yourself, but the real you is far more beautiful," she smiled, giving me a reassuring hug.

The following day I was seated in history class. The teacher's voice droned on and on in the front of the room. I could hear a group of kids whispering behind me. A paper airplane whizzed by. Someone kicked the back of my chair. The next thing I knew, the tall boy seated behind me reached out, yanking the extension from my head. The room filled with laughter.

Clutching the wig, I slowly made my way out of the classroom. As I passed the teacher's desk, I knew I'd never forget the look of compassion on his face as long as I lived. He remained silent, sadly shaking his head in the direction of the class.

I spent the entire class period in the restroom feeling alone and humiliated.

That night I sat encircled in Mom's loving arms in the center of her quilt-covered bed, as I shared the day's humiliating experience with heart-wrenching sobs. We prayed together and Mom shared a few embarrassing memories of her own. As I wiped another tear away, Mom grew thoughtful.

"Don't you think it's time to let go of this silly wig?" she asked, lifting the extension into the air.

I had to admit, I was pretty sick of the sorry looking thing. It was starting to resemble a woodchuck anyway.

Suddenly Mom reached into the drawer of her bedside table for a pair of scissors. Before I knew what was happening, she snipped the shoulder-length fall into pieces.

Next she wrapped her arms around me, anticipating more heart-wrenching sobs to come.

I took one look at the bits and pieces of fake hair scattered over the bed and experienced an overwhelming sense of relief and freedom. Freedom from grief, freedom from insecurity, freedom from worrying about what the following days would bring.

Sudden laughter rose to my throat as I tossed a strand of fake hair into the air. Soon, we were both laughing so hard the entire bed shook.

"What's so funny?" my brother asked from the doorway.

"You could say we've just had a hair-raising experience," I cried.

"Women," he mumbled shaking his head and disappearing once more.

The following day I wore my favorite outfit... including my favorite head of hair.

"I like your haircut," a new friend complimented over lunch. I couldn't help smiling at my reflection in the window beside us.

I had to admit, it did look kind of great.

~Mary Z. Smith

Chicken Soup
for the Soul

The Unexpected Roommate

In the cookies of life, sisters are the chocolate chips.
~Author Unknown

"**H**ow many bedrooms?" I asked my mom. "Five," she said over her shoulder as she shoved the last suitcase under the front passenger seat. We had just managed to load all our bags into the shuttle and were in the process of piling in ourselves. It seemed like hours since our plane had landed in Brazil, and it seemed like years since the last time we had slept. At last we were on the road and headed to our new apartment. My dad was busy trying to give directions to the driver in Portuguese. My older sister, Ona, was staring wide-eyed out the window. My brother was busy with his Game Boy, and my little sister, Abby, was leaning against my mother and sleeping.

I know I probably should have been more excited about being in a foreign country. I should have taken that time in the shuttle to look around and absorb all the new sights and sounds. Truthfully, all I could think about was our new five-bedroom apartment. Five bedrooms! That meant that I would get my own room. I was overjoyed. My own room—I wouldn't just be sharing a room with my big sister anymore. I would have a room all to myself. I could decorate it however I wanted. I could have my own bedroom rules that all guests had to follow. My bedroom would be a symbol of my growing individuality, my maturity. I was ten years old, after all. "Ten years old and with my own room," I sighed happily.

I was beyond upset when my family arrived at our new apartment and I learned that I would be sharing a bedroom with Abby. I was furious.

Our apartment was a little different than the houses I was used to. On one side of the apartment there were four bedrooms and then in the complete opposite corner of the apartment — past the kitchen, pantry and laundry room — there was a little bedroom for the family's *empregada*, or housekeeper. We didn't have an *empregada*, and so I asked my mom why Abby couldn't move into that little room.

My mom, weary from the many hours of travel, simply told me, "No."

"Why not?" I demanded.

"Abby isn't going to be by herself in a completely different part of the apartment every night," she explained. "She's only seven!"

"So!" I mumbled.

"Would you like to sleep out there?" she asked me.

I thought about the little room way in the back of the apartment. "No," I admitted, but quickly added, "but I'm older. I should get the bigger room."

My mom again told me no.

"Well then I can share a room with Ona. Abby can have her own room."

My mom said no again. "Ona is the oldest, and she needs her own room."

I couldn't believe my mother. Sharing a room with Abby after sharing a room with my older sister felt like I was being demoted, like I was being sent back to the kids' table at Thanksgiving. It was ridiculous, especially since I was on the cusp of my teenage years. Ona was a teenager. If I had to share a room with anyone, it should be her. It was obvious.

"I'm not sharing a room with Abby! You told me there were five bedrooms, so I should have my own room!" I was becoming hysterical—partly because of jet lag and partly because I wasn't as mature as I believed.

My mom continued, "Amy, I'm sorry, but you and Abby are sharing a room. And that's final."

Poor Abby. It wasn't her fault. Eventually, everything smoothed out, but things were rocky at first. I was anything but sisterly. I was actually quite bratty—hiding Abby's favorite toys, making her play games that were completely unfair, locking her out, demanding that she remake her bed again and again because she was doing it "wrong."

Despite all of this Abby still wanted to play with me and hang out. She wanted me to join in whatever she was doing. This was a welcome change. I was used to begging Ona to play with me. The best I could do most of the time was convince her to read aloud from one of her books while I cleaned our room. Abby, on the other hand, was up for anything—making Halloween or Christmas decorations for our windows, hide and seek, dolls, tea parties, toy parades, and playing with stuffed animals.

We played with our stuffed animals a lot—making up stories, having adventures. I adored my stuffed animals, particularly a little brown and pink plushy elephant named Hosey. Hosey was my little buddy. He would snuggle with me as I attempted to read a book that was "too old" for me, and occasionally he would cuddle with me while I read one of Abby's books that was perhaps "too young" for me. He would watch movies with me, do homework with me, and always slept in late on Saturdays with me. Hosey would play with Abby and me, and it was okay. Abby didn't tell me that I was too old to have an imaginary friend. She didn't laugh at me when Hosey started talking about his little sister Peanut or his uncle Fred who was forever breaking things. Abby never told me to "grow up," and she never pointed out that Hosey "wasn't real." He was just a fellow well-loved playmate. No problem there.

I shared a room with Abby for the entire three years that my family lived in Brazil. Somewhere during those three years I realized that Abby was pretty cool—not just because she didn't tease me when girls my own age probably would have, and certainly not because she was star-struck by her big sis. Abby very quickly grew out of that phase. No, I just began to see Abby as Abby and not my little sister. We became best friends. To this day no one can make me laugh or smile like Abby. And there is no one more fun to hang with.

During the whole experience, I always thought how lucky Abby was. If we hadn't been in Brazil, sharing a room, then Abby wouldn't have been able to hang out with me as much. I doubt we would have spent even half as much time together, and I know we would not have become best friends.

Now that I am older and wiser I know that I was the lucky one. I realize now that I wasn't exactly my little sister's first choice when it came to playmates. Sure I was her big sister and a certain degree of admiration came with the title, but little sisters will only take so much brattiness before they stop inviting you to tea parties and toy parades altogether. If it hadn't been for Brazil, I would have totally missed out on my best friend. Luckily, I didn't.

~Amelia Hollingsworth

The Best Lesson

When you find peace within yourself,
you become the kind of person who can live at peace with others.
~Peace Pilgrim

oing solo into seventh grade at a new school? I would've rather had all of my teeth pulled. Without anesthesia.

My family lived in a different school district, which meant I was forced to attend Kennedy while friends from elementary went to another junior high. To make matters infinitely worse, my height registered a lanky five feet eight inches. Forget about boys liking me, they didn't even come up to my shoulder.

I walked to class alone on my first day. Girls with too much make-up and guys with backpacks slumped over one shoulder dotted my path. I was lost, but not brave enough to ask for directions. While wandering around the concrete corridors lined with clumps of angry orange lockers, I heard people talk about me.

"Could she be any taller?"

"She needs to get a tan."

"What a freak."

It's hard to hide when you're several heads taller than everyone else, so I tucked my chin into my chest and kept searching for the right room. The insults continued to follow me. I finally found where I needed to be and settled into a seat in the middle row, not wanting to appear nerdy or stupid, when Brandon Thompson sat next to me.

One part bad boy and the other part slacker, he oozed of mystery. He was one of the few guys my age taller than me (I later found out he was held back a grade or two) and he had this "I-just-rolled-out-of-bed-and-I'm-still-hot" look. I attempted to ignore him and failed as he leaned toward me.

"Do you have a pen?" The corners of his mouth twitched up as I gawked at him.

"Uh, oh, yeah. Sure. Here." I thrust the ballpoint I was holding toward him.

Brandon raked a hand through his messy hair and took the proffered pen. Without thanking me, he returned his focus on the front of the classroom. My eyes betrayed me several times by glancing back at him.

When the period ended, I shuffled out of the room and stumbled toward my next class. Hours went by in a haze of boy crazy daydreams until I found myself with nowhere to sit for lunch. No friends called to me and no groups offered an invitation. Yet again, I paced the halls alone. As I strolled past a cluster of cliques, an arm jutted out to block me. A boy with big muscles and, from what I could tell, little brains, squinted at me. He pushed his face closer to mine and said, "You are so ugly."

To my horror, Brandon stood beside him wearing a smirk.

I ran to the nearest bathroom and locked myself in a stall. Tears prickling my eyes and nose dribbling, I leaned against the wall and counted down the minutes. Fifteen until class. Two more hours to go. With a sigh, I wiped my face and pushed myself to leave the lonely bathroom.

Weeks passed with no end to the rudeness, but I began to ignore the mean kids around me. I couldn't change my height or my pale skin; the only thing I could change was my attitude. Eventually, I found solace in art class and in the accomplishment of getting good grades.

Mrs. Vierra, my English teacher, pulled me aside one morning to ask for my help. A new girl named Carmel had come to Kennedy and she needed someone to show her around. My heart fluttered first with hope and then with apprehension that this new girl would treat me as poorly as the others did. I took a chance and promised to escort Carmel to her next class. Mrs. Vierra nodded her head and introduced me to the girl who would become my best friend.

I never conspired to win Brandon's affection or to change the minds of those who thought me freakish, but by the time I entered high school, I didn't care. Sure, the mean comments and ostracizing hurt, but I became stronger because of the criticism. My see-through skin and long extremities are what make me who I am. And they're not so bad. Maybe time provides perspective, or maybe some people in seventh grade need to make fun of others to help them cope with their own insecurities. Whatever the reason, as an adult, I now appreciate everyone's uniqueness. Maybe that's the best lesson I learned at Kennedy Junior High.

~Hilary Heskett

Just for
Preteens

Learning Lessons and Doing What's Right

When I do good, I feel good.
When I do bad, I feel bad.
That's my religion.

~Abraham Lincoln

Kali's Gift

The only gift is a portion of thyself.
~Ralph Waldo Emerson

"Okay," our Sunday school teacher, Mrs. Woodland, said. "It's time for the gift exchange." I was actually sort of excited. Not ecstatic or anything. But I knew what a lot of the girls had brought, and any of those gifts would have been really great. Especially my best friend Sara's gift. She had made fudge and put it in this super cute bear mug. I love fudge and figured it would be fun to have the bear mug for drinking hot cocoa over Christmas.

And rich Megan Perkins had wrapped a bottle of expensive perfume. Her favorite kind, she said. Megan always smelled really good. I wouldn't mind smelling like her for the holidays.

Actually, all the girls had brought cool gifts. Mrs. Woodland had us put them all on our classroom table, next to the manger scene she had set up. Mrs. Woodland had just finished telling us the story of Jesus's birth, something she did every year before we had our class Christmas party.

We opened the gifts like a game. We each drew numbers and we got to go up to the table and choose a wrapped gift when our number was called. Or more accurately put, we could choose a wrapped gift—if we wanted to. But we didn't necessarily have to. We could take a gift from somebody else that had already had their number called—if we thought we'd like that gift better than the wrapped ones.

Some of the gifts really got passed around. Like Sara's. Everyone likes fudge.

Still, everybody seemed to like the gift I'd brought. I was relieved, since I hadn't paid much for it. It was just some cheap nail polish—but in a cool color—and I'd tied a fingernail file to it with a pretty ribbon.

I'd hoped the girls would like it—but I'd been worried they wouldn't. After all, I hadn't had very much money to spend. I was basically broke and I still had my mom's Christmas gift left to buy. I wanted to get her something special. Something cool. But that was the problem. Cool things seemed to cost a lot of money... and I just didn't have any.

When it was my turn, I didn't take a wrapped gift from the table. And I didn't take Sara's either, though I really wanted to. Just being around fudge was making me hungry. But I took the perfume Megan had brought instead.

"Bummer," Beth groaned as I took the bottle from her.

"It's for my mom," I wanted to explain, but I didn't bother. It was none of Beth's business. It was no one's business. I didn't have enough money to get Mom something as special as she deserved, but the perfume was really nice. She might really like it... and maybe she would let me borrow it sometime.

I was busy thinking about the perfume and whether Mom would like it or not. I guess that's how I missed how the incident happened. But suddenly there was a big commotion. It had been Hannah's turn to choose. She was the last one. And no big shock, she didn't go for the last wrapped gift on the table. Instead she'd taken Sara's gift from Lauren.

Well, that meant Lauren had to take the wrapped gift. She'd huffed all the way up to the table. Everyone knew the last gift was from Kali. That's why no one had chosen it. Kali was really poor. I mean really poor. And she always brought lame gifts—gifts no one ever wanted. I guess everyone knew today would be no exception. And it wasn't. The gift Kali had wrapped? A pair of crocheted potholders. Potholders!

"I don't want to be stuck with these," Lauren whined. "I want my fudge back."

"No way," Hannah protested, keeping the mug of chocolate out of Lauren's reach.

"Then I want Megan's perfume." Lauren came over to take my perfume. "Come on, Melanie, trade with me."

I shook my head. The game was over. I had gotten the perfume fair and square. No way was I giving it up.

Mrs. Woodland cleared her throat. "Melanie, why don't you trade with Lauren?"

She was always doing this to me. Making me take the dorky gift. Last year I had to take the broken gingerbread house, and for Valentine's Day I had to settle for the messed up valentine. And I always, always got stuck with Kali's lame gifts. It wasn't fair.

I was about to tell Mrs. Woodland off. Tell her I was tired of being the nice guy and getting stuck with the lame stuff and stinky deals. I was about to tell her what she could do with her potholders.

Then I noticed Kali sitting silently in the back of the classroom. She was sitting there all alone with her head bowed. Suddenly I felt ashamed of myself... and the rest of the class. Poor Kali. She had obviously worked hard on the potholders. And they were really nice... as far as potholders go.

And she probably didn't want to give them to us any more than any of us wanted them. Probably her mom had dragged her to church this morning. Probably she had tried to fake sick or something so she could stay home and not have to go through this. I know that's what I would have done.

"Sure—I'll take the potholders," I said to Mrs. Woodland. I gave my best effort to smile. But it was kind of hard. I felt sort of sick. "They're really pretty." I glanced over at Kali—wanting to say something nice to her. Wanting to make up for how horrible Lauren and Hannah and I had acted. "Did you make them yourself?"

Kali nodded, but I already knew she had. Our class had learned to crochet as a craft project last year. None of us other girls really got the hang of it. Obviously Kali had.

"They're really pretty," I said again.

"Here," I told my mom after church, handing her the potholders as soon as I hopped into the car. "They're an early Christmas gift. I'll get you something else too—something real."

"They're beautiful," Mom said, actually beaming.

She seemed so delighted with them, I was worried she was confused or something. "I didn't make them," I confessed quickly. "Kali Harris did."

"I know," Mom said, still beaming. "Mrs. Woodland told me what happened in class today. She says she relies on you to keep peace in the class a lot." Mom gave me a hug. "Mrs. Woodland said you handled the situation wonderfully. You're growing to be a very thoughtful young woman—that's the best Christmas present a mother could ask for."

I rode home from church with a happy heart, knowing next year I would be honored to get Kali's gift.

~Melanie Marks

Chicken Soup for the Soul

The Birthday Party

It's nice to be important, but it's more important to be nice.
~Author Unknown

I love parties. I always have. I love planning for them, making the invitations, planning the games and decorating my own cake. The only thing that I don't like is deciding on the guest list. When I was in grade school my mom would tell me the maximum number of friends that I could invite and it was always a number too small for my list.

I also liked all different kinds of people. I never quite fit into one of the many little groups at my school, so I just kind of floated around, accumulating friends from various cliques. There was an "in" crowd made up of the cool kids who had the power to rule the school—if a cool kid wore two different colored socks to school one day, everyone thought it was great. But if an uncool kid did the same thing, the other kids would turn away in disgust. It made getting dressed in the morning a very scary thing. Without knowing exactly what the rules were, I never knew if I would inadvertently cross the line of "uncoolness."

Shannon was one of my friends who seemed to unknowingly break the rules all the time. I don't know why she was targeted, but people found it acceptable to make fun of her. Shannon was a nice girl and wore pretty clothes, but was somewhat overweight and didn't talk much. She was picked on a lot. Whenever there was an odd noise or smell in the classroom the kids would giggle and point at her. Shannon never said anything, but it made me feel sick inside and I was relieved that the kids hadn't pointed at me.

One year, to celebrate my birthday, my mom told me I could have a party at our house. I struggled for days deciding on which girls to invite to keep the number within the specified limit. Once I had chosen all the names, I made the invitations and handed them out to my friends at school.

"Why did you invite her?" asked one of my cool friends when it was discovered that I had invited Shannon. She insisted that I had made a big mistake and pressured me to tell her not to come. There were other people I could add in her place who would be more acceptable. I wasn't sure what to do; I liked Shannon, yet I was afraid that I would become the target of the girl's ridicule if I admitted that Shannon was my friend. I knew the right thing to do, but I struggled with the fear of having to live with my decision.

I decided not to say anything to Shannon and let the invitations stay as written, but I worried about what would happen. The day of my party, both Shannon and my other friends came, and all that happened was that we had a lot of fun together. It was not unlike other parties I had been to and none of the things I had worried about came to be. More parties and events followed that one and the memory of it was whisked away almost as quickly as the colorful paper plates on which we ate our cake and ice cream. In fact, it was many years later before I thought about that particular party again.

I was at my high school twenty-year reunion when a beautiful, slim, very professional-looking woman walked up to me. She said, "Lindy, I am so glad you came tonight. You're the reason I am here."

"Oh?" I replied, not recognizing her face at first. She pointed to her nametag that read, "Dr. Shannon Chatzky." We hugged and laughed and caught up on the years that had passed since we had last seen each other. She was now a wife, a mother and a doctor!

Then she told me something that stayed with me. She said, "Grade school was awful for me. I hated to get up each morning, dreading the ridicule that would come each day. I struggled all the time with thoughts of ending my life. I came tonight to thank you for being my friend. You made my days bearable and I will never forget that you invited me to your party."

Shannon cherished the memory of that birthday party from so many years before. It was important to her that I had welcomed her into the fun, and it was a day when she felt accepted and part of a group. She talked about the games we played and the cake we ate, remembering all the details. For me, it was just a simple party, one I hadn't even remembered. But for Shannon, it was a party she would never forget. And now, neither will I.

~Lindy Schneider

Feeding the Soul

Act as if what you do makes a difference. It does.
~William James

hite puffs of bread lined up in front of me, with seas of mayonnaise spread over them. How many times had I done this? How many more times would I be forced to do it?

The pink circles of meat and perfectly square blocks of cheese made slapping sounds as I threw them down. My dad would soon be leaving to feed the homeless.

Every afternoon we went to the store, and the people there would give us things that were past the expiration date but hadn't gone bad. Usually we received things like sliced vegetables, pieces of fruit, bread, and slices of cake or pie. We gave these to the homeless along with the sandwiches and tea.

My father and several volunteers from the church gathered every day in the park to feed the hungry and teach anyone who was willing to listen about God.

Boy was I glad I didn't have to go to the feedings. It was enough trouble just getting everything ready. I really didn't understand why my father bothered with it. I couldn't wait for him to leave. I looked forward to a whole Saturday by myself. I planned to watch some television, talk with my friends on the phone, and maybe do some shopping during the afternoon.

It didn't take long for my plans to change and my happiness to dissolve. Dad came in while I was finishing and stood behind me.

"I'm going to need your help today. Some of the others that usually help me won't be able to make it."

"Dad, I can't today," I whined. "I have plans, television, friends, shopping, and I was maybe going to go to the pool."

He just gave me the you-should-be-ashamed-of-yourself look.

"Fine." I pouted. "It's not like I have a life."

"I really appreciate it. It will just be us today."

He left the room.

That's probably because everyone else finally realized that it's all just a waste of time, I thought to myself. You're not really helping anybody.

I was really upset my day was now ruined.

I finished packing the sandwiches and followed Dad out to the van. I wanted to cry. This was going to be the worst day ever. My dad always drove the church van, which also contained clothes and small bags filled with personal items such as combs, toothbrushes, toothpaste, razors, and deodorant.

He pulled out of the driveway to head downtown. I looked out the window and watched as we drove past kids playing in their front yards. I felt like a prisoner forced to perform community service.

When we arrived at the park, people were already gathered under a tree waiting for us. We opened the back of the van and pulled out a long cafeteria table and some chairs. I put the table on one side of the van with the food on it, while my dad lined up chairs on the other side for them to sit in.

In between the table and the people was a single chair for my dad to sit in. I watched as he opened his guitar case. He smiled at me and turned to his congregation to play, sing songs of praise, and read from the Bible.

I couldn't believe how many people were there, and all of them homeless. I was surprised to learn my dad knew most of them by name. He also seemed to know what each one needed and what they had suffered through that landed them on the street.

One man told me if it hadn't been for my father he didn't think he would have found Jesus.

"Even when the weather is bad and the shelter has closed its door to us, your dad is still here. It's the one thing folks like us can count on, and we don't soon forget his kindness."

After the sermon we put what food we had left into bags and handed them out. That's when I noticed a man still sitting in a chair. He had a badly swollen, purple face.

My father noticed my stare and explained a member of a gang had found the man sleeping in the street and thought it would be fun to throw bricks at him.

While my father went to talk with him about the Lord, I climbed into the back of the van and started handing out some articles of clothing.

A girl about my age came up to me from across the street. Her face was stained with dirt and her dark hair was a mass of stringy curls. I noticed right away that she was barefoot.

"Do you have some shoes, about a size six?" she asked meekly.

I stared into her blue eyes for a moment, unable to believe someone so similar to me could live like this. I had never thought about the possibility of homeless children.

She didn't look me in the eye for very long and I was worried I had made her uncomfortable.

I looked back into the van and saw only one pair of shoes left. Please let them be a six, I thought. I picked them up and turned them over. Exactly a six.

"Thank you!" she cried happily. She slid them on and ran back across the street. I felt all warm inside as I watched her leave.

When everyone was gone, we loaded things back into the van. Now I understood why my father did so much to help the homeless. I could tell he loved seeing their smiles of happiness. I did too.

I was so worried that morning about missing out on my fun day. I realized I should have been thankful for everything I have. That day with my dad taught me that there will always be someone smarter, prettier, or richer than me, and there will also always be someone less fortunate. The difference is in the individual willing to take the opportunity to help others, even if it means sacrificing something of their own.

~Sylvia Ney

"Hi Carol!"

Kindness is the language which the deaf can hear and the blind can see.
~Mark Twain

i Andrea... Hi Anthony... Hi Cristina... Hi Tommy... Hi Steve."

Every day, we heard a sputtering voice from the top of the brick wall we passed in the morning, a few steps from school. The voice was Carol's, a mentally disabled girl who went to our school. She called out to be our friend.

I gave a slight wave. As time went by, I said, "Hi."

Then after more time passed I said, "Hi Carol!"

The others only gave a sideways glare and went on giggling with their friends.

One day at lunch, Carol began to inch her way closer to my group of friends, who were all classroom representatives and popular. I smiled at her as she stood there and listened to our jokes. I was happy she joined in laughing. She never said anything, but day after day she stood there and listened and laughed.

Finally I said, "Carol, sit down with us."

She did.

"Did I tell you about my brother?" Carol finally spoke.

"Hey, did you hear Kyle got a cell phone?" Tommy said.

"Yeah, well my friend's sister is only seven and she already has one." Everyone was off on another subject. Carol didn't seem to mind that no one had listened to her.

"He used to play lacrosse but now my brother likes to swim. I do too...." Carol continued.

It wasn't long before kids didn't want her talking or sitting too close to them.

"Carol smells," one kid would say. "Leave our table," said another. But Carol wouldn't leave.

Eventually, one of the kids started nasty rumors about Carol.

Everyone acted grossed out, with bursts of, "Ugh" and "Ewww." When I heard this rumor I couldn't believe someone could be so mean. I quickly changed my group of friends. Carol did not deserve to be treated like that!

I continued to be nice to Carol when I saw her in the hallway or on the playground or at lunch.

"How's your teacher Mrs. Stringer?" I'd ask.

"She's great. How are you, Andrea?" Carol asked.

"I'm good."

I felt good talking to Carol. I was her friend and she was my friend. I noticed after some time passed Steve started to say "hi" to Carol too. Then at lunch he helped her carry her food tray when her arms were too full with books. I was impressed at how nice he was being.

One day after school, I checked the mailbox and there was an invitation from Carol. It was to her eleventh birthday party at the skating rink. When I went to school the next day, all of the classroom representatives were talking about Carol's invitation and her birthday party.

"No way. I wouldn't be caught dead at her party," Kendra said.

"She probably can't even skate," another kid said.

I realized I would probably be the only one going. But I figured it was better than no one going. I couldn't do that to Carol. I would show.

My mom dropped me off on time for Carol's party. As I walked in I saw Carol and her mom and dad and brother smiling. Carol ran to me.

"Andrea! Hi!" she said.

"Happy Birthday, Carol. Should we get our skates?" I asked.

Her mom and dad smiled as we walked to get our skates.

When we turned around I almost crashed into Steve. Carol was ecstatic to see him. So was I. The three of us headed out to the music-filled rink.

Steve asked us, "Hey can you guys do this?" He did a zigzag with his legs.

We tried to copy but laughed instead. Carol went on to have a super birthday. Steve and I did too. We both agreed we were glad we went.

When we got back to school on Monday the jokes started.

"Andrea and Steve went to Carol's party? What losers."

"Who would want to go to Carol's party?"

Steve and I ignored the jokes and blew off their comments. They weren't nice kids, so we didn't care what they said.

A few years later Carol died. I was so sad when I heard the news. She was a rare girl with a true heart. All she ever wanted was friends. A mean word never left her lips. I wish every kid could have a friend like Carol. I'm glad I did. I will never forget her.

~Andrea Q. Verde

22

Chicken Soup for the Soul

Standing My Ground

Courage is not the absence of fear,
but rather the judgment that something else is more important than fear.
~Ambrose Redmoon

It was the summer of my tenth year, and I was enjoying a carefree morning with nothing much that I had to get done. I walked barefoot through the grass, carrying my flip-flops as I headed for the neighborhood park and swimming pool.

Being ten was not always easy—it was a time when I felt stuck awkwardly between childhood and adolescence. I remember experiencing intense and unpredictable emotions that would come and go in waves. At times I still wanted to "play" and embrace the privileges of childhood, and at other times I resented being treated as a child and could not wait until I reached that magical age that included the word "teen." It seemed this small detail might help confirm that I had entered a new stage of life and end the confusion about how I should feel and behave.

As I approached the park that summer morning, I saw that swimming lessons were well underway. I casually strolled toward the fence surrounding the pool and sat down on a bench to watch for a while before continuing on my walk. Not far from where I was sitting I saw a boy about my age fiddling with his bike lock. I felt a wave of self-consciousness when I recognized who he was. He was popular for all the usual reasons. Most of the girls I knew thought he was really cute, and I was no exception. Good looks weren't the only thing he had on his side—he also came from a family that was quite wealthy, and they were well known for having the newest, coolest things, including a motorized scooter that he had proudly showed off earlier in the summer to an envious crowd of admirers.

But popularity based on appearance and money alone is sometimes accompanied by pride and arrogance, and that was the case for this boy. He was also known for teasing kids who were not as popular as he was, and that made him much less appealing to me. Still, knowing he was that close to me with no one else around, I felt extremely self-conscious and aware of my every move. As I contemplated slipping away invisibly, I noticed he seemed to be working very hard to get the bike unlocked, as if he were racing against some deadline that was fast approaching. He kept looking up at the kids who were in swimming lessons before frantically returning to his work. His behavior struck me as odd, and I had the feeling that something wasn't right.

I took a closer look at the bike, and suddenly I realized what was going on. You see, the funny thing about being ten and spending endless summer days at the pool is that you begin to remember the bikes and towels of the other kids, who spend as much time there as you do. I knew whose bike this was—it belonged to another boy who was younger and whose family didn't have a lot of money. And this "popular" boy was going to steal it!

The injustice I was witnessing overpowered my desire to slip away unnoticed. Without even thinking about it, I walked towards him. He looked up from his criminal work, annoyed by my disturbance. I just stood there for a moment, hoping that just my wordless presence would deter him from his crime. No such luck. I had to take the next step.

"That's not your bike. I know what you're doing."

He half-smiled, but it was an unfriendly sarcastic snarl. "Oh, really? And what are you gonna do about it?" He looked bored, almost cruelly entertained by my concern.

"You don't even need that bike. I know whose it is, and if you steal it, I'll tell who did it."

He looked shocked and laughed mockingly. "You don't even know my name."

"Sure I do. Everyone knows your name," I fired back.

He showed a little pride at the fact that I knew his name and he had no clue who I was, but then it faded and his look became angry and intimidating. He stood up and moved towards me.

"Oh, look," he sneered, "it's little-miss-goody-two-shoes trying to save the world." Then he moved even closer. "You're not going to say a word to anyone—do you get it?"

It was painfully obvious that in his mind, there wasn't an option for me to disagree. At that moment, I found myself at a fork in the road with two clear choices. I could back down and let him steal the bike, or I could stand my ground and face the potential consequences of standing up to a bully. I took a deep breath and braced myself, trying not to show my fear. "I told you, if you steal that kid's bike, I'll tell that you did it."

He looked shocked and caught off-guard for a few seconds before his face contorted into a look that told me exactly what was going to happen next. He charged at me and knocked me to the ground, and the fight was on. Adrenaline and my survival instinct helped me to defend myself with everything in me as he threw punches at me without any sign of mercy. My only experience with fighting was light-hearted "play" fighting with my sister or brothers where there were never any injuries or any true sense of fear. For this reason, my pathetic moves were limited to pulling his eyes down and twisting the parts of his bare chest I could get to in a desperate attempt to get him off me before I really got pummeled.

Miraculously, he did stop his attack, leaving me lying in the dirt but relatively unharmed. He laughed at me, called me a few more names and said something about me not being worth his time. And then he turned and left.

I stood up and brushed the dirt off myself, straightened my clothing and watched him walk away. A grin spread across my dirt-streaked face as I looked at the bike, still waiting for its rightful owner. Sure, he might have thought he won the physical fight, but I felt certain that I had won the larger, more important battle. I had stood my ground and stopped him from stealing the bike. And I couldn't have felt prouder!

~Julie A. Havener

Chicken Soup for the Soul

23

The Gift of Giving

The manner of giving is worth more than the gift.
~Pierre Corneille

During Christmas vacation one year, my mom, my seven-year-old sister and I went on a two-week trip to India. I was really excited because I couldn't wait to see all my cousins, aunts and uncles. The last time I had visited them was when I was only three years old. I also wanted to purchase souvenirs and outfits for myself, go sightseeing, see the Taj Mahal, ride elephants, and much more. I imagined India to be a beautiful place, with palm trees swaying in the air and humongous shopping malls. Before I left, I bragged to my friends about riding elephants and buying exotic jewelry.

But oh, was I wrong. The moment I stepped out of the airplane, the entire airport smelled like... I can't even describe it, but let's just say it was something you probably never smelled before. It was like a mix of body odor and exhaust. I couldn't stand it! Plus, the airport was packed with people! I had never seen anything like it. People were shoving and pushing each other and yelling at the security guards. I thought I was dreaming. There was no way this could have been the India I had imagined. I couldn't wait to get out of the airport. Maybe the city would look more like my India, I thought. By the time we collected our luggage, it was already one in the morning, so I didn't really pay much attention on the ride to my grandma's house.

A few days later, a lot of things happened. My Aunt Joyce and my thirteen-year-old cousin Michelle came to keep us company. Michelle, my sister Samantha, and I played games, made tie-dye pillowcases, and much more. Soon, I was ready to see the country; I wondered what adventures were in store for us.

"Mom?" I asked. "What are we going to do today? I really want to go shopping and buy some new outfits."

"Stephanie, today we are going to one of the public schools in town. Remember the hundred-dollar bill Aunt Lila gave us before our trip? I decided that we are going to use the money to buy school supplies for the children there. And I am going to use an extra hundred dollars of my own to help the children," Mom said.

"But I wanted to go shopping today! You said before our trip I could get some new clothes!" I whined. I did not want to spend my entire vacation helping the poor. What would I tell my friends when I got back from my trip?

"Stephanie, we can go shopping some other time. But we need to put a little time in helping these poor children. Now go tell your sister to get ready because we will be leaving in ten minutes," said Mom.

"Oh all right," I told her. Boy, what a vacation I was having. I came to India to go sightseeing, not do charity work.

Ten minutes later, we were on our way. The city was smoky and smelled like car exhaust. We didn't even have our own rental car. We traveled in a rickety old rickshaw over the bumpy road.

When we arrived at the school, I couldn't believe my eyes. The school looked like a dump. There was a lot of dust in the air and there was only one building, which looked as if it were a hundred years old. There was no playground, no parking lot, nothing. Just a big, brown, dusty, old building. Oh well, I thought. Maybe it was only an intermediate school. But I soon found out that this was an elementary school. It was so small; the school I went to back home was a million times bigger.

The classroom we arrived at was unbelievable. There were about forty students in the class and they looked so weak and malnourished.

All the students stood up and said something to us in another language. Later, the teacher told us that they were welcoming us to their school. Their school backpacks were very small plastic bags, the kind you get after a trip from the grocery store. They had very few school supplies and most of the students had only one pencil. Can you even imagine writing with only one pencil for the entire school year? I probably wouldn't even last a month. In addition, there were three students sitting at every desk. Just then, I felt like my heart was torn in half. That morning, I had felt like spending money on clothes and souvenirs, when these were the people who really needed the money.

I was amazed at what two hundred dollars could buy. Each student received a coloring book, crayons, two brand new pencils, and some candy. You should have seen the expressions on their faces as Samantha and I passed the supplies out to the children. They looked at us as if we were angels sent from heaven. Every child who received the supplies was so grateful for everything. Some of them started eating their candy and coloring in their coloring books right away. I was so happy about making the students smile that I felt like getting all my money and purchasing supplies for every classroom in the entire school.

I learned a very important lesson that day. Life isn't always about receiving. When I first arrived in India, I was feeling sorry for myself. All I ever thought about was sightseeing and riding elephants. There are millions of people all over the world who don't have enough food, and who are very ill. I think every human on earth should make it a point to do something for someone else. It could be something as simple as tutoring a student who is failing, as long as you do something. When it is our turn to die, nobody is going to ask us what car we owned, what degrees we got, or how many times we were in the newspaper. What will really matter is how much we gave to other people.

~Stephanie Downing

The Right Thing

Character is doing the right thing when nobody's looking.
There are too many people who think that the only thing that's right
is to get by, and the only thing that's wrong is to get caught.
~J.C. Watts

"Hey, Sharon," I heard as I got off the school bus. "Did you get your math homework done?"

"Yup," I said. I'd spent over an hour getting it done, and only caught the end of my favorite TV show because of it.

"We had company, my dad's business partner." Julie's toe shuffled in the playground gravel. She wasn't a friend of mine, but I'd known her since kindergarten. "Can I copy your answers?"

"I can't...." I began.

"But I couldn't get mine done. I'll get a zero."

I thought of the hot chocolate I didn't have with my mom because of this homework. Fourth grade math was hard. It was my worst subject. I had to work hard to understand long division. Each problem took a half page in my notebook.

"You have to help me out."

"I can't." I turned and walked toward the school.

"I need you!"

I kept walking. I knew if I copied someone's answers it would be cheating. But if I let her copy mine, was that cheating too?

The first bell rang. There was Julie with her best friend. She looked at me and whispered to her.

Later, at recess, she stood in a group of girls on the playground and I heard her say, "I asked her and she said no!"

"How selfish."

"If I was in your class, I would."

"Me too."

"Let's not talk to her any more."

"Yeah."

"Come on Sharon, let's teeter-totter," said my best friend, Cindy. I ran after her and we both got on.

"Don't like her any more Cindy," Julie called over from her group of friends. "I asked her to help me with my math and she refused."

Cindy looked at me for a moment with a funny look on her face, then jumped off the teeter-totter and ran after Julie.

By lunch recess, nobody would talk to me. Words like mean and selfish drifted to me from their huddled, whispered conversations.

Right after lunch was math. I'd still have time to let Julie copy my answers before the bell rang. Then my friends would play with me. People would like me again. I sat on the playground bench to consider it.

I'd had trouble learning to tell time in the second grade. Cindy and I did our homework together on the phone until I understood it. Was that cheating? Was it any worse to let Julie copy my answers? Was I being selfish just because I'd missed most of my TV show and hot chocolate with Mom? Was Julie right?

When we were back in the classroom, Julie began to copy the answers from another girl's paper.

The teacher walked in. "Class, hand in your homework."

Julie had run out of time. Hurriedly she passed her paper forward with the rest. I wondered if I had done the right thing or not.

That night, as I lay in bed, I realized that Cindy had helped me understand how to tell time. She didn't give me the answers. She helped me to figure them out. I'd had to find the answers on my own.

That wasn't cheating. That wasn't the kind of help Julie had asked for.

As the days passed, Cindy listened to my side and started to play with me again. Other kids did too.

Julie never liked me again because I had refused to cheat, but I was okay with that. I was glad I had done the right thing.

~Sharon Palmerton Grumbein

The Prize

Envy is a waste of time.
~Author Unknown

The gym was stuffy for October. A teacher had pushed the double doors wide open, but the heat from one hundred kids wearing Halloween costumes soaked up the fresh air.

"How do I look?" I asked my friend, Gina.

"Old," she said.

"Perfect."

I tugged at the eyeholes of my wrinkled, rubber mask and adjusted my spectacles. My mom and I had worked on my costume for two days, and I looked grandmotherly. Padding in all the right places. Little gray curls. Pantyhose, shoes, handbag, and dress from my grandma's own closet. I'd even been practicing my walk.

Gina tugged her skirt and twined her fingers through her long blond ponytail. "The parade's about to begin. Here's the music."

The music sounded in the gym, and the procession began. I steadied myself in Grandma's shoes and grabbed my cane.

The costume contest was a big deal in junior high school. It took forever for the big, round clocks to strike one o'clock on Halloween day. But when they did, the fun began. There was a half hour for costume preparations and then a parade in the gym. The teachers judged the costumes and there was a gift certificate prize taped to a jumbo box of candy.

I'd been thinking about my costume for a long time. I wanted to win. I didn't care so much about the gift certificate. I wanted the recognition. I wasn't one of the popular girls, though I had a fair number of friends. Winning the contest wouldn't be a ticket to being popular, but it would sure make me look cooler.

"Can you move faster?" Gina asked from behind me.

I really couldn't. Marie was in front of me, and she moved like a snail, though she was dressed as a ladybug. She took tiny steps in her red knee-high socks. Even I moved faster with my grandma-like shuffle.

Marie. Poor Marie. I felt bad for her. She never seemed to have what she needed. She had a hard time with schoolwork. She had many brothers and sisters but I'd never seen her with a friend. Her hair was often unkempt and either stuck out in wild tufts or was matted to her head. Her clothes didn't fit. Even her ladybug costume had seen better days. From behind I could see that her spots were frayed and were pulling loose. Her antenna was bent. Her red tights had a long snag.

But I stopped thinking about Marie as we neared the judges' table. "Almost there," I whispered. Several teachers laughed as I shuffled by, and I was quite confident that I'd win. I'd done a pretty thorough assessment of the costumes before the parade began. Lots of ghosts. Plenty of ghouls. My costume was, by far, the most authentic.

We'd gone full circle around the gym when the music stopped. The judges came out from behind the table and walked in a slow circle, taking one last look at the costumes. A low buzz of conversation spread across the gym as vampires and musclemen talked about who would win.

"You've got it," Gina whispered. "They laughed when you walked by."

"I think so, too," I said. "But hey, your costume is great."

Gina smiled and the teachers walked to the center of the gym.

I was about to burst with excitement. It was getting sticky behind that mask, but I'd take if off after I claimed my prize. Mrs. Bronner blew a whistle and the crowd hushed. It was time.

"I'd like to compliment all of you on your great costumes," she said. "They are wonderful this year."

I wasn't surprised when she started to walk in my direction.

"But we have one costume that is really, really special."

My heart started to race.

Mrs. Bronner continued to walk. The clack of her heels came closer and closer. She stopped in front of me. "This year's Halloween costume winner is... the ladybug. Marie, congratulations! You've won!"

I looked at Gina to see if I'd heard right. She shrugged. Mrs. Bronner gave Marie a hug. Everyone clapped. Marie jumped up and down. She jumped and jumped and jumped until one of her wings fell off.

Marie had won? My costume was better. I pulled the rubber mask from my face and drew some fresh air. Then I bent to pick up Marie's wing. "Good job, Marie," I said as I handed it to her, though frustration filled my heart. Marie took the wing, but she didn't hear me. She was just too excited.

An hour later, after we'd gulped punch and munched the many cookies that the room-moms brought, I sat on the school bus. I was still disappointed. I knew better than to think one Halloween prize would elevate me to cool-girl status, but I'd really wanted to win. I felt a sense of injustice as I looked at my costume, balled in a shopping bag under my seat.

Our bus moved over the windy, country road. The leaves had turned harvest orange and gold, something I normally would appreciate. But I couldn't escape my sullen mood.

After a mile or so the bus slowed and stopped in front of a well worn home—Marie's. She moved up the aisle, toting her costume bag. Then she nearly tripped down the steps. The driver waited patiently then snapped the door shut when her feet hit solid ground outside the bus.

As the bus began to creep forward again, I sighed and looked out my window. I saw the front door of the house open, and Marie's mother came out and stood on the landing. Marie ran up the sidewalk, dropped her bag, and rushed into her mom's arms. They clasped hands and jumped together. Then Marie let go to fish through her bag for the prize. She retrieved it and there was more celebration.

I craned my neck to see more but the bus picked up speed. Marie and her mom became tiny people, then little specks lost behind the trees. All of a sudden it didn't matter that I hadn't won. I didn't care that the cool girls hadn't clamored around me in my victory, and I felt a little ashamed for wanting it so much.

Marie needed to win that contest, and I was so glad that she had. Funny thing was, I felt that in witnessing such a tender scene, I'd been given a prize, too.

~Shawnelle Eliasen

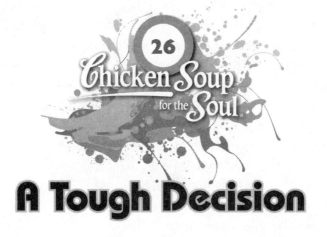

26

A Tough Decision

I would prefer even to fail with honor than to win by cheating.
~Sophocles

hen I was in my first year of junior high I was an average student. I got all A's and B's and had many friends. I had one secret, though: I cheated. I cheated starting from about halfway through the fifth grade, which was when the work started getting difficult. I didn't want to get held back or fail the grade and have to see all my friends move on without me. So, I did the only thing I could think of—I cheated. The real fact was I just couldn't pay attention and learn the new subjects. I cheated all through the rest of fifth grade, even on the TAKS (Texas Assessment of Knowledge and Skills). And it didn't stop there.

As I moved into sixth grade I was making new friends and leaving old ones behind. I seemed like a regular sixth grader. None of my friends knew I cheated, mainly because I cheated off their papers too. As junior high went on and teenage drama started entering my life, I found it harder and harder to pick up and learn the few things I did learn. So I began cheating on everything. It became more difficult to cheat, since the teachers began to put me in the front of the class, possibly to watch me more closely. Because of this, my grades started to drop quickly. Some of my teachers asked if everything was okay. Of course, I just said I hadn't been sleeping well, which was the only excuse

I could think of at the time. When I thought things couldn't get harder, I started getting picked on by the other kids.

I thought my life would never get cleaned up and I would never go to college or be a zoologist (my dream job). That's when I started to consider telling someone. The first person I told was my best friend, Sherry. She was really smart and she was the person I told all of my secrets. Of course the one thing she said was, "Elizabeth, you need to stop. You need to tell the teachers and clean this all up." Of course, I really didn't plan on telling because I was scared. I thought that the teachers would never look at me the same way again, that they'd never be able to trust me.

I was gravely wrong. I continued cheating all the way through the semester exam. But after that I got seated by the kids who also failed, so I couldn't cheat off the smart kids. My grades plummeted. I didn't know what to do, so I went back to Sherry. She told me the exact same thing again, but this time it meant something to me. I took it to heart and thought, "My teachers will forgive me. It's not like they're going to hold this against me forever."

That time I was right. Sherry and another friend, Taylor, who I also told, finally convinced me to come clean. It was the longest Thursday of my life. Finally, the dreaded fourth period came around, which was when I had Mrs. Burnum, my science teacher. She was the teacher I felt most comfortable around, so she was the one I had decided to tell. Right after the bell rang, I walked up to her and asked if I could talk to her outside. At that point I was sweating and shaking. She asked what was wrong.

I just poured everything out. I explained why I had failed the mock TAKS test. I emptied everything I had bottled up. Mrs. Burnum said that the teacher I took my mock TAKS with, Mrs. O'Conner, should hear my confession. Mrs. O'Conner, who taught reading and language arts, was the strictest teacher I had. Mrs. Burnum accompanied me to her classroom and, with a reassuring nod, eased me into telling Mrs. O'Conner. She nodded while I was explaining and when I finished I could tell she wasn't happy. But all Mrs. O'Conner said was, "Elizabeth, you know cheating is wrong. It is never the right decision. Why did you do it?"

First, I sighed with relief that I wasn't getting detention, and then I explained how I would have most likely gotten held back and hated to see my friends move on without me. I just couldn't let that happen.

Mrs. Burnum gave me an unhappy look and said, "Elizabeth, if you had told someone, you know you would've gotten help."

I nodded, fighting back tears.

The next thing my two teachers did surprised me. They told me they weren't happy, but they weren't angry either. They were proud of me for telling them, even though they were shocked and surprised I'd been cheating for an entire year. But they also said I wasn't giving myself enough credit—they didn't believe I could've gone a whole year without doing any of the work myself.

Again, they were right. It turned out that as I had been looking at the other kids' papers, I had been learning.

Mrs. Burnum and Mrs. O'Conner ended up holding a conference with my parents about the whole matter. After the conference the teachers started helping me a little bit more and I ended up catching up on things quickly. I only cheated one time after that and I got caught. But that time it wasn't because I didn't understand; it was because I didn't finish my science review the night before. The teacher told Mrs. Burnum and I got detention for it, but I learned my lesson and I haven't done it since.

I am still in sixth grade and still learning and preparing for the TAKS test coming up, but now I do my own work and I no longer have wandering eyes. I am happy I confessed, otherwise my life would still be miserable. Sometimes when I get home my mom will ask me, "Haven't done any cheating today, have we?" And I will always reply, "Mom, you know the answer." Whenever I hear teachers talk about kids who cheat, I am proud to no longer be one of those kids. The decision to tell my teachers and my family the truth was difficult and frightening, but ultimately it was the right thing to do.

~Elizabeth M.

27

Found

*You can easily judge the character of a man
by how he treats those who can do nothing for him.*

~James D. Miles

I've spent the last seven years teaching seventh grade. Just between the ages of twelve and thirteen, my students crash land into the most wonderfully awful age—not kids anymore but not teenagers either. They're constantly tested by one puzzling question on a repeating loop: "Who are we?" No one exemplifies this more than a student I had four years ago....

"Class, please welcome David. He's new to our school." The class silently scanned him, trying to decide if he was worth more of their attention.

Paralyzed by fear, David looked down at his shoes, letting his straight brown hair fall in front of one eye. In an attempt to calm his nerves, he reached into his jeans pocket and clenched two smooth pebbles he had found outside on the blacktop that morning.

The one benefit to being the new kid is no matter where you come from, no matter what your past, you get a chance to start over—a clean slate.

"Mrs. Solej, he can sit over here," Dante said firmly. Dante and his buddies had made a claim on him already. All the girls whispered and straightened up in their seats as they looked in their direction. These boys, wearing their basketball championship jackets, were among the most admired. Dante had just handed David a winning lottery ticket and the prize: instant popularity.

As each forty-two-minute period went by, David had gotten more confident that life here was going to be different. No one here knew what he had gone through at his last school, but at the same time, he didn't fully realize what he was getting himself into here.

"Dave, meet us after practice," Dante called out when the bell rang. And he did. An hour and fifteen minutes later the boys were shooting hoops in the driveway of one of the players. "Did you see that scrawny kid on the bench?" Dante asked David. "That's Tim. He's such a freak. He didn't make the team, but he still comes to all the practices and just sits there. It's pathetic."

"And he tries to talk to us as if he knows us," added one of the others. "We laugh in his face and he just doesn't get it. He keeps coming back around." David missed the basket but kept moving. He said nothing.

"Yeah, someone needs to put him in his place." They all laughed.

The next couple of weeks were eye-opening for David. Being suddenly popular definitely had its advantages. He had the attention of girls, and friends to hang out with after school, which made him overlook how mean some of his new friends could be. As they walked down the hall, the guys on the basketball team would knock the books right out of some poor kid's hands, start humiliating rumors, threaten the smart kids to let them cheat, and draw disgusting pictures of the teachers. David didn't know how long he could get away with just following along instead of participating in the mean actions.

At 8:15, just before the morning bell rang, Dante caught David's arm and whispered, "Follow me." He led him down the cold cement steps to the boys' locker room. The whole team was there standing in a circle. David stood on his toes in back of the crowd to see what was going on. He saw Tim on the ground crying. "You fool, get up!" one of them taunted. He didn't move.

Someone from the back shouted, "Go!" and the next horrifying moments were a blur. The new corduroy pants and striped shirt that

Tim's mom bought for him were being stuffed in the toilet, his books and the contents of his lunch bag were flying through the air, the guys ran around turning all the showers on full blast, and Dante showed up with a large mesh gym bag used to hold the sports equipment.

"Get him in there!" Dante commanded, and the others followed. They knotted the strings at the top of the mesh bag with Tim trapped inside and tossed him in the shower stall. Shivering beneath the forceful stream of ice-cold water, Tim lowered his head and hugged his knees.

As the boys laughed, David looked around for help. They had gone too far this time. He noticed a button on the wall that the teachers use to contact the office. He wondered if he should push it.

David hesitated and thought to himself, *I don't want to go back... to how it used to be. Made fun of. Lonely. Tortured. Not good enough...* Suddenly David's mind reeled, and he was back at his old school. He recalled the day his mom had to pick him up at the office after the incident....

Shaking his head back into focus in the locker room, David slowly raised his hand toward the button, fully conscious of all that he was about to lose if anyone saw him, but it was something he had to do. "Yes, may I help you?" the secretary's voice echoed through the intercom into the damp underground chamber.

In a sea of chaos, the other boys bolted in every direction to avoid capture. All except Dante. He stood there, glaring at David and then at the button, rage shooting from his eyes. "You're not the kid I thought you were. You're going to regret this," Dante threatened as he ran off, too.

David turned his back to Tim, knowing there was nothing more he could do. He turned his back, realizing that he had just lost everything. He turned his back, letting Tim have one moment without anyone staring at him.

Tim rubbed his hands together, raw and blistered from unknotting the mesh that had imprisoned him. He moved in slow motion as his skinny bare legs carried him across the cold cement floor. His head hung low as he noticed yet one more offense: they had gone so far as to use the toilet after his clothes had been cruelly stuffed into it.

Knowing the room would be filled with adults in a matter of minutes, Tim reached down, retrieving his soaked shirt. His beige corduroy pants were as heavy as his heart. As he slipped each leg in, he held his breath, trying to ignore the stench of ammonia. His drenched sleeves clung tight to his clammy skin. He just stood there with arms and legs slightly apart trying not to feel, barefoot, dripping with humiliation. David, his back still turned, whispered something inaudible.

The next day, David walked through the halls hearing chatter of the incident and how sixteen of the most popular boys got suspended, but no one spoke to him directly. Some kids were scared of him; others were disgusted. It was like a giant black cloud had followed him around from that moment on. It was hard to believe that with 108 kids in his class, he was so alone... again.

I often wonder about David and others like him who were made to feel like they were nothing. But in my experience, it is those kids who grow up to be responsible, successful, happy, kind adults. It is my hope that sooner rather than later, they awake to realize what they thought was white is black, and black is now white—that what's popular isn't always right, that doing what is right is sometimes difficult and doesn't always bring immediate reward, and that loneliness doesn't have to last forever.

~Erin Solej

Chapter
4

Just for
Preteens

Crushed

Love puts the fun in together, the sad in apart, and the joy in a heart.

~Author Unknown

Heartbreaker

First love is only a little foolishness and a lot of curiosity.
~George Bernard Shaw

I met Brett when I was in third grade and he was in fourth. Our parents were friends (thank God for that!) and we often doubled up and vacationed together. We went to the same small private school year after year together and I could honestly say I don't think he ever noticed me. Looking back, I completely understand why. I was tall, skinny and dorky. He was tan and muscular. I understand why he didn't want to be with me. Pretty girls always get the hot guys; it's just a rule of nature.

Sometimes when my mother forgot to pick me up from middle school, she called her friend Margie (Brett's mom) to pick me up instead. I always loved this because I thought it gave me a chance to flirt with Brett. I would sit in the car, legs crossed and silent, waiting for him to ask me a question or talk to me. Silence. Always. No matter what I asked him he'd always respond with "Uh-huh" or "Yeah." Just once I wanted him to be enthusiastic about talking to me. I didn't understand. I was throwing myself at him and he didn't even see the signs!

"Don't waste your time on boys at your age, especially ones like Brett. He's a real heartbreaker," my mom always said, but I never listened. Every time I knew I'd see him I split my hair up into two pigtails because I thought it looked cute and it would make him notice me. But, yet again, he couldn't care less. My obsession with him continued all the way to the end of my seventh grade year, his last year at my junior high. I knew I had to make a move, so I built up enough courage to tell him that I had liked him for the previous four years.

My mother took me to the beauty store where I bought a flat iron, make-up, and nail polish. I tried to straighten my hair and make myself look prettier but yet again he didn't notice. So one time, while on vacation at the beach, I just came out and said it: "Listen, I know you don't know this but I really like you, Brett." Every hope I had in the world hung on this statement, because this is when I thought he'd admit the feelings were mutual. I fantasized he would tell me he loved me and grab me with his strong arms and lay a passionate kiss on me. No, none of that happened. Instead, he broke out in laughter and told all his friends. I was humiliated. I felt pretty miserable and worthless.

For months after that I just tried to ignore him but that seemed impossible. He was always in the hallway with his friends, mocking me or making kiss faces and winking at me. It was so embarrassing and every time I looked at him I thought about the way he looked so repulsed when I told him I liked him. Was I that ugly? I didn't understand. I did everything I could to look like what I thought was his type of girl and he just rejected me flat out.

Middle school came to an end and I was lucky I hadn't been cursed with having to share another humiliating vacation with Brett. But just before school ended our families decided to throw one last, big trip. We all rented one large condo and shared rooms. No matter what, I was stuck seeing him every day. At first, the trip was admittedly awkward. No one seemed to be having fun and I couldn't wait to go home so it could all be over.

To my surprise, one day he confronted me.

"Listen Carley," he started, "I really like you and I just don't understand why you haven't been talking to me or even noticing me."

Was he kidding? I was trying to avoid him only because I knew he probably couldn't stand me, and because I had been so humiliated. Instantly I was filled with happiness.

"You like me? But, I thought you didn't," I said.

He explained, "I didn't like you when you acted like you were obsessed with me, but now that you've shown me who you really are, I like it. I like you."

At that moment he leaned in, grabbed my back, and kissed me. It was one of the happiest and most confusing moments of my life. I didn't know what to feel, but I knew that his kiss felt good.

After I recovered from the shock and confusion of that day, I learned a very valuable lesson. Being a young girl is tough. We change so much during our preteen years, it's hard to keep track of feelings and emotions. Looking back, I agree with my mom; I shouldn't have cared so much about boys. Whether he liked me or not, Brett was a heartbreaker, and I was the naïve girl who tried to change who I was to make him happy. In the end, it was being myself that really got his attention—no matter how confusing that attention was.

~Carley Jackson

In Nick's Arms

The best way to mend a broken heart is time and girlfriends.
~Gwyneth Paltrow

For two years, I was in love with an older boy. Nick was fourteen, two years older than me. Tall, with curly brown hair and dark brown eyes, I thought he was perfect.

Too bad he acted as if I didn't exist.

That wasn't easy since there were only about a dozen senior boys at summer camp and fifteen senior girls. When Nick wasn't playing sports with the other boys, he was reading or playing chess. I didn't mind as much when I was only eleven, but the summer I turned twelve I decided he was going to take me to the end-of-camp dance.

Since we spent so much time on the beach, I made sure my bathing suit flattered me. My white and turquoise bikini, with its rows of white ruffles across the chest, gave me the illusion of a bigger chest. The other girls in my bunk said it made me look very mature.

Nick never noticed. I consoled myself with the notion that he ignored all the girls. At least I didn't have any rivals.

At night, I would whisper to my best friend, Patricia, who had the bed next to mine. "What can I do to get him to notice me?"

"I don't know why you bother," she'd say. "I don't think he's that great."

I'd sigh. "But he's so smart and cute."

"And stuck up," she'd add.

It didn't matter what Patricia said, my heart was set on going to the dance with Nick.

By the end of the first month at camp, several couples had formed—Shelley and Sammy, Ashley and Mike, Gail and David. Nick remained alone, as did I. That only left me one month.

I borrowed a book on chess from one of the counselors, determined to show Nick we had something in common. After the first few pages my eyes glazed over and all the words ran together. Okay, so I wasn't going to learn chess.

Less than a week before the end of camp, Patricia bounded into the bunk just before lights out. She hurried into bed and then tapped me on the shoulder. "You'll never guess what happened," she whispered. Without waiting for me to guess, she continued. "Nick asked me to the dance."

"But..." I started to say.

She didn't give me a chance to finish my sentence. Although she chattered non-stop for another ten minutes, I don't know what she said. My brain couldn't take in anything after "Nick asked me to the dance."

When her voice finally stopped, I turned my face into the pillow and grabbed a corner between my teeth to stop myself from crying out, "But you knew I loved him." She knew. She just didn't care. In that moment, I lost both my best friend and Nick. I let the tears slip down my cheek and dampen the pillow.

The last four days of camp were busy as we divided into three teams for Color War. I was co-captain of the blue team with Sammy. Patricia was co-captain of the red team and Nick of the green team. It was easy to stay away from both of them.

Between athletic events, making posters, and coming up with a team song and skit, I had no time to feel sorry for myself during the day. The nights were different. My pillow held my tears and my heart felt as if it were broken into a million pieces.

On the last day of Color War, Sammy and I were in the arts and crafts building, putting the finishing touches on a backdrop for our skit. As co-captains, we spent a lot of time together. One of the quietest of the senior boys, I discovered he had a good sense of humor. We'd often kid each other. I also liked the way he treated everyone with courtesy.

"So, what do you think?" I said, pointing to the finished project.

"I think you're really nice," he said.

I swiveled towards him. "Oh," I said.

"I'd like to invite you to the dance."

My mouth dropped open. "But..." I stopped to think. I really liked Sammy. In working with him, I had begun to realize how much nicer he was than Nick. But he and Shelley had been going out for a month. Even if he hadn't actually asked her to the dance, she would have assumed they were going together. We all did.

I was tempted. I had brought a new dress to camp that summer, hoping I would wear it when dancing in Nick's arms. It was easy to substitute Sammy's face and arms for Nick's.

Then I thought about Patricia and Nick. Did I really want to do to Shelley what Patricia had done to me? "I'd like to but can't," I said. "It wouldn't be fair to Shelley."

Sammy nodded. "You're right. I shouldn't have asked you. I guess I just wanted you to know that I like you."

We finished cleaning up and then went to our bunks to get ready for that night's performance. Hours later, when our team was declared the winner of that year's Color War, Sammy and I hugged. For an instant, I regretted turning down his invitation.

The next night the girls going to the dance spent the afternoon doing their hair. About half an hour before the dance began, they started putting on their dresses. I sat on my bed, a book in my lap, but not reading. A loud cry caught my attention.

Patricia stood in front of the bunk's only mirror, trying to pull her dress over her body. Unfortunately, after two months of camp food, there was too much body and not enough dress.

A minute later, Patricia was at my bed. "Harriet, since you're not going to the dance, can I try on your dress?"

First Nick and now my dress. I almost said no. Then I realized I didn't want to be in Nick's arms. Suddenly the dress, and Nick, didn't seem quite that important. "Yeah, sure," I said, though not very graciously.

Patricia ignored my tone and ran over to my cubby. After wriggling out of her dress, she pulled mine over her head. It fit. She even filled it out better than I had.

Late that night after the dance, I felt her standing next to my bed but I kept my face to the wall, pretending to be asleep. I might not have been in love with Nick anymore, but I didn't need or want to hear about Patricia's evening.

The next morning I found my dress crumpled up in my cubby, a stain on the front. I stuffed it into my suitcase with the rest of my clothes.

I never spoke to Patricia again or wore that dress, even though the dry cleaners removed the stain. My decision not to go to the dance cost me a lot of tears and a new dress, but I knew I had done the right thing in not making Shelley suffer the way I had. And I was rewarded, when my next boyfriend was a lot more like Sammy than Nick—and my next best friend was a true friend.

~Harriet Cooper

My Online Crush

A lie may take care of the present, but it has no future.
~Author Unknown

I had never actually seen a picture of Austin James. All I knew about him I learned from his profile information and my friend Whitney.

Whitney had gone on a cruise over spring break. We got together after she returned and she told me she had met a boy while on the cruise. My group of friends had a code: no dating until high school. I had broken the rule once, not only dating, but having my first kiss. When my friends found out, I had to break it off. But Whitney? How could she have a boyfriend?

Ironically, two days after the cruise, Austin got an online profile on a chat website. Whitney set us up to be friends and so we were. The two of us talked every day. He didn't have a profile picture, but he had plenty of information in his profile description. I knew he had brown hair and blue eyes, he was captain of his football team and the lead guitar player in his band, as well as taking drum lessons. Austin was perfect.

I began to develop a little crush on him. I had my own idea of what he looked like. He told me every day that he thought Whitney was "so pretty," and I thought I was prettier than Whitney. I hoped Austin would realize this and begin to like me instead. It was rude to Whitney, I knew, but it was so unfair. This guy was perfect.

The next time we talked, I insisted we talk about him instead of Whitney. But he still wanted to talk about her, and said he had something to tell me. This had to be good.

"Did Whitney ever tell you I kissed her?" he typed the words and I read them in horror. Whitney had been kissed? I had to tell someone.

So I told my mom. She wanted to see who this Austin James was. I said he didn't have a profile picture. She then said I couldn't have any online friends I didn't know in person, especially if they didn't have a profile picture. No. No. No! I wouldn't let that happen. I blew up and started telling her that Whitney knew him. I was careful, and I never even talked about myself.

Then, something clicked for both me and my mom. Whitney was Austin James.

It made so much sense, I felt like an idiot for not catching it sooner. Whitney would never have a boyfriend or let him kiss her. She was much too shy. The two were never online at the same time and though I never did talk about myself, he seemed to know a lot about me. He was also just too perfect. Football, guitar, drums — all at thirteen. No way, Austin was too perfect.

That night, I didn't go online at my usual time to talk to Austin. Whitney texted me, asking me to get on the computer because Austin was waiting to talk to me. I texted back that I would no longer be talking to Austin, because my mom wouldn't let me. As bad as I wanted to, I didn't call her out on her lie.

At school I refused to participate in any conversation involving Austin James. Whitney had already gotten a lot of attention from her made up boyfriend, and I wasn't going to give her more. No one seemed to remember that I had dated and been kissed first. My friends had all been mad at me when they found out about my boyfriend, but they didn't say anything about Whitney's boyfriend. Some friends.

Either way, I had had a crush on a made up person — the idea of a dream boy. Though I never called Whitney out on the lie, I am sure she knew I had figured out who "Austin" was, because he didn't talk to me or get online to chat anymore. The end of the school year was the last I saw of both of them: Austin and Whitney.

~Kyra Payne

Chicken Soup for the Soul

Beauty Is as Beauty Does

Remember that the most beautiful things in the world are the most useless;
peacocks and lilies for instance.
~John Ruskin

I had just turned twelve when I realized I wasn't young enough to be a carefree kid anymore but also not old enough to be a "cool" teenager. I was also unlucky enough to be a twelve-year-old with thick glasses and orthodontic braces. In spite of the "four eyes" and "metal mouth" name-calling I had to endure, my mother insisted these temporary impediments would all be worth it someday. She reminded me of Hans Christian Anderson's story, *The Ugly Duckling*, to make her point. However, back then, even imagining straight teeth and contact lenses in my future wasn't enough to convince me I would ever turn into a beautiful swan, especially since I had the additional drawbacks of being overly tall for my age and twig thin to boot.

My misery was especially amplified every Friday at Walgrove Elementary School, which was coed day in my gym class. That was the one day of the week when the boys and girls had combined physical education classes. Most of the time that meant girls playing foursquare or dodge ball with the boys, which was bad enough since I wasn't particularly adept at either game. However, the worst activity for me was the Friday coed dance class that rolled around about every third week. On those days, we would march single file into the gymnasium and the girls would line up against one wall with the boys facing us from the other side. Most of the time, the teacher put dance partners together but occasionally she let the boys choose their own. Needless to say, I was usually one of the last to be chosen and almost always ended up with a freckle-faced red-headed kid named Pete who was having his own rejection problems.

Of course, as in every grade school there are those kids who never seem to go through any awkward stages—the popular kids—who everyone else envies. In our coed dance class, those lucky ones were Veronica and Robbie. Veronica was blond and pretty with a bubbly personality; Robbie was a developing athlete with a friendly grin and dark curly hair. When it came time to choose partners, they always picked each other and it was understood by the rest of us that they always would. After all, they were a perfect match and obviously belonged together. Since I, like many other girls, had a serious crush on Robbie, I often wondered what it would feel like to be Veronica—one of the beautiful people, one of the chosen ones. The day came when I received a small taste of that feeling.

It happened during one of those dreaded Friday dance classes. Once again the teacher suggested the boys choose their own partners. As I waited, leaning up against the wall with the other girls, I noticed Pete wasn't in the boys' line across the way. Then I watched anxiously as one by one the other girls were chosen until I was the only one left. No boys remained to choose me even if they had wanted to. As I stood by myself, enduring the looks of pity, my lips trembling, tears ready to fall, Robbie suddenly walked over to me and took my hand. "I'll dance with you," he said. Maybe not the most endearing words, but good enough for me. I glanced over at Veronica in surprise but she just smiled and waved as she stood alone while Robbie led me out onto the gym floor to where the others were waiting.

Soon after that incident, I graduated from sixth grade and there were no more P.E. dances to contend with. I transferred to another junior high school and lost track of Veronica and Robbie for good. I don't know if they ended up together or not. However, I never forgot the two of them and the kindness they showed me that day.

Years later, when my straight body turned curvy and my tallness became an asset, I, with my contact lenses and Crest toothpaste smile, became the swan my mother had predicted I would. While I enjoyed my new popularity and more desirable appearance, I found they didn't bring me the happiness and satisfaction I had expected. I think that's when I realized that Veronica and Robbie had given me so much more than kindness that day. They had given me the truth—that beauty on the outside isn't nearly as important as the beauty that comes from within.

~Christine Stapp

How Not to Impress a Boy

Be kind, for everyone you meet is fighting a hard battle.

~Plato

The seat by the big, front window at Mayhew's, an old-fashioned ice cream shop, was where everybody who was anybody in the sixth grade at Boyd Middle School wanted to be. My friend Anna and I liked the front because you could see everybody who strolled by. That way, if a boy you liked came up the sidewalk, you'd have time to take a deep breath and think about what to say if he came inside.

Anna and I were sitting in front of the window one spring day when her eyes got big and she said, "Don't look now, but Allen Keyes just walked by! Invite him in, Ruthie."

Anna had had a crush on Allen since he'd moved to town right after Christmas that year. To tell the truth, Allen was really cute, and he was in the seventh grade, so that made him even cooler. His family went to our church and his mom sang in the choir with my mom. That's how I knew him.

Anyway, Anna knocked on the window and waved to Allen. He looked up and squinted at her and then smiled when he saw me waving, too. His smile made my heart beat faster too. I could see why Anna liked him.

"Come inside," I mouthed, and was kind of surprised when he nodded and walked through the door.

"Hi Allen," Anna drawled. He didn't even know her name, and she was acting like she'd known him since first grade.

"Hi Ruthie. Hi, umm..." He looked at me for help.

"This is Anna," I said. "She's been to church with us a few times, but I don't think you've ever met."

"Want to sit with us?" Anna asked, and he did.

I scooted over so my back was to the window.

Allen looked around. "This is a cool place. I've never been in here before."

"Oh everybody hangs out here," Anna said.

She was gushing a lot and getting on my nerves, and I swear she actually batted her eyes at Allen. She was my best friend, but sometimes, especially when it came to boys, she was clueless.

"Do I order at the counter or does someone come over?" Allen asked.

That's what I liked about Allen. He wasn't afraid to ask the questions that some people might feel like a dork asking. He just seemed to have more confidence than any of the boys I knew.

"You can order at the counter," Anna said, smiling and batting her eyes (again).

I watched Allen walk to the counter and whispered, "Quit acting like that or he's going to think you're an idiot."

She looked at me blankly for a second and then her eyes got big and she said, "Oh. My. Gosh."

"What?" I asked. "Do I have something in my nose?"

"No," Anna replied, rolling her eyes. "But look behind you. There's the strangest looking woman over at the Taylors' yard. She just now walked up the sidewalk with a lawn mower and... look at her, Ruthie. I mean, who in the world would mow the grass dressed like that?"

The woman looked fat and matronly, but she wasn't that old. Her dark hair was pulled back in a long ponytail, and she had tucked a pink azalea blossom behind one ear. She wore a red T-shirt about two sizes too big for her and a full, denim skirt that stopped right above her lavender socks and black high-tops. Before I could say anything, though, Allen was back, taking a bite of ice cream as he sat down.

"How is it?" I asked.

"Great," he replied. "It's my favorite."

"Well you get dinner and a show today," Anna said. "Ice cream for dinner and that," she nodded out the window toward the lawn lady, "is your show. Have you ever seen anybody so weird?" She laughed like she had just said the funniest thing in the world. "I mean, where has she been shopping? At every garage sale in town?"

Allen scooped up the last bite of his ice cream and looked out the window toward the woman mowing the grass. "She's a live one," he said, raising his eyebrows a couple of times. Then he smiled and stood up. "Wish I could stay longer, but I was on the way to help my sister with a project and now I'm late."

"I didn't know you had a sister," I said. "I've never seen her at church."

Allen smiled again, and I felt my stomach do a somersault. He was really, really cute.

"She lived in Florida but she's had some problems and just moved here. Now she's getting settled into an apartment and trying to start her own business, so I told her I'd help her out this afternoon."

I thought he might be kidding, but then I realized he wasn't. Allen was just too sincere to kid about something like that. And I could picture him helping his sister unpack boxes and put things away.

"I wish you didn't have to go," Anna said with a sigh.

"Hate to be late," he said. "Bye Ruthie. See you around." He waved at Anna and walked out the door.

"He is so fine! And I'll bet there's a really interesting story about his sister, don't you?" Anna asked.

I shrugged my shoulders. "I doubt it," I said, watching Allen as he held the door for two little girls coming into the shop. "They're a nice family. She might even be as cute as Allen."

"You're probably right," Anna answered. She glanced over my shoulder and her eyes got big again. "Oh. My. Gosh."

"What?" I was tired of her dramatics, but I turned just in time to see Allen talking to the lawn lady as he tied a bandanna around his head. And then he hugged her, kissed her cheek, and started pushing the mower up and down the Taylors' yard, helping his sister out with her new business. Just like he'd said.

~Ruth Jones

Chicken Soup for the Soul

Countdown to a Kiss

A kiss seals two souls for a moment in time.
~Levende Waters

"**S**o, who's it going to be?" Julie inquired. Everything was different this summer now that we were the oldest juniors in our summer camp. We were nicknamed "OOTH" which stood for "Oldest On The Hill." The hill was where all the junior girls lived, and finally we got to live in the biggest bunks at the bottom. A lot of the girls in the age group had already gotten kisses from boys, and Julie, my counselor, wanted to know who I had my eye on. It was like having a big sister at camp, since she was nineteen and I was only twelve. We made the perfect pair.

"I'm not sure," I confessed, "although..." There was one guy that I could see myself getting closer with. The only thing holding me back was that I was terrible at talking to boys, and usually got scared or tongue-tied around them. The last thing I wanted to do was say something stupid in front of yet another boy.

"Although what?" I had done it—caught Julie's attention. That was the other reason why she was just like my big sister; annoying her was my favorite pastime.

"Nothing... it's nothing important..." I teased. But, of course, she wore me down like a pro. After several minutes of talking in hushed whispers Julie convinced me to talk to Chris.

"I don't think I can, Julie. I'm no good with boys," I confessed.

"It's easy. During free play just ask him about whatever he's doing."

I followed her advice, not that I had a choice anymore. Any gossip spreads like wildfire through the girls' camp and soon I had a whole throng of supporters practically tailing me to make sure that I didn't chicken out.

I didn't.

"Hi," I said, walking up beside him. I was so surprised that my voice wasn't shaky. My breath was steady too, and you could probably be fooled into believing that I had confidence. I didn't, but he didn't have to know that. I was fine so far, and didn't want to mess up.

"I'm Rachel," I said.

"Chris," he said, giving me a smile. I returned it with a weak smile, thrilled that this was working so well.

For the next couple of days we continued to have conversations, and he (attempted) to teach my uncoordinated self how to use a Chinese yo-yo. His patience amazed me, and I realized I loved him, even if it was only for the two weeks before he had to go home.

In the days that followed our conversations grew longer, our topics differed, and we began to look more into each other's eyes. I had a feeling we were both thinking the same thing: almost every girl and guy pair that talked at camp ended up kissing. Would we be next?

Our question was answered soon after. Apparently, our friends believed we were taking the whole thing a bit too slowly. That night they practically pushed us into each other, hoping that they were giving us a sign. It only made me embarrassed and hurt. I ran away in tears, but somehow Chris found me within minutes and brought me out of my hiding place.

"They're jerks for doing something stupid like that," he told me.

"Yeah, what right do they have to make decisions for other people? All of them should just go get a life or find some other people to annoy," I said, bitterly. Being next to Chris wasn't a foreign or nerve-racking thing anymore. I felt at ease with him now.

"Come with me," he said. "I want to talk to you."

Suddenly, all my ease melted away and I was jittery. What did he want to ask me? My heart was racing. What did he want to say?

We walked all the way to the baseball diamond. It was late at night and the moon was full. It seemed to be spotlighting the pitcher's mound: the exact place where Chris stopped walking.

He looked at me, and said, "Rachel, do you want to go out with me?"

"Of course!" I said, throwing my arms around him. It felt good, like my arms belonged there.

Two days passed and blurred together. It was nearing the end of his stay at camp, and soon he would have to go back home. Living several states away from where I did, it would be next to impossible to see him before the reunion in six months. We hadn't kissed yet, and our window of opportunity was getting smaller and smaller. In fact, we hadn't even decided if we wanted to kiss in the first place.

But the "general public" had another idea. Mobs and mobs of both boys and girls followed us everywhere we went, telling us to kiss or asking us about how much we liked each other. It was madness and I was starting to realize why celebrities hated paparazzi so much. Finally we got away and hid behind the hockey rink at the back of the camp.

"Would it kill them to leave us alone?" I asked, annoyed and out of breath from running.

"I bet it would, but a person's got to wonder why they follow us all the time," Chris told me; he seemed out of breath as well.

"I think they'd die of boredom. After all, they're so boring that they need us for entertainment." I laughed at my own joke, and I saw Chris chuckle. I could tell we were both happy just to be alone.

A couple moments of silence passed between us. We were trying to be as quiet as possible so we wouldn't be discovered.

"It's just so funny, everyone chasing us and everything," he said.

"I bet I know why they're doing it," I said after a couple of minutes.

"Why?"

"Because they think we're going to kiss."

Another minute of silence passed between us. He seemed to be very calm, as was I on the outside. But on the inside I was anxious and excited. I did want to kiss him. After thinking for several minutes, I finally selected the right words to say, and though I was confident, talking seemed like a challenge.

"Well, would you, if they didn't find us?"

"Would I what?"

"Kiss me?"

Another second of silence followed, but then everything happened at once. Almost like we were reading each other's minds we turned to face each other. Then, slowly, he leaned in and kissed me.

The moment was magical, and time seemed to stop. It was like everything fell into place that day, and the world was perfect.

Three days before he left, he gave me a little note, telling me how he was happy that I wanted to go out with him, and that I was the first girl he had ever wanted to be his girlfriend. Now that I think about it, he was truly the perfect boy to be my first boyfriend. He was smart, sensitive, and an all around great person, and that was why I loved him.

~Rachel Davison

My First Crush

No, there's nothing half so sweet in life as love's young dream.
~Thomas Moore

The summer I was twelve, I vacationed at my Aunt Alice's farm, an hour's drive from home. Her house boasted a grand porch with comfortable wooden rocking chairs and an unspoiled view of the surrounding farms. I remember the air, so pure and country fresh, and Rex, her reliable rooster, crowing at the crack of dawn. A small but inviting apple orchard always beckoned me to zigzag in and out of its orderly rows.

On Sunday morning, I collected eggs from the freshly white-washed henhouse. As I set the basket on the sideboard, Aunt Alice asked, "Could you pick some green beans and summer squash after breakfast? They're for my vegetable casserole. We're invited to the Lindsays' next door for Sunday dinner."

"I'd be happy to." Thinking about all her country fare, fresh from vines, plants and trees that tasted so much better than city offerings, I donned a wide-brimmed straw hat and headed for the garden. The soft breeze offered relief from summer's intense heat. I snapped the green beans easily and cut the sun-yellow squash from its thickening vine. A luscious tomato, heavy with its juicy meat, needed rescue before it rested on the ground. Aunt Alice's grand flower garden, a kaleidoscope of bright color, was a stone's throw away. Three long-stemmed gladiolas caught my eye. They would be perfect for the dining room table. I made a mental note to wear gloves after encountering two snakes slithering half concealed in the dirt.

Early that afternoon we arrived at the Lindsays' farm to a warm reception. I was introduced to the family and quickly took note of a boy about my age and height, freshly scrubbed and lanky, with budding biceps and a hint of an Adam's apple. A strand of light brown hair casually hugged his forehead. He had deep blue, widely set eyes hooded with long, curly lashes. His voice was velvety like a fine-tuned cello. The corners of his mouth curled up like a sliver of moon when he smiled. His name was Vincent. He was confident and comfortable. I was shy and smitten.

After dinner, Vincent, blushing, asked, "Would you like to see our farm?" I smiled and he reached for my chair. "We have a new litter of puppies."

I thanked his mom for the delicious meal as we left the room to tour the outbuildings. He showed me the animals he fed, groomed and loved, talking enthusiastically about the workings of the family farm as we passed precious pups back and forth. I hoped he didn't notice me hanging on his every word. The afternoon passed too quickly. Animals always dictated their keeper's schedules. My aunt called out, ending our visit for the evening.

Vincent visited my aunt's farm often, but only after he delivered papers and completed morning chores. I daydreamed in the rocking chair on the porch, reflecting on the stirrings in my heart, waiting for him ride up the driveway on his bike. When he did, we'd walk through the orchard and the flower gardens, then through the pasture, usually deep in conversation. We shared our interests, compared city to country life and discussed our families and school experiences. I loved listening to his stories. Occasionally Vincent brushed my arm or grabbed my elbow to direct me away from a gopher hole or cow pie.

Such was my introduction to puppy love. I was impressed with his unassuming presence and his attitude. Vincent was focused. He possessed a strong sense of himself. I felt safe. His visits were too short as his chores were always waiting.

On the last day of my vacation, Vincent handed me a wallet-size picture of himself. "I'm looking forward to seeing you next summer,

Colette." His eyes caught mine in a lingering, fond farewell. He gently took my hand in both of his, squeezing tenderly. He turned around, picked up his bike and pedaled down the gravel driveway.

I thought about Vincent often. I shared his picture with my best friend, but kept it in my nightstand away from my twin brother's teasing eyes, and counted the days till next summer. School and good grades were important, since ninth grade was only a year away.

Summer finally arrived. I was eager to see Vincent again. We'd take long walks and catch up on our lives. Then maybe... possibly... hopefully... eventually... we'd experience our first kiss.

Aunt Alice welcomed me with a big hug and her home-baked cookies. We sat at her kitchen table and chatted easily about family and school. She seemed preoccupied. I asked about the Lindsays. There was an immediate change in her demeanor. She took my hand and took a deep, steadying breath. She looked directly into my eyes and spoke quietly, carefully measuring her words. "The Lindsay family is very sad these days. Vincent was delivering newspapers on Van Dyke, close to home. There was a horrible accident. A car hit him. He died—instantly. I'm so sorry dear." She stood up and gathered me in a heartfelt hug.

Shock rushed in. Thank goodness. I responded with a barely audible one-syllable noise like air leaking from a tire. My brain fuzzed up, my heart imploded and my eyes brimmed wet. I stood, looked away and staggered to the guest room, burying my head in a pillow to muffle my wrenching sobs. It took a while to wrap my mind around Aunt Alice's words.

I half-heartedly walked myself through life's everyday motions, managed some chores and rocked aimlessly on the porch, where I replayed pieces of my conversations with Vincent.

At the end of the day, when the sun slipped over the horizon, I lost myself in the colors that splashed across the sky. I knew he was there. Over time, the pain of losing my dear friend Vincent became easier to bear. But that year, I learned about loss and how precious life is.

~Colette Sasina

Hard Truth

We are so accustomed to disguising ourselves to others that in the end we become disguised to ourselves.
~François Duc de La Rochefoucauld

I picked through the jumble in my locker. Only a few students clustered in the hall. The class bell was about to ring. Where was that science book?

"C'mon," I said. My heart was beginning to beat a little fast when I saw the blue binding at the bottom of a pile of books. I tugged hard. The book slid from the stack. I pushed it under my arm, slammed my locker door, and bolted down the hall to Mr. Countryman's room.

As I walked through the door, my heart beat a little harder still. My eyes scanned the room. Our sixth grade classroom had short brown tables and cream-colored plastic chairs. Two kids per table. And the seats were assigned.

I cleared my throat and trudged toward my table. My tablemate was already there, twisted backwards in his seat, visiting with someone at the table behind him. His thick blond hair hung over the collar of his sweatshirt. I felt that I could melt into a puddle, just being so close.

The bell rang as I reached my seat. I dropped my books to the tabletop and created a sharp "Slam!" Scott turned in his chair and flashed a smile. There he was. Golden boy of the junior high school. Handsome. Athletic. Strong. And nice.

"Tough morning?" he asked.

I plunked into my seat and conjured my best growly voice. "Stupid science. It smells like frogs in here. I just hate science."

Scott produced a sad, crooked smile. I set my jaw and flipped my book open as Mr. Countryman made his way to the front of the classroom.

Unsettling. That's a good word to describe my first year of junior high school. In our town, three elementary schools, two from town and one from the country, fed into the junior high. I was from the country school. We were a tight group, and it was different to be sprinkled in with the kids from town who all seemed to know one another well. There was a lot of new stuff to keep up with. A cool crowd. Nike athletic shoes. Just the right brand of jeans. Talking the right talk. Then my best friend became best friends with a town girl—one who didn't care for me. I felt overwhelmed and insecure. I masked my uncertainties behind an angry exterior. My new class-mates had no idea I was like Jell-O inside.

Mr. Countryman began to talk about different types of rocks. Several students opened their notebooks, tipped their heads, and scrawled notes. But I was distracted. It was hard sitting at the same table as Scott. I wanted him to like me. I daydreamed about being his girlfriend—another big, new thing that was customary in junior high. I could picture myself in the bleachers watching him rule the basketball court. I'd cheer at all the right times and maybe there'd be pizza at Joe's Pizzeria after the game. Many of my classmates were allowed to walk there after sports events.

A jab on the arm brought me back to reality. A boy from the next table thrust a rock sample in my direction. From the corner of my eye, I saw Scott watching me. I held the crumbly rock with distaste, poked my nose in the air, and passed it to him.

The remaining forty-five minutes of class flew by. Science class always did. I didn't have any other classes with Scott, and I enjoyed every minute of sitting there, though no one would have known that.

When the bell rang to end the period, the science students

screeched their chairs back and bolted out the door. Scott hung back a bit. It appeared that he wanted to talk. I was hopeful and excited. But I was also scared, so I was sure to not smile.

"Shawn?" Scott said. His eyes were so blue.

"What?" I answered a little gruff.

"Well, I just wanted to say something."

I acted annoyed. "Go ahead."

"I think you're a real pretty girl," Scott said. "Nice to look at. It's just too bad you don't act nice, too." Then he pulled his red sweatshirt from the back of his chair, shrugged his shoulders, and walked out.

I stood beside the table for a minute or two. My face felt hot and I knew tears were close. I wanted to yell at the top of my lungs. He was wrong! I was nice! Didn't he know that I was just scared? The answer was no. He didn't see my fear—only my grouchy attitude.

I learned a lot from Scott that day. I wish I could say that the honest, hard truth caused me to do a fast 180. It didn't. In fact, for a while, the words may have made me feel even more insecure with who and where I was. But later, when middle school anxiety melted away and I didn't feel the need to protect myself with a grizzly exterior, I found honesty and kindness in those simple words.

Scott never became my boyfriend. And he never treated me to pizza at Joe's. But he had given me something of value. Though it had been hard to hear, he'd given me the truth.

~Shawnelle Eliasen

The Kindness of Others

When I was young, I admired clever people.
Now that I am old, I admire kind people.

~Abraham Joshua Heschel

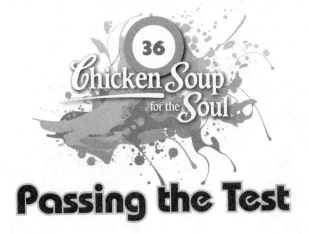

36

Passing the Test

You can teach a student a lesson for a day; but if you can teach him to learn
by creating curiosity, he will continue the learning process as long as he lives.
~Clay P. Bedford

hat happened?" asked Mrs. Sharpnack. I shrugged. Pre-algebra was my last class of the day. Mrs. Sharpnack had asked me to stay after to discuss my mid-term exam. The red marks covering the test said everything. Without even seeing the grade, I knew I had failed. I had felt lost while taking the test, but still I had hoped that by some miracle I had passed. My shoulders slumped as I realized the consequences that would come from this.

My failing score would mean my grades wouldn't be high enough to be on the honor roll that semester. In just a few weeks, the names of the honor roll students would be read during class. Those on the list would be excused to go watch a movie and have treats. I wasn't as upset about missing the party as I was about having to explain to my friends why I wouldn't get to go. My friends always got good grades, and usually, so did I.

"I know you can pass this test," said Mrs. Sharpnack. I didn't respond. "What if I let you take it again? I'll give you a week to study."

I just wanted to go home and forget about the test and never think about math again. "Thanks," I said sadly, "But I'll just take the score I earned." A week, a month, a year—in my mind, it didn't matter. I just wasn't good at this kind of math and no amount of studying was going to change that.

Mrs. Sharpnack had given me an opportunity for a second chance, and I had turned it down. She could have left it at that. But she didn't. Perhaps great teachers just can't be satisfied with students falling short of their potential. "I know you can pass this test," she repeated firmly. She said it with such resolution that it almost felt like a vow. For a brief moment, I wondered if she could be right.

"What time does your bus come?" she asked. I had thirty minutes from the time school let out until my bus came, and I told her so. She asked if I would be willing to use that time to go over the problems I had missed.

"I guess," I replied timidly. We started right then and made plans to meet each day for one week, after which I would take the test again.

After going over a few problems, my friends, Valerie, Madena, and Charity, came looking for me. We always wandered the halls and just hung out while we waited for our bus. They stuck their heads in the doorway and when they saw me, they walked in.

"There you are," said Madena. "We've been looking everywhere for you."

"What are you doing?" asked Valerie.

I could feel my cheeks redden as I prepared to tell my friends why I was there. But, before I could say anything, Mrs. Sharpnack flipped my test upside-down, hiding its contents. "Amanda is helping me with a special project," she said. And that was all the explanation my friends seemed to need. By then, it was time for our bus to come. I gathered up my things and the four of us left.

For the next week, I stayed after class with Mrs. Sharpnack. She would go over each problem, carefully explaining their solutions. Sometimes I still wouldn't understand, and I would get frustrated. She stayed calm though and would think of a different way to explain it. Inevitably, while working through the problems, my friends would saunter in. Mrs. Sharpnack would pull out some puzzles for them. That kept them busy while we quietly went over my test.

The day designated to take the test again came quickly. I remained after class, as I had all the other days, but this time I sat at my desk alone. Mrs. Sharpnack gave me a new test and let me start working. I was nervous since it was a different test than the one we had gone over. The questions were hard, and I almost handed the test right back to her. But, then I remembered how hard we had worked and how she had told me that she knew I could pass. I settled into answering the questions, trying to remember the examples my teacher had used.

It wasn't long before my friends arrived. They didn't come over to talk to me, but left me to my work. I'll never know if they knew what I was really doing each day after class. If they knew, they never said anything. I heard Mrs. Sharpnack talking with them. She was asking them about their lives and seemed genuinely interested, even though she wasn't even their teacher.

Mrs. Sharpnack graded my test while I waited. She smiled as she recorded my new score, ninety-seven percent. A near perfect score; I had only missed one question.

Things were different after that. Maybe I could do math after all. Maybe it was possible. The day after I took the test, I was surprised to discover Charity, Valerie, and Madena walking into Mrs. Sharpnack's class after school. I had assumed that once I had retaken the test that I wouldn't be spending any more time outside of class there. But my friends had discovered something—a teacher who cared. And so we went to Donna Sharpnack's classroom every day while we waited for our bus. It became our spot. She would talk with us, let us play with her games, and she even helped us with our homework.

Not long after my second chance, Mrs. Sharpnack stood in front of the room and read names from the honor roll list. She turned and smiled at me as she read the last name, "Amanda." I happily met up with my friends and we all walked to the honor roll party together.

That was the only year I had Mrs. Sharpnack for a teacher. She moved on to a new school, but she had given me something far greater than a party with a movie and treats. Somehow, Mrs. Sharpnack made middle school, not just math, a little bit better.

The influence of a good teacher is far-reaching. A good teacher makes you feel like you matter. Good teachers motivate, inspire, and elevate us, and not just for the few moments when we are in their classes, but for our lifetimes.

~Amanda Yardley Luzzader

37

Chicken Soup for the Soul

Solving a Fifth Grade Problem

Never be bullied into silence. Never allow yourself to be made a victim.
Accept no one's definition of your life, but define yourself.
~Harvey S. Firestone

"**H**ey Alena, nice leggings!" Britney yelled from atop the slide. Her voice carried mockingly to where I was swinging. Then, with a burst of laughter, she glided to the sand to join her posse of girls.

Britney Palmer was the elected point person of The Pink Ladies, a group of elite fifth graders to which I desperately wanted to belong.

Shoot. They were all wearing jeans. The Spandex I wore hadn't been in style in five years. Aside from the fact that my mother proudly dressed me in my cousin's hand-me-downs, I was chubby. Thus, I was The Pink Ladies' favorite target.

"I told my mom they are stupid but she made me wear them anyway." My attempt to explain my embarrassing choice of wardrobe just encouraged more laughter. I stared down at my swinging feet.

They joined hands and skipped to the corner of the playground where they plopped down in a circle. I couldn't decide which felt worse, when I was the object of their scorn or when they forgot I existed.

"Okay, so tomorrow we all have to wear pigtails," Britney

addressed the six girls who circled her. "And if you don't, you can't play with us all day. This way, everybody will know who is a Pink Lady and who is not."

The next morning, it was clear what I had to do.

"Mom, can you put my hair in pigtails?" I stood in the dark at the edge of her bed, looking intently at her sleeping face.

"Alena, I'm sleeping. Maybe tomorrow," she muttered.

"But I need them today."

"Then you'll have to do it yourself," she replied, turning over. I left her room in defeat and headed for the bathroom.

I studied my reflection, comb in one hand, two hair ties in the other, trying to see what it was that caused The Pink Ladies to explode in laughter every time I smiled in their direction. I could understand my round face and straggly hair, but why didn't they like my blue eyes or the beauty mark next to my mouth like Cindy Crawford's? I placed one hand on my stomach and the other on the small of my back, making a hasty measurement of my waistline. Would they like me if my hands were closer together?

I had never made pigtails before, and I knew it would be no easy feat. I pulled, pushed, maneuvered, tightened and loosened, but my efforts were fruitless. My pigtails were hopelessly lopsided. After a ten-minute struggle, I had to surrender to my fate and run to the bus stop.

As soon as I entered the classroom that day, I felt the burn of The Pink Ladies' stares on me. If I had been fortunate enough to possess telekinetic powers, I would have willed the hair ties to the floor.

For the first half of the day, despite the many superficial compliments I gave them, they ignored me. Not exactly the reaction I had imagined. I was discouraged, but too proud to relent and untie my hair.

At snack time, I sat in a corner, chewing on peanut butter crackers and bemoaning my situation to my friend Amy, when I noticed Emily Kaplan and Elizabeth Hawkins approaching. Sure that I was about to be reprimanded for my false indication of popularity, I swallowed hard and prepared myself for verbal war.

"We know you are wearing pigtails just because we are, and you aren't allowed to. Pigtails are the way we are wearing our hair today and you aren't one of us," Emily said, propping her hands on her hips and pursing her lips.

I wanted to tackle her to the carpet. It could have made me a legend, exalted at Mill Hill Elementary for my courageous act. I could have formed my own army—The Red Ladies or The Blue Ladies—the strongest social force in the academic district. It would be I who had the power to proclaim the fashion for each week. Every fifth grade girl would beg her mother to take her shopping to purchase Spandex leggings in a variety of colors and fabrics. They would all have to rush to Goodwill since stores stopped carrying leggings three seasons before, but still! That stupid Emily Kaplan would have begged for mercy. That moment had potential for greatness.

At the very least I could have said something to the effect of, "Emily, who made you queen of the world?" But those types of lines only seem obvious later that day. At that particular moment, my mind went horrifyingly blank. My eyes darted around the room, looking for any inspiration. Nothing. The only pathetic words I could manage to choke out were, "Oh. Sorry. I didn't know," as I sheepishly tugged the hair ties at either side of my head and stole an embarrassed look at Amy.

"Oh, you knew. You are just a poseur." Emily issued a satisfied sneer, spun around with a pompous toss of those stupid pigtails, and sauntered away with Elizabeth at her heels.

Emily was right, I was an imposter—a desperate, pathetic mimic. All of my rage and shame gathered in my stomach. I felt nauseous. The moment reeled over and over again in my mind, a mental documentary of my fifth grade tragedy.

"She can wear her hair any way she wants!" Amy shouted.

Emily and Elizabeth slowly turned. "What?"

"She can wear her hair however she wants," Amy repeated with just as much confidence.

The two girls were stunned. Never before had anybody dared to question their authority. They looked at each other, hoping the other knew what to do. But no protocol was established for such a circumstance. Finally Emily stammered, "I-I guess so. Sorry."

I was baffled. For months I cowered beneath the power of The Pink Ladies, hungry for their approval, accepting their pressure, never realizing there was an obvious solution. Stop—stop caring about what they think or say. My thirst for acknowledgment was what fed them. They didn't torture me because I was chubby. They tortured me because I let them. I gazed at Amy in awe. This ten-year-old girl with freckles and spunk held the answer all along. I just never looked in the right place.

"Thanks," I managed.

Amy shrugged. "Can I have a peanut butter cracker?"

~Alena Dillon

A Promise to Mrs. Parsons

A teacher affects eternity; he can never tell where his influence stops.
~Henry Brooks Adams

After the brief school break, I stepped back into Mrs. Parsons' class. She was a heavy-set woman with kind eyes and a raspy voice, and from the moment I met her there was no doubt that she cared very deeply for me. It didn't take long for me to fall in love with her as well. She was the perfect teacher who listened with concern and was quick with praise or encouragement. "What a wonderful poem," she'd whisper, or "I know someday you'll make me very proud." And how I wanted to! We all did. I soon learned that the saintly woman was equally quick with the truth. It was the greatest lesson I could have ever learned.

I was walking home from school when I spotted three neighborhood bullies waiting. My heart jumped into my throat. The Benoit brothers were frighteningly tough, but nothing compared to their huge sister who had worn a cast on her right arm for as long I could remember. My nemesis, Roland Benoit, was swollen with the courage provided by his sneering siblings. With a dry mouth and sweaty palms, I forced my rubbery legs to flee but it was no use. Roland cut me off and, without a word, threw one shot at me before his brother and sister jumped in. I went down and curled up into the fetal position. The Benoits pounced and inflicted their damage.

Bleeding and ashamed, I returned home to hide my battle scars from my proud father. I even made Grandma promise not to tell.

"It better not happen again," she said.

As the weeks rolled by, the thought of the Benoits loomed over me like a five-ton anvil. The memory of the unanswered beating, however, hurt so much more than the lingering cuts and bruises.

I was at morning recess when a grinning Roland Benoit approached. He was alone. I started to tremble.

"Ready for another beatin'?" Roland barked, loud enough to ensure my public humiliation.

I swallowed hard, amazed at how small the world had just become. With Abby (my childhood crush) looking on though, it was time to redeem my honor and I knew it. Though a circle of excited spectators awaited the blood sport, before long it was only me and Roland Benoit. Everything else became darkness.

Roland started with the name-calling: "Chicken."

"You're the chicken," I countered.

"How 'bout I punch your head in?" Roland threatened.

"How 'bout I punch yours in?" I matched, my knees quivering and a string of sweat beads forming across my forehead like a cruel crown. Everything seemed to be happening in slow motion. I could hear my heart beating hard in my ears. My breathing was quick. For the sake of saving face I knew I wasn't going to cower. While our peers cheered us on, I felt like I was going to vomit. It was a living nightmare. Roland was still grinning. I couldn't take it anymore. As the crowd began to chant, panic made me lunge.

There was a brief scuffle and in one strange, syrupy moment, I had Roland on the ground. I looked down and to my surprise, I'd pinned my enemy. Roland stared me straight in the eyes. He looked scared. With the bully's arms pinned behind him, I went to work.

With each blow, I ignored Roland's girlish pleas for mercy and cut up his face like a skilled surgeon. And with each blow, I felt my fear lighten. I was now a man—in my mind, anyway.

While the crowd chanted for more blood, I leaned into Roland's swollen face and screamed, "Who's the boss now?" Before my nemesis could answer, I worked my fists again like two deadly pistons. I didn't let up until I realized that Mrs. Parsons was trying to pull us apart. I let go right away.

The crowd erupted in cheers. The vicious beating was a victory for anyone who ever feared Roland Benoit. Everyone celebrated—everyone but Mrs. Parsons and Abby. Both of them looked completely disgusted and it made my stomach queasy. Mrs. Parsons grabbed my ear and forced me to look down at Roland. The frightened boy had folded himself into the fetal position and was crying. "I hope you're proud of yourself, Mr. Manchester," she said.

While my hands ached something awful, a sea of emotions raged inside me. The angry mob was no longer cheering for me. Abby's face looked contorted in pain. I felt confused. I looked up at Mrs. Parsons and the disappointment in her face broke my heart. I'd never felt so bad my whole life. She shook her head disgustedly. "I thought you were better than this," she said. "I really thought you were a bigger person." At that moment, something inside me changed.

I was escorted to the vice principal's office, where I received the strict punishment deserved by any violent kid; a severe reprimand coupled with a three-day suspension. My aching body was then carted home where I suffered my father's wrath.

Collectively, and even if multiplied a thousand times, none of this could have ever compared to the pain I suffered from looking into Mrs. Parson's disappointed face. She was the nicest person I knew and I'd let her down. In turn, I'd let myself down.

Days later, I'd drummed up enough courage to approach Mrs. Parsons. I made her a promise: "I'm sorry for what I did... and I'm going to prove it."

With a simple nod, she accepted my apologetic vow and watched me walk back to my desk.

Though I had to avoid several potential fights, the remainder of the year passed without further trouble. On my last day of school,

Mrs. Parsons gave me a hug. "I expect big things from you, Mr. Manchester," she whispered, "so don't let either of us down, okay?"

I nodded, contritely. She wasn't the only one who felt that way. I realized that because of Mrs. Parsons, I expected more of myself.

~Steven Manchester

Gifts

The art of teaching is the art of assisting discovery.
~Mark Van Doren

I once met a teacher who taught me to read
And how to spell words that I someday would need.
She had no idea where that someday would lead
When she shared her gift with me.

I once met a teacher who taught me to draw.
She opened my eyes to the beauty I saw.
She taught me to see there is beauty in us all
When she shared her gift with me.

I once met a teacher who taught me to play
As part of a team—not only my way.
He taught me a lesson on sharing that day
When he shared his gift with me.

I once met a teacher who taught one thing in life—
To believe and have faith during good times and strife.
I wonder if he knew how his words would give light
When he shared his gift with me.

All of my teachers shared gifts that were free.
What I do with these gifts now is all up to me.
If I share them with others, how glad they will be
That they shared their gifts with me.

~Tom Krause

Chicken Soup
for the Soul

Finding Friendship

Don't wait for people to be friendly, show them how.
~Author Unknown

n middle school I was the shy, quiet girl who always did her work, sat in the back of the class, and never raised her hand for fear of giving a wrong answer. My shyness was a problem when it came to meeting new people, but I had a small group of friends who I had grown up with, and I believed they would always have my back. Emily, Vicki, and Michelle were my three best friends in the whole world; they were also my only friends.

Vicki was the leader; she took it upon herself to always invent games and take charge, and she absolutely hated anybody standing up to her. Put simply, she was bossy, and if something didn't go her way, she wouldn't hesitate to fight.

Michelle was Vicki's sidekick, and she was much more passive. She followed Vicki around like a puppy dog, and went along with whatever she said.

Emily was quiet and not as bossy as the others, but she was also more assertive than I was. She never picked fights with anybody for disagreeing with her, and she never had anything bad to say about anybody. I trusted her the most of my three friends.

I was in sixth grade when I finally saw my friends' true colors, and it felt like a slap in the face. I had just finished gym class, and I was walking to the cafeteria with Vicki, Michelle, and Emily. It was time for lunch, which was my favorite part of the day.

We walked in as a group, with Vicki and Michelle in front, while Emily kept pace directly behind them. I brought up the rear, walking slowly and silently. Without warning, the three sat down at a table nearest the entrance, and I suddenly noticed that there were no empty seats for me to sit in.

"Very funny, guys," I said softly, hoping they would move to another table. The one where they had chosen to sit was already full with a group of boys that I barely knew.

"Can you make room for me?" I asked, and I could already feel the flush of embarrassment creeping up my cheeks.

"There's no room," Vicki said simply, looking me straight in the eye.

"Can't we just sit at a different table?" I pleaded. I felt humiliated. I was being abandoned by my best friends, my only friends.

"No. We're sitting at this one. You should just walk faster next time."

"Yeah," Michelle piped in.

I looked desperately at Emily, my last hope, but she stared down at the sandwich in her hands instead of meeting my gaze. She acted like I wasn't even there.

The hurt and embarrassment of this betrayal was enough to shatter what little self-esteem I had, and I could barely make my voice audible, much less keep it from breaking.

"Wow, thanks guys," I choked. I had tried to make it a sarcastic, biting comment, but I couldn't maintain my composure. I wanted them to feel a fraction of the pain I was feeling, I wanted them to regret this. But Vicki had already moved on and was starting a new conversation with Michelle.

I shuffled away from the table, holding onto my lunchbox for dear life. I refused to let myself cry, but I couldn't stop my face from turning what must have been an unsightly shade of red. I glanced at every table I passed, skimming each one for a single friendly face. I just needed someone to sit with, just for today. Sadly, this was the moment I realized I really had no other friends. There was nobody else I could sit with. I finally made my way to an empty, dirty table in the back of the cafeteria.

I wished desperately that someone would join me, and I angrily wondered why my friends couldn't have simply sat at this empty table.

Halfway through lunch, a teacher walked over to my table. I wondered frantically if I had done something wrong to draw his attention. I didn't want to get in trouble.

"Hey, Brianna," Mr. Hickey said to me kindly. His voice was soft and comforting, but that didn't stop my anxiety. "Did you and your friends have a fight or something?"

I shook my head vigorously, "No, we're fine."

"Then why are you sitting all alone?" he seemed concerned, and a small part of me was thankful that somebody was taking notice, but I didn't dare say anything about my friends.

"I just felt like sitting here for a change, I guess. I don't really know." I shrugged and bit into my sandwich like it was no big deal.

He nodded slowly, and started turning away. "Okay, well, if that's all. Enjoy your lunch." He looked back at me over his shoulder, but only for a moment, before a group of boys shooting milk out of their noses drew his attention and he was gone.

The next three days followed a similar pattern, only it soon became a race not to be the last to the table. I was desperate, but somehow, I was always last. For three days I sat by myself at the dirty table in the corner. Mr. Hickey didn't approach me after that first day, but I never missed his glances in my direction.

One day this pattern was broken. I was sitting alone at my table, like always, when a small voice asked, "Can I sit here?"

Startled, I looked up to see a girl named Stephanie who I only vaguely knew. She had ridden the same bus as me the year before, but other than that I had never really had much contact with her.

"Yeah, sure," I said, eagerly making room for her.

Suddenly, lunch didn't seem so miserable. We talked all period, and my heart felt like it was going to burst. Stephanie's act of kindness was hugely important to me, and I have never stopped feeling entirely grateful to her. I also didn't miss Mr. Hickey's quick smile as he watched us from over his shoulder.

The next day, it wasn't just Stephanie who joined me for lunch. Emily came over, as well as three other girls who were friends with Stephanie. A few short days later, my entire table, once empty, was almost completely filled.

Finally, there was only one person missing.

"Can I sit here?" Vicki asked softly.

I looked at her for a long moment, and Stephanie opened her mouth to deny her.

"Yeah, there's a seat next to Michelle." I cut in.

Vicki scurried over to the indicated seat, and Stephanie turned to me, asking why I had let Vicki join us.

I had no answer other than sometimes a little kindness can go a long way. I had learned a lot over those few days, and finally I saw who my real friends were. Stephanie, who was practically a stranger, had seen me when I needed help, and she was the only one to come to my rescue when my "friends" abandoned me. Now I want to reach out to others, to spread kindness and love, just as Stephanie did for me.

~Brianna Abbott

The Gift of Dignity

I like a teacher who gives you something to take home to think about besides homework.
~Lily Tomlin as "Edith Ann"

don't remember her name but I remember the day as if it were yesterday. I don't remember what day or time of year it was, but what my teacher did for me that day was etched in my memory and changed me for the rest of my life.

It began when I entered my classroom and the teacher announced for us to clear our desktops as we were going to have the math test she told us about the day before. Having never had trouble with math before, I hadn't bothered to study and I thought I was ready. When I took a look at the paper full of what looked like hieroglyphics to me I began to panic. The first few problems were easy but I was stumped when I got to the middle of the page. I did the best that I could, then left my seat to put my paper in a pile on the front desk with a sigh. I knew I had blown it.

I returned to my seat and then an idea popped into my head. I checked where the teacher was before I made my move. She was strolling in the back of the room with her back turned. I left my seat and went back to the pile of test papers already handed in and when I picked up my test I also included the test right below it before returning to my seat. When I looked at the extra test I had taken I discovered it was the work of the smartest girl in our class and I felt great about my luck. I went to work with my eraser and copied her answers to my paper. I checked that the teacher was still not paying attention and returned both papers to the top of the pile on the front desk. I made it! Nobody was paying any attention. I figured I was home free.

The next day the teacher handed back our tests turning them face down on everyone's desks, smiling at each student and raising her eyebrows at me over her smile. When I turned my test over I was shocked to see an "F" on it, with, "Does not know material" written across the top. Wow, the person I had copied didn't know the answers either. At recess I approached the girl whose test I had copied and said to her, "Boy, that math was tough. I failed it. I guess we need to study more." Her happy reply was, "Not me, I got every one right and got an A."

The teacher knew. I forgot teachers have eyes in the back of their heads! How could I be so stupid? The teacher never said a word to me about cheating but I got the message loud and clear. She never embarrassed me in front of the class, but her smile said everything to me when she handed me my "F." She allowed me to keep my dignity. The turmoil was in my own heart and I made a promise to myself never, ever to cheat again. I would remember to always be honest in the things I do and—first and foremost—study, study, study! I never forgot that teacher who failed me when, really, I had failed myself.

~Mary Grosvenor Neil

Surprise Visitors

How far that little candle throws his beams!
So shines a good deed in a weary world.
~William Shakespeare

My eyes focused on a long sidewalk that stretched out of sight. As I sat by the window and waited, nothing moved. I saw no girls with backpacks, tossing their hair, happily chatting on their way back from school. I'd only been in my wheelchair a few weeks, following an illness with a high fever that left me weak. It was all so new to me—home all day, unable to attend the opening days of school, studying with a tutor.

My life had centered on my girlfriends because boys had seldom paid any attention to me. I thought of guys as interested only in their sports, their friends, their lives. I couldn't remember the last time a boy from school said or did something nice for me.

I wondered why the girls weren't visiting. We had spent so much time together, riding double on bikes, falling over onto the grass in laughter, and running fast around the baseball diamond while the whole team cheered. Now I couldn't even run at all. I wheeled away from the sunroom window, usually a place of sunshine and light, but on that day it was overshadowed by doubt.

"Here's a snack, dear." My mother's voice startled me out of my thoughts. With my only brother away at college and Dad off on a long business trip, Mom did her best to lift my spirits... but I needed my friends. Desperation began to rise in me.

Surely they would come.

Then one day I saw two small figures on the sidewalk, not quite as bouncy as I had expected. As they kicked the fallen leaves, I realized they were not girls, but boys.

Boys wouldn't visit someone stuck in a wheelchair. I watched disinterested, certain they would go right past my house, until, shock of shocks, they turned up my walkway. With my neck stretched forward to see better, I recognized them as guys I barely knew from school — Phil and Mike.

I did wheelies as I sped to the front door.

"We just came by to see how you are," they said.

I couldn't believe it. Girls might go out of their way to visit me, but never boys.

"Well... come in."

Mom served them cookies and I asked them about sports and school. Even though long pauses dominated the conversation, they didn't seem eager to leave, and they came again... even when Mom had no cookies to serve. It really blew my mind. Why would boys do this?

It couldn't have been because they had a crush on me, since I was already a couple of inches taller than them. It couldn't have been my popularity, since I didn't hang out with the popular girls anymore. It couldn't have been because I was a lot of fun in my wheelchair — clearly I wasn't.

My girlfriends soon visited and apologized that activities had kept them busy. "We just don't have much extra time," they said. The boys, however, seemed to make time. Then and there, my mind did a 180 — maybe boys could be nice after all, even go the extra mile, literally. After all, they could have walked the mile to my house, once, and thought that sufficient. But Phil and Mike walked another mile, and then another. Perhaps they didn't even know it, but their faithful weekly visits until snow set in gave me something to look forward to and hope to carry on.

The second term, I felt strong enough to be on my feet and return to school. Phil and Mike couldn't be spotted in the swarm of students that buzzed through the hallways between classes. But I never forgot them and their acts of kindness that brightened my loneliest days.

~Margaret Lang

Ravioli Rescue

The best portion of a good man's life —
his little, nameless, unremembered acts of kindness and love.
~William Wordsworth

s soon as I walked into school, I knew something was horribly wrong. "Marla wore her uniform to picture day!" My classmate's outburst announced my mistake to everyone before I even figured it out on my own. I turned red. I'd been wearing the same uniform — navy skirt, white blouse, navy vest, white socks — to Catholic school nearly every day since kindergarten. It wasn't exactly crazy that I'd forgotten to dress up, but I still felt humiliated.

"So?" I sang in response to the taunts. "My mom wanted a picture of me in my uniform to send my granny in Louisiana!"

The lie just popped out before I could stop it, but it was better than letting everyone think I was stupid, even if I was. In my head, though, I was beating myself up. How could I have forgotten something so important? All the other girls were dressed in dainty dresses and had their hair fixed perfectly, and here I stood, in Catholic school navy and white, wishing more than anything that I looked as elegant and nicely dressed as my friends. Lisa had curly hair for the first time ever and Gloria wore a beautiful green velvet dress that made her look like a movie star.

The bell rang and most of the teasing stopped as everyone settled into their desks. First thing after roll call, our teacher announced that we would not have our pictures taken until after lunchtime recess, so we were to be very careful with our nice clothes until then.

Even without nice clothes, that was not as easy as it might have sounded.

At lunchtime in the cafeteria, we had ravioli and green beans and applesauce and a roll, my favorite meal of the week after fish sticks. My friends and I usually ate quickly because every minute spent eating took time away from recess. We had forty-five minutes total for lunch and then recess. If we spent twenty minutes eating, we only had twenty-five minutes left to play, but if we inhaled our lunches in ten minutes, we got to play for thirty-five minutes. Today, though, good pants and frilly dresses motivated everyone to eat slowly.

I got my tray and walked to the table I shared with my friends.

"Mystery meat wrapped in pasta," my friend said next to me. We all laughed. I stabbed a piece of ravioli with my fork and opened my mouth. Before I even had time to react, the ravioli fell from my fork and splattered heavily onto the front of my clean, white blouse.

The other girls didn't even laugh. Everyone knew this was a horrible thing. Not only had I forgotten to wear dressy clothes for picture day, now I had ruined the uniform blouse I was wearing. My picture would be ruined.

I got up and ran to the girls' bathroom. Looking in the mirror, I could see there was no hope of hiding the stain. I grabbed brown towels from the dispenser on the wall and scrubbed at my blouse furiously, trying to clean up the mess. It was no use. I sat down on a bench in the bathroom and started to cry. My mother was going to kill me. I hung my head and bawled, great drops of tears soaking my face.

"What happened? Are you crying?"

When I looked up, I recognized the girl speaking to me as a seventh grader, but I didn't know her name. I pointed at my shirt. "I didn't even remember today was picture day," I wailed. "And now I've ruined my uniform blouse."

"It's a pretty big mess," the girl agreed.

"I want to go home! I can't get my picture taken looking like this!" I dropped my head into my hands again and sobbed.

"Stop crying," the girl said. "I have an idea." She tugged on my arm. "Hurry, or you'll miss the whole recess!"

The girl pulled me into one of the bathroom stalls and said firmly, "Take off your blouse!"

"The sauce won't wash out," I said. "I already..."

"Just hurry!" she urged. "We'll swap for the day. But hurry up, because Sister Margaret will be looking for me." And right there in the bathroom, this seventh grade girl took off her blouse.

"What if we aren't the same size?"

"We'll be fine. Just hurry."

So I did. I took off my stained blouse and handed it to the girl. "But what about your school picture?"

"Seventh and eighth graders went first thing this morning."

I couldn't believe my luck. I slipped the seventh grade girl's top on quickly. It fit perfectly, and it felt like silk. It was a white blouse, like mine, but it had white flowers embroidered into the collar and cuffs. It was beautiful.

"Wow," I whispered.

"You look great!" the girl said. "So don't cry anymore, okay?"

I nodded.

The girl smiled. "Maybe leave your vest off for the picture," she said. "I gotta run." And she was out the door.

"Wait," I cried. But she was gone. I didn't even know her name. How was I going to give her blouse back after the picture?

I took a minute to look at myself in the mirror. I looked good. I felt grown up and pretty in the girl's soft blouse. Happy for the first time all day, I walked out into the sunshine.

"What took you so long?" my friend Lisa asked. "You missed almost the whole recess!" She didn't even notice my shirt.

Just then I saw a line of boys and girls getting on a school bus. The girl who had given me her blouse was in that line.

"Where are they going?" I asked the playground monitor, Sister Helen Clare.

"The seventh and eighth grade children are going to sing for the people at the nursing home today," she answered. "They're off to make some folks happy."

One of them had already made me very happy, but I didn't say so.

I had a thought and I gasped out loud. The seventh grader still had on my dirty blouse! She must have forgotten she was going on a field trip. She would hate me!

I looked at the bus, full of older kids, and suddenly I saw that very kind girl waving happily at me through the bus window. She stuck her head out and screamed, "Have a great picture day!" The girl was laughing with her friends as the bus pulled slowly away.

She knew what she was doing all along, I realized. She was just a very kind girl who didn't seem to care at all what her friends thought of her dirty blouse.

As I watched the bus pull out, I thought, "I want to be like her."

The next day, I gave the girl's freshly washed and ironed blouse to a seventh grade teacher to give back to the girl. I didn't even learn her name, but I never forgot her kindness to me on what could have been a very bad day.

~Marla H. Thurman

Chapter
6

Just for
Preteens

When the Going
Gets Tough...

When the world says, "Give up,"
Hope whispers, "Try it one more time."

~Author Unknown

Still a Winner

The best teachers teach from the heart, not from the book.
~Author Unknown

bright red apple fell out of my knapsack and bounced against each step before landing at the foot of the stairs. I stared at the broken apple with tears in my eyes, desperately holding onto my knee, hoping to stop the pain.

"What's wrong, honey?" my mom asked, running to me where I'd fallen at the top of the stairs. I was unable to speak as I sobbed in her arms. She held me tenderly and stroked my hair. My body trembled as I blurted out my story between gasps for air.

"My knee hurts when I run, jump and play with my friends! Last week I fell down during hopscotch. Sometimes, I have to grit my teeth to stop the tears. I didn't want to tell you because you'll take me to the doctor."

Despite my protests, my mother convinced me to go to the doctor. But nothing prepared me for what the doctor had to say.

"You have Osgood-Schlatter disease. It's a knee disorder that affects athletic kids between the ages of nine and sixteen. It could create permanent damage and pain if you don't take it easy for a while. If you're having pain, it means you have to stop what you're doing and rest."

"Can I still do sports and track and field?"

"You better stop doing organized sports for now. You can

participate in Physical Education class if you don't feel pain. It's not track and field season yet. Let's wait until spring and see how you're feeling."

I sat in her office, speechless. I thought my life would be over if I couldn't compete in track and field. I was only eleven years old but I'd been the best runner, high jumper and long jumper in my school since kindergarten! I always won first prize in those three events. But the one hundred meter race was my favorite competition. Nothing boosted my ego more than my schoolmates cheering for me as I sprinted across the finish line. I said a silent prayer that God would heal my knee by spring.

When Mom brought me to school the next day, we met with my teacher, Mr. Lewis, and explained the situation. The doctor said I should elevate my leg and ice it whenever it hurt. It seemed like a big hassle, but Mr. Lewis made me feel more comfortable by sharing my story with the class. At first I was embarrassed about my injury, but soon realized it was a great way to get attention from other kids.

It was hard to stop playing with my friends and sit down, but there was always someone willing to get ice or an extra chair. The hardest part was being a spectator on the sidelines. I tried to be strong, but there were times when I'd get so mad I wanted to smash everything in the gym and curse God for doing this to me. One evening, while alone in my bedroom, I got so mad at the pain that I yelled "You stupid knee!" and actually whacked my knee with a book. Of course, that made it throb more and I had to ice it for the rest of the night.

Spring eventually came and the fateful return to the doctor was scheduled. I prayed she'd tell me everything was fine. But my hopes were shattered when the doctor explained that competing this year would put too much strain on my knee. Then the final blow hit me like a knockout punch that left my ears ringing in disbelief.

"You may never run competitively again, possibly for the rest of your life. I'm sorry."

I was crushed. I stared out the window of the doctor's office and wished I had lied to her. I should have told her my knee never hurt during sports. I should have run all year through the pain. I never should have told my parents. The conversation between Mom and the doctor grew faint as I daydreamed about winning the one-hundred-meter dash.

Nevertheless, the next day I was stuck inside, while the other kids were outside running. Mr. Lewis told me I could write for extra credit while the others practiced track and field. He had always encouraged me as a creative writer and told me I should enter the town poetry contest that year. Every day, I worked on different poems to enter in the contest, constantly revising and perfecting the rhyme and rhythm. But the sadness of being excluded from track and field was overwhelming.

One day I was in the classroom writing when I overheard Mr. Lewis talking to the boys in the next classroom. While he explained the rules of track and field, several boys moaned and complained about participating. They were tired of running every day and wanted to quit. Until that moment, I'd never heard Mr. Lewis get so animated and loud.

"I'm ashamed of you boys! At this moment there's a girl in the next classroom dreaming about competing in track and field! She'd do anything to take your place, but because of a bad knee, she can't! You able-bodied boys should be embarrassed! You should be happy you can run every day without pain! Now get out there, start running and stop your whining!" Then he blew a loud whistle and the boys scurried outside with their cheeks flushed and their heads hanging low.

I sat in my seat in shock. For the first time since this happened, I felt valued and appreciated. Mr. Lewis understood how much I'd lost because of my impaired physical condition. Through the tears, I smiled and thanked God for my teacher. From that day forward, I wrote my poetry with a deep conviction that I would win the poetry competition, for me and for Mr. Lewis!

That year, I did win first prize in the poetry contest of my small town in Ontario, Canada. I have Mr. Lewis to thank for pushing me to strive through difficult times.

During the last class of the year, Mr. Lewis gave everyone a special quote to take with them to ponder throughout their lives. This is what he said to me: "Kathy, people look up to you and respect you. Never lose their respect."

Before leaving the classroom for the very last time, I walked to the front and placed a big red apple on Mr. Lewis's desk.

"An apple for the best teacher in the world," I said. "Thank you Mr. Lewis. I'll never forget you."

~Kathy Linker

May's Story

Cancer is a word, not a sentence.
~John Diamond

I knew that cancer was an awful disease. Cancer killed my dog. Some of my mother's friends have had breast cancer. I've read books about people with cancer. But I never really knew how scary cancer could be until sixth grade.

I go to a private school—an all-girls middle school that goes from grades five through eight. On the first day of sixth grade, I was excited to see my friends who I hadn't seen all summer. Some new kids had come to our grade, so I wanted to meet them too. The first thing I did was find May, a good friend of mine. We hugged each other; I went to greet my other friends, as well. People made friends with the new kids and greeted old friends. The teachers were friendly. Sixth grade was shaping up to be a good year.

In November, May wasn't feeling well. She was tired. Her back and stomach hurt. One day, May wasn't in school. It wasn't like May to be sick. She never got sick, not even a cold. I got worried. When I got home from school, I called May right away. Her mother picked up the phone.

I asked her what was wrong with May. She told me they didn't know. May was in the emergency room. I hung up and told Mom what Hannah, May's mother, had said. Hannah called again because she thought I was worried and my mother talked for a while with her. My mom said they thought it wasn't anything serious and that I shouldn't call May so they could have a day to themselves.

The next day, Thanksgiving, I called and left a message. I was worried. My mother was baking Thanksgiving dinner while I played around. We were eating dinner when the phone rang. My mother answered it and sent me away. I heard something like "There is a high cure rate." I knew it was about May. What did May have? I pondered the illnesses it could be. She could have anything. Mom got off the phone. "What does May have?" I asked.

My mother replied "May's parents want May to tell you."

"Is it cancer?" I said

"I can't tell you that," my mother answered.

"Does it have to do with organs?" I questioned. If it was cancer it would have to do with organs.

My mother went to ask my dad. Then she came back. "No, it doesn't have to do with organs."

I was puzzled. What could May have? The phone rang; it was May. I went into my room and asked her what she had. "Well," May said, "I have leukemia."

I was shocked, but my voice remained calm. I could not believe it. Out of all the possible illnesses, this was the last one I had thought of. We talked about how boring it was at the hospital and how disgusting the food was. Tears streamed down my cheeks, and my eyes turned red. I was so scared that May would die—the most scared I had ever been in my entire life. My dog had died of cancer; would my best friend die too? My parents comforted me. I thought of the good things I could do.

I visited her once a week. One day we tried to get lost in the hospital. It didn't work, so we went to the cafeteria. May's parents were irritated. It seems that we weren't supposed to go out of the unit that May was in. That was just one of our hospital adventures. May was trying to find hats on the Internet, so we looked at hats too. Most of the hats that May wanted were funny, like one with cat ears and a red pom-pom on top.

I wasn't allowed to tell any of my classmates or friends that May had leukemia, and it was hard. Nobody noticed that May was gone for the first two days. Izzy was suspicious and wanted to make a get-well card for her. I got scared and told her that maybe she shouldn't do that. On the fourth day May was absent, I almost told another friend about her. Teachers were kind to me, and I ate with my science teacher before she went to visit May in the hospital. My fifth grade teachers hugged me and told me that I was welcome to come back to their classrooms if I ever needed a break.

During the second week, the teachers told the class that May had leukemia. People cried and gasped. The class was surprised. A nurse came in and told us what leukemia was. Some people came up to me and asked me questions. I said I didn't know the answers to any of them. It was awful.

Later, the head of our school talked about how May was doing. I made a split-second decision and described to the class what happened when I went to the hospital to visit. I told them about trying to get lost in the hospital and the time when May had a little snowball fight with the nurse. Some people were laughing. Everyone felt a little better.

It has been four months now, and since then, May has been in school and having fun. A group of us made a video for her. We found out that another classmate has cancer, and we will support her, too. My sixth grade class is doing a project called Bike4aCure. We will raise money for cancer patients and improve cancer awareness.

~Mariah Eastman

46

Chicken Soup for the Soul

Against All Odds

Turn your wounds into wisdom.
~Oprah Winfrey

I faced the struggle of conquering the difficult preteen years of my life without a mother to guide me. My mom died very suddenly when I was eight years old, leaving me, my dad, and my twelve-year-old sister without the glue that had held our lives together. Although this tragedy was very difficult for me because I was so young, I can't imagine what my sister must have felt, losing her mother at such a crucial time in her life. And, a few years later, it was my turn to experience the pain of crossing the threshold into my teenage years without the invaluable guidance of my mom.

Many days, I would listen to my friends at school complain about what, to me, seemed to be such petty problems. It was different for me. Often, I would lend an ear as they vented about various issues, including how much they hated their parents or their mothers. Deep down, I wished I could shake them and tell them how lucky they were to have a mom, even if they didn't always get along. I would have given anything to have my mom there to give me advice about "girl things" during that time—I would even have gladly welcomed the occasional argument or disagreement, just to have her around. Sometimes, I wanted to tell my friends that their problems were nothing—try getting your first period or going shopping for your first bra without your mom there to help you. I felt lost, to say the least.

Don't get me wrong—my dad did a wonderful job of raising my sister and me on his own, and I was lucky to have an older sister to turn to who could give me advice. But it just wasn't the same. Everyone knows that nothing can replace the presence of a girl's mother in her life—and the loss leaves a void that can never truly be filled, by anyone or anything.

I remember one particularly difficult day at school, when a peer in my Spanish class made a joke having to do with my mom, apparently not knowing that she had passed away. I ran to the bathroom, locked myself in one of the stalls and cried. On another occasion, I was online and received a message from someone with a very hurtful user name having to do with my mom. It even had my name in it, so I knew this was an intentional attack on me by somebody who knew me—not an innocent joke made by someone who didn't know better—and I was heartbroken at how hurtful people could be. I didn't want to go to school the next day because I was so upset and had no way of knowing who had played this cruel joke on me. I was afraid I might end up having a conversation with this person and not even know it, or that people might be making fun of me behind my back.

I always felt that having lost my mom made me different from everyone else—that it would always brand me as being an outsider, the girl without a mom. I often wondered if it occurred to my schoolmates when I passed by—"There goes the motherless girl...." Some days, I would have given anything to just wake up with a pimple or have worn an ugly outfit—those seemed like such simpler problems. Most days, I felt very much alone.

Despite the challenges of navigating the trials of life as a preteen girl without a mother, I learned a lot about myself from this experience. I realized at a fairly young age just how strong and independent I was, and how much I was really capable of. While I knew that nothing could ever ease the hurt of being forced to live these years of my life without my mom by my side, I realized eventually that I would be okay one way or another. My dad always told us that we had already been through the hardest thing two young girls could ever be faced with, and if we could get through that, we could do anything. At some point, I finally began to realize that he was right and adopted this attitude myself.

Life makes no guarantees—not to any of us. The only thing within our control is how we choose to handle the obstacles life places before us, whatever they may be. The thing to remember is, with the right attitude, you will never meet an obstacle that is insurmountable. No matter what happens today, there will still be tomorrow—and you will make it through. I'm living proof.

~Julia K. Agresto

47

Chicken Soup
for the Soul

Feathers on My Wings

*Hope is the thing with feathers
That perches in the soul
And sings the tune without the words
And never stops at all*
~Emily Dickinson

All the girls in our school were waiting to run, and for the most part they all looked miserable. Still, no one could have been more frustrated than me. See, I decided I'd do whatever it took to earn the President's Patch for Physical Fitness. Of course, that was before I knew I was a crummy runner.

Before we began the running part of the test, my gym teacher grinned when she watched me do more push-ups, pull-ups, and sit-ups than anyone twice my height and weight. See, even though I was little, the requirements stated I had to play with the big boys... uh, big girls. But I overcame that problem. Plus, I had freakishly strong arms, which meant I did great in arm strength tests. But running—well, not so much. There was a reason I wasn't a great runner. I had been in an accident.

When I was little, I was outside playing with the neighbor's kids. There was a whoosh of movement, and the others dashed away. I stared at them and didn't see a black car loom over me. It knocked me to the ground, squishing my legs under a giant tire. Children screamed and the driver panicked.

He jerked his car into drive, and ran over my legs a second time. My body twirled under the car. The crunch of gravel was loud—but not louder than my mother. Her scream joined the kids' yells and confused the driver. He was certain he was still on top of me.

I could hear the gears shift. Just as the car rocked into reverse, something fell to the ground next to the car. It was my mom. In a firm voice, she ordered me not to sit up. We waited.

The third grinding run over my legs left me quivering on the ground, unable to speak. I was in shock.

Now, standing waiting to run, I was again in shock. The day before, I ran in the sprint race for the physical fitness test, and it ended up feeling like a horror movie. Before that race, I had forgotten I even had damaged legs. So when the whistle blew, I charged forward with the others, fully expecting to win.

Too quickly, I was near the end of the pack. I looked down at my legs and screamed at them to move. But something between my brain and legs was disconnected. It was devastating.

And then there was the look on my teacher's face. She was confused. She looked at her chart and said I could eliminate two things and still get the patch. I'd already failed the high jump, so this was number two. However, the final test was another race. This time it was a mile-long run. I felt sick.

Because my parents didn't want me to focus on what I couldn't do, we rarely talked about my legs. They're parents, so what do you expect? However, that day when my dad saw me scowling and chewing on my braids, he decided to refocus me. He pointed through the window at a bird's nest and asked, "Why aren't the baby birds flying?"

I said, "Because they don't have feathers."

He nodded. "Still, do you see how they stretch and pump their wings as they try to fly? They mimic their mother and work their muscles until they get feathers on their wings. Your wings are different, so it may take a while until you fly. Until then, you need to keep flapping."

The next day, while waiting to run, I thought of what my dad said. But I wanted that patch right now, and this hurt.

I needed to be close to my older sister so I searched the crowd for her. When I got close, she knew I was totally miserable because I hung my head. She squeezed my hand. One of her friends piped up, saying that we needed to stretch. She apparently was a runner. All I could think of were baby birds stretching to fly, so I stretched. It was awful. I watched the others go nearly to the ground as they relaxed into their stretches. Not me, I barely looked like I was leaning down. Scar tissue was to blame.

Next, she told us to breathe through our noses and out through our mouths. Then, she said the most remarkable thing: "We should jog—not run."

I perked up. Could I keep up with a jog? Nonchalantly, I wiggled through the crowd to the front of the pack. I knew I would need every inch.

The whistle blew and we were off. It was horrible. In a dead run, almost all the kids passed me. Clearly, no one but me got the memo about jogging.

But then, something amazing happened. I passed a girl—then two others—and then a whole clump of kids. It was weird. Most were clutching their sides in pain. Those hares that had run super fast past me were left in my tortoise dust.

Steadily, I moved forward. When I got close to my sister, I stared. Her pasty white skin startled me. She had allergies and I was worried. I told her to breathe through her nose and out her mouth. There was a part of me that wanted to stop, but my legs had a mind of their own. I chugged on.

With each person I passed, I became even more confused. How could everyone be dropping like flies, and I wasn't even breathing hard?

I glanced back, and nearly stumbled. Yep, my legs were still my legs—totally clumsy and uncooperative. I forced myself to focus on the skill of running.

Ahead of me was the leader of the pack, my sister's friend, the runner. She pumped her arms close to her side. So, like the baby birds mimicking their mother, I pumped mine close to my side. I inched closer.

She turned and saw me. The day before, she must have noticed my shocking failure in the short run, so no doubt she was surprised that I was the one right behind her. Still, she grinned and yelled for me to hurry and run with her. No competition here, she just loved to run.

With head down and quick pumps, I joined her. We were on the home stretch.

I'll never know for sure, but I think she slowed just enough to let me cross the finish line first. My gym teacher grabbed me in a bear hug. "You did it, you did it."

There was a big hullabaloo when she told everyone I had won the race. Girls cheered and patted my back. My biggest cheerleaders were my sister and her friend the runner.

Yep, I had earned the patch, but it was strange. Getting it was great, but learning never to quit was huge. Maybe even better was realizing there were lots of people ready to help a klutz like me.

After the award ceremony, someone asked how I could be so slow one day, and so fast the next. I grinned and said, "Because I've got different kinds of feathers on my wings."

~Sandy Lackey Wright

Equally Beautiful

Share our similarities, celebrate our differences.
~M. Scott Peck

"Hey, do you want some fried rice-ee?" I bit my lower lip and pretended I didn't hear. "What's wrong? Don't you understand any English? Eee-ngrish?"

I slammed my locker shut, clutching my science textbook to my chest. Rooted in front of locker 163, I blinked furiously to prevent tears from spilling down my face and giving them the satisfaction of seeing me cry.

"Stupid, what are you staring at?"

I stood still. The pretty, teal blue that the school had painted the lockers with in the beginning of this year was peeling, revealing a dreadful, bleak gray—its true colors.

When I was eleven years old, I was teased for who I am.

Prior to entering middle school, I had never been self-conscious about my differences; I didn't understand why my classmates teased me about my "Engrish" when I spoke English like everyone else. As far as I knew, I was just as American as anyone else. I was born in the United States. I wore jeans, T-shirts and sneakers; I liked hot dogs, mashed potatoes and ice cream. I giggled on my hot pink phone to my best friends and developed crushes on cute boys. I listened to Britney Spears, *NSYNC and was in love with Nick Carter from the Backstreet Boys. The only differences that I could see were in my appearance; my hair was black while my friends' hair was blond, red, and brown; my eyes were chocolate and theirs were green, blue, and honey-colored.

One spring afternoon, I hopped into the passenger seat of my mother's Jeep and hid my bloodied palms underneath my legs. Earlier, a group of seventh grade girls had followed me down the hall during lunch break, yelling one particular derogatory term. When I didn't respond, they snapped. "Don't you know it's rude to not respond when someone's calling your name?" They pushed me onto the asphalt, where I scraped my hands.

"How was school?" my mom asked.

"Fine." I looked out the window.

"Lots of homework today?" she cast a quick glance at my dirtied backpack.

"Some," I muttered.

As soon as my mom pulled into the garage, I hurried into my bathroom and washed the brown, dried blood off my hands. Sneaking into my parents' office, I uncovered a roll of gauze, which I carefully wound about my hands. When I returned downstairs for my afternoon snack, my mother was standing in the kitchen waiting for me.

"Pearl," she began angrily, her left hand on her left hip. "Why didn't you eat your lunch? You just wasted food that I took so long to prepare for you."

I hid my hands behind my back and sat down in the dining room chair. "I didn't have enough time."

My mother stared at me for a moment, as if deliberating whether this was worth a reprimand. Finally, she exhaled. "Eat your snack," she said quietly. Relieved that the discussion was over, I forgot about my hands and lifted them to the table. My mother suddenly gasped.

"What happened to your hands?" she cried, rushing over to the table.

"I fell," I began, watching helplessly as my mother unwound the gauze.

My mother stared at the scrapes piercing diagonally across my palms. "How?"

I lowered my head, pausing for a moment to make up an excuse. I could have said that I tripped during physical education. Or that I tripped over untied shoelaces. But I heard myself whisper, "Some girls pushed me."

My mother's gentle, steady breathing abruptly ceased. I looked up at her quickly, out of concern and curiosity. She was standing over me, concentrating her eyes on my face, with an expression that I've seen only during the rare moments when she accidentally slices her finger while preparing vegetables.

Suddenly, she was kneeling in front of me, holding onto my wrists so tightly that the pink beds of her nails turned into a milky white. "Listen to me," she began fervently. "And listen to me well. Do not let others hurt you in any way, and if they do, do not allow them to think that they can get away with it. Do not believe that you are somehow less than them, because you're not. We are all equal, each blessed with a brain that keeps you going, hands to do your work and feet to carry you far. These years are difficult because you've been given something different and others around you don't know how to respond to it. But do not despair, even for one moment, for I can assure you that this too shall pass, and if you keep your head on straight and embrace the person that you are, you will go far."

Seven years later, I graduated high school at the top of my class and chose to attend a prestigious university in Southern California. I made lifelong friends, whose hair colors varied from blond, brown, and black to red, purple, and green. I learned that appearance was only skin deep, and personality, intelligence and humor are the true treasures of each soul. I met people who not only tolerated differences, but also embraced them, and I have learned to embrace mine. My black hair-brown eyes-fair skin is just one combination in a vast melting pot of physical features, all of them equally beautiful, equally valued, and equally respected.

~Pearl Lee

Better to Have Loved

'Tis better to have loved and lost than to have not loved at all.
~Alfred Lord Tennyson

Unita, my cat, had diabetes, but we found out too late. We had taken her to the vet for a sideways tooth. After the tooth was pulled, the vet asked if there was anything else bothering her, and my mom brought up the fact that Unita was always thirsty and we had to refill the water bowls every day to keep her happy. The vet had a feeling it was diabetes and did a quick test to see if it was. It came back positive. A blood test would make it definite, so blood was drawn. That was positive as well. Unita had diabetes. I got Unita to go back into the carrier, and it nearly fell off the table with her weight. My mom and stepdad, Mike, were going to be gone for a week and I was staying with my grandma while they were gone, so we decided not to treat her until they got back.

I was home after school feeding the cats during the week, but I didn't notice any difference until we were all home again that Friday and I saw that she was lethargic. We all knew that there was another trip to the vet coming up.

On Saturday, when my mom and Mike got back from the vet, I was cleaning the litter boxes. The mood in the apartment had darkened drastically. My parents said they would tell me what was going to happen to Unita when I was finished cleaning, but I still wouldn't let them say anything until Unita was beside me. As I stroked her fur, my mom told me that Unita was very sick and that we would have to put her to sleep. It was going to happen the next day, so I would have one last night with her.

"No," I cried. "Isn't there anything we can do?" My pleas were met with a solid no. I was lying on the couch crying into Unita's fur, like I had so many other times before, when my mom came over and asked me to bring Unita to my room. I figured she just wanted to get rid of me. I was wrong.

"This isn't her space; your room is," my mom explained, and I agreed. My mom picked up Unita, carried her into my room, and set her down on my bed beside me. "Lie down and say goodbye."

Later, my mom told me that she could tell by the way Unita's head was lolling that she had gotten worse and would probably slip into a coma before morning. The appointment we had made for the next day was moved up a few hours. It was nearly time to let her go.

The next morning, I picked up Unita and held her to my chest. We figured it would be less painful for us if we carried her in than if we brought home an empty carrier. We went down to the car and piled in. With a few final sniffles, we were off. Once we got to the animal hospital we were told to go into the first room on our right. I didn't want to let Unita go, but I had to. I set her down on the blanket that was on the table and gave her more affection. Then, the vet told us what would happen. All it was going to be was an anesthetic overdose, quick and painless. The drugs were to be administrated through Unita's rear leg, so we had to turn her around and put her facing away from us.

Unita was sitting with her back end on its side and her front paws resting flat with her head up. Once the vet put the needle into her leg Unita shifted so that she was lying on her side with her eyes closed. It was like she knew she was going to die. We were told that we could leave if we needed to. I nodded but I knew I'd stay until the end. When we were as ready as we could be, the vet injected the drugs. In a matter of moments, she stopped moving.

"She's gone," my mom said, and the dam broke. Looking back, I think I cried more that day than in all of fourth, fifth, sixth, and seventh grades combined. "She loved you most of all," my mom told me as she held me. The dam was completely smashed at this point. I couldn't—wouldn't—believe she was gone, but one look at her still body and I just knew.

Mike left and it was just me and my mom in the room. Once I had calmed down, my mom suggested we leave. Tears threatened to fall once more, and with willpower and the knowledge that she would always be with me no matter what, I held them back until I was sure they wouldn't fall. The drive home was sadder than the drive there by many degrees. Leaving Unita there was one of the hardest things I've ever had to do, and I hope my other two cats' lives end on a better note. Questions like "Would she still be here if we had started treatment earlier?" and, "Why didn't we go to the vet sooner?" have made the wounds deeper and even more painful.

Even though Unita's with me every day, I still miss her and love her with all of my heart. No matter what, Unita has shown me how to love without fear or questions, and she taught me that it is better to know how love feels than to have never experienced it before.

~Sara Drimmie

Chicken Soup for the Soul

Making a Mark

Pain is inevitable. Suffering is optional.
~M. Kathleen Casey

I was consumed with happy thoughts about my sister Theresa and her upcoming wedding. It was only three months away. She asked me to be her maid of honor and I was thrilled. She chose a soft lavender gown with a white organza overlay for me to wear. I looked lovely in it. When I tried it on, my long brown hair cascaded over the shoulders and hid the pretty ruffled neckline.

"Hold your hair up," Theresa said. "Pretend you are wearing your hair in an up-do." She twisted my hair into a braid and held it high. "You look like a princess."

Our mom walked in the bedroom and saw us. "You look stunning," she said. She stood there for a moment taking it all in. Then, her smile faded and a look of concern washed over her face. "What is that on your neck?"

I looked in the mirror that hung over Theresa's dresser. "I don't see anything. What are you talking about?" I kinked my head to one side, then the other.

"This," she clamored, pointing to a huge, round lump in the front of my neck at the base of my throat. "What is this right here?"

I ran my fingers over it. "I never noticed that," I said. "It doesn't hurt." I swallowed hard and watched to see if it moved.

Mom walked straight to the kitchen, picked up the phone that hung on the wall, and dialed the doctor's number. I stood beside her listening to everything she said. I knew whatever I had was not normal. I wondered if I needed surgery. My mind ran wild with thoughts of not being able to stand up for my sister's wedding and I began to cry. Theresa hugged me tightly and reassured me that it would all be fine. But I was worried sick that nothing about my throat would be fine.

That summer was filled with doctor's appointments, blood tests and ultrasounds. I had X-rays and nuclear medicine scans. I was poked and prodded. In the end, the doctor announced that I needed an operation to remove that lump. I could only think about being a bridesmaid in August and that beautiful lavender gown that I wanted to wear so much. How good would I look at Theresa's ceremony with an enormous Frankenstein-like scar across my throat? I envisioned the worst and was angry that something so terrible was happening to me.

I was only twelve and about to start high school. I couldn't go to class with a scar across my throat. What would my classmates think if they saw something so gross and disfiguring? I knew I couldn't wear turtlenecks because the weather would still be too warm. How could I hide a hideous scar? I imagined no one would want to be my friend and I couldn't bear it. I sobbed hysterically every time I thought about it and my parents were concerned.

The doctor gave me a choice. I could postpone the operation until August and be a bridesmaid without a scar, but that meant I would have to walk down the halls of my high school with a fresh surgical wound on my neck. Having the surgery immediately meant I would have a nasty red scar in all of Theresa's wedding photographs. But, I would be able to start high school with a wound that had time to heal.

After struggling with the dilemma, we reached a tolerable compromise. I would have surgery the day after Theresa's wedding. The doctor reassured me that there was enough recuperation time before school began in September and it wouldn't be as bad as I thought.

Every morning that summer when I woke up I would run my

fingers over that lump to see if it was still there. I examined it in the mirror to see if it had shrunk during the night. But it never changed. Theresa kept me occupied with bridal showers and other wedding plans. There was so much to do and it was a lot of fun pulling it all together. When the big day finally arrived, I looked and felt like a princess and never thought about the lump.

The surgery and recovery period was very traumatic for me, probably because I was so young. I remember feeling afraid going to school with a big white bandage across my throat, but no one seemed to care. I made friends and adjusted. I was so worried about a silly scar when I should have been concerned about having cancer or losing my voice. That experience made me decide to devote my life to working as an X-ray technician.

I did become an X-ray tech, and I enjoyed looking at films, awed by the way I could see the inside of the body. Some of the most difficult images to interpret were nuclear medicine scans. They looked like a galaxy of stars in outer space. The equipment used to obtain the images looked like it was rolled off the Starship Enterprise.

But I still remember how scared I felt when I was twelve and that equipment was wheeled over me to obtain images of the lump in my neck. I tried to become a compassionate technologist who cares more for the individual on the table than the film that needs to be taken. The tumor in my neck taught me that.

In the end, I beat cancer and have only a tiny mark on my neck to show for it. I laugh when I recall how I fretted over a scar. I have vowed never to let a mark on my body control or interfere with my life. I have promised to instead care more about the mark I leave on society, because that is the most important thing.

~Barbara Canale

51

Chicken Soup for the Soul

The Normal Girl in a Not-So-Normal Chair

The hardest struggle of all
is to be something different from what the average man is.
~Charles M. Schwab

s a twelve-and-a-half-year-old American girl, I like doing girly things. But many people aren't aware of that because they only see a twelve-and-a-half-year-old disabled girl who sits in a wheelchair. When I was in second grade, I was a speaker at an after-school program for children my age. In the beginning, the children were curious about my tubing and alarms. By the end of the program, when it was time for questions, they didn't know what to say to me. I guess they felt embarrassed. Instead of trying to talk to me, they ended up walking away and ignoring me. Unfortunately, this is a typical occurrence. Often, people would rather act like I am not there.

I use a wheelchair that has tubing to control my breathing and alarms to signal for assistance. To explain why I use this chair, with all of these devices, I need to explain my diagnosis. Before I was born, I had a stroke that affected my brain stem. It's as if my brain is a computer, and the circuit board shorted out. My muscles don't always do what I want them to, and most definitely not in a timely manner. I can breathe but not enough to stay alive, so I use a ventilator. I can stand, but I cannot control my muscles so I would wobble around or fall over. With a ventilator I am unable to use my voice to speak, so instead I blink yes or no with my eyes. To say yes, I blink twice, and once to say no. My mom also helps me by holding my hand while I type, which takes a very long time. My alarms notify my moms that my devices are having a problem. There are different sounds for different alarms, and sometimes they can be noisy. Now you understand what it is like to be in my chair.

As a preteen girl, I enjoy putting on make-up, dressing trendy, reading about anything I can, and being outside in nature. I need a ventilator to breathe and a wheelchair to move, but I have the same interests as any other preteen girl. People seem to forget this when they see me.

Often, when I go into a store with my family, people will stare and then avert their eyes. They don't think that I see them, but they are wrong. I am aware of a lot more than they think. People are afraid to be out of their comfort zone. They feel threatened by someone like me because they don't know what to say or do. What they don't realize is that not saying anything at all is more hurtful than anything they could have said. I want people to know that handicapped people have feelings too. If you walked into a place and everyone walked away from you, would it hurt your feelings? Well, that is how it feels for me.

By saying a simple "Hello" or asking my name, a stranger can brighten my day. This simple gesture makes me feel welcomed. I want people to know that being a preteen is hard enough, but sad stares from strangers makes it even harder. Don't feel sorry for me — my life is great! The next time you see a person in a wheelchair remember that a simple hello can go a long way. After all, a wheelchair doesn't make a person — what's in the chair is what's important.

~Dani P. d'Spirit

52

Chicken Soup for the Soul

Remembering Brian

There are things that we don't want to happen but have to accept,
things we don't want to know but have to learn,
and people we can't live without but have to let go.
~Author Unknown

I liked Brian. Not in the typical "I'm a girl, you're a boy" way, but just as friends. We were both in the same fourth grade class at Municipal Elementary, but the only time that our worlds really collided was at recess.

I didn't like to play with the other girls at recess, mostly because they didn't do much playing. I'm not that into drama and gossip, and the swings got old pretty fast. That left soccer. I'd never played soccer before, so I sat on the hill above the soccer field with my knees tucked under my chin, studying the game. I watched as I always did—on the outside looking in—until I had the basics figured out.

I didn't have to know much about soccer to recognize talent when I saw it. Brian was really, really good at it. His blond hair, left a little long in back, flew behind him as he ran and ran and ran. He never seemed to get tired. The other boys watched Brian, too—watched the way he ran with the ball somehow magically attached to his foot. He played soccer outside of school and wore that fact with distinction on the field.

I knew that if I wanted to play, I'd have to ask Brian. I waited until I'd practiced kicking some in the backyard and was pretty sure I wouldn't embarrass myself if he said yes.

"Hey Brian," I said one day. "Can I play soccer with you guys at recess?"

He looked at me with his blue eyes, shrugged and nodded. And that was that. After all the agonizing, I was in. Brian let me in.

I quickly settled into my new role of designated goalie. I think I earned my position by having no regard for my pants. My mom complained about all the grass stains, but I thought it was a small price to pay to have a spot on the team. I threw myself into soccer with abandon—lunging, kicking and hollering. I came in from recess every day dripping sweat, but triumphant. Save by save I was gaining respect and friends, and I liked that feeling.

I wish I could remember the last day we played, the last time my screams of "go Brian, go" echoed from the far end of the grass. What I do remember is Mr. Henry saying the four most horrible words in the English language—"There's been an accident." I'd heard Katie whispering about an accident before class started and I had passed groups of teachers whispering in the hallway. I knew something was up and I was waiting for Mr. Henry to give us details. My stomach hurt, but all I was hungry for was details, facts to reassure me that everything was okay and the scary "what ifs" in my head weren't coming true.

I didn't get them. Instead we got information like which hospital Brian was at and that his mother had been in the car too. At the very end, my teacher added in a casual voice, "Brian hurt his head." It was that statement that brought the chaotic events together for me. The phrase I'd heard as I passed a cluster of teachers in the hallway was "brain dead." And I knew. I knew that Brian was not okay, and my teacher just hadn't figured out how to break it to us yet.

Mr. Henry passed out construction paper and told us to make get well cards. I stared at my paper for a long time coming to grips with the powerful feeling I had that Brian wasn't coming back. How could I write a get well card to someone I knew wouldn't? What could I say to Brian so he'd know how much his friendship meant to me? In the end, confused and a little angry, I wrote something like, "I hope you can come back to school soon."

He didn't. He died.

My dad took me to Brian's funeral. I needed the chance to say goodbye. I shuffled along behind my dad in the receiving line tracing the outline of the roses on my skirt and brushing the suede patches on the elbows of my dad's jacket — anything to avoid looking at Brian. I only glanced once when Casey reached out to touch Brian's hand. "He's cold," he said, turning to all of us standing in line. I looked to my dad — waited to see if he'd comment on the wrongness of it, but instead I heard him murmuring words to a woman in a dress.

I looked up into the kind, blue eyes of Brian's mother. She took my hand in hers and asked, "Now who are you, honey?" She searched my face as if it were the most important thing to know. The ice that had built up around my heart and stomach for those past awful days thawed and I found the words that I had wanted when I'd stared at a blank piece of construction paper, numb with hurt.

"I'm Jill," I said, "and I played soccer with Brian at school."

The tears came then, and Dad led me away to find seats for the service.

It's been years now since Brian died. When I close my eyes, I can still see him running, always running, chasing a soccer ball a few inches in front of his feet. In my mind, I see a smile stretching across his broad, freckled face. No one needed to tell me about the strength of his heart, how it had continued to beat for minutes after life support had been removed. I had experienced it already firsthand. Thank you, Brian, for letting me in. I will always remember you.

~Jill Hansen Fisher

53

Chicken Soup for the Soul

Scarred But Not Different

Being happy doesn't mean that everything is perfect.
It means that you've decided to look beyond the imperfections.
~Author Unknown

When I was fifteen months old, I was burned by hot grease falling on me from an electric skillet on the stove of my parents' home. This was an accident caused by a precocious, strong-willed, or as my sisters would say, bratty child who wanted her way and wasn't getting it. In plain terms, I pulled a pan of hot grease on myself that caused first, second and third degree burns on my face, arms and chest, leaving me with permanent scars, the worst of which is having one breast. Growing up with scars was and has been all I have ever known. My body as it is now is my "normal."

Going through grade school I never saw myself as different, other than the fact that I was overweight. The boys teased me of course, and some girls did too, but my parents taught me that these kids didn't feel good about themselves so they didn't want anyone else to either. These words always helped me get through the teasing and find friends that liked me for me.

My scars followed me from elementary school to junior high school and at eleven years old I learned that not all kids are cruel.

On the first day of school we found out that we would be required to take showers in the open locker room during physical education. This meant that I would have to undress in front of the other girls and shower with them. They would see my scars.

"Would you feel better if I talked to your teachers to see if you can take your shower after the other girls are gone?" my mother asked.

"Yeah," I said quietly. "I'm afraid they'll laugh at me."

My mother looked at me. Even though she may have been hurting for me inside she didn't let me see it. "Remember Stacie, anyone who would make fun of you because you have scars isn't worth the worry. They just do that because they think that will make them feel better about themselves." The next day my mother went to the school and met with my P.E. teacher and together they worked out a solution: I would wait until the other girls showered and went to the next class and then I would shower and be allowed to be late for my class. I was relieved. I would avoid all of the stares and ridicule that I knew would come from my scars.

But that night as I lay in bed I felt like a coward. I didn't want to be different and I didn't want to be picked on because I was allowed to do things the other girls didn't get to do. It was then that I knew what I had to do.

The next morning as I got ready for school I had a talk with my mother. "Mom, I think I might go ahead and shower in P.E. like everyone else."

She looked at me surprised. "You don't have to, honey. The teacher has already worked the schedule out for you."

I nodded, "I know Mom, but I don't want to be different because of my scars."

She hugged me and said, "I'm proud of you, but Stacie, if you change your mind, you don't have to." I hugged her back. I knew that no matter what happened, my mom would always understand.

That day I dreaded P.E., not just because it meant running, but because I knew that no matter what, I was going to shower when the other girls did. "Okay girls, it's time to go in and shower!" the teacher said, blowing her whistle. The one hundred yard walk to the locker room felt like one hundred miles. I went inside the locker room to my locker and stood there, taking deep breaths. It was now or never. As I undressed and picked up my towel, I saw some of the girls looking at me. To my surprise, not one of them laughed or made fun of me.

After we showered and dressed, all of the girls in my class walked over to me and asked how I got my scars. I told them my story and one girl asked, "Do they still hurt?"

I shook my head. "No, I can't feel anything," I said, which was true — I didn't have any feeling in my scars — not then, not now. They walked with me to our next class, talking about school and boys, but none of them talking about my scars. From that day on, P.E. was not the class I dreaded... math was. I didn't worry that I was different from the others. We were all the same; we were friends.

That day is when I realized I didn't have to be different. I just had to be me, and in doing so, friendships that began then followed me into my adult life. We all finished high school together as friends, and none of them ever made fun of me for my scars or my weight. As for the boys, when any of them tried to make fun of me, I had a whole class of friends to set them straight.

That P.E. class taught me that even though my body is different, I'm not. My scars don't make me who I am — my heart does.

~Stacie Joslin

Chapter
7

Just for Preteens

Finding Your Passion

Follow your passion, and success will follow you.

~Terri Guillemets

54

If My Heart Had a Voice

Music is what feelings sound like.
~*Author Unknown*

Some preferences you can't explain, like choosing vanilla over chocolate ice cream, or marmalade over strawberry jam. It's like that with me and the oboe. I can't tell you why I fell in love with the instrument at age seven but I can remember the exact moment when I did. My sister Kris and I were playing with Barbies as we listened to one of my parents' records. The smell of meatloaf with its melted cheese and ketchup crust floated through the house. Kris and I debated which shoes went best with Barbie's miniskirt when I heard a breathtaking sound.

I ran to the kitchen and tugged on Mom's blouse. "What's that?"

She listened. "A saxophone."

"Not now—before. Play it again and tell me."

We waited until I heard the mournful wail. "That's an oboe," Mom said. "Pretty, isn't it?"

She returned to the kitchen while I stood transfixed, listening to the passage while repeating the word. Oboe—it felt good in my mouth. I knew one day I would learn to play one.

I hadn't forgotten my promise when I entered fifth grade. On the contrary, I'd memorized every oboe passage in my parents' record collection. The sound washed over me in luscious waves. I heard it in my dreams.

On the first day of music class I couldn't stand still. The new music teacher was a short, swarthy man with an infectious grin. Mr. Burke raced around separating children into groups for each instrument. When everyone but me was in place he asked if I needed help deciding. Kids tittered behind me.

I stood up tall. "I want to play the oboe."

The room fell silent. Mr. Burke was so proud of my selection he was speechless. Eventually he cleared his throat. "You don't want to play the flute or the clarinet?"

"No. I like the sound an oboe makes."

He tugged his tie. "The problem is fifth graders can't play the oboe. The fingering is too complicated and the embouchure too difficult."

I knew there was a reason the oboe sounded so beautiful. When I asked how old I had to be, Mr. Burke said I could learn in seventh grade. "Okay," I said. "What do I play to train for the oboe?"

Mr. Burke gave me a funny look and suggested the flute. I happily complied because I was an oboist-in-training. For two years I sat with the flute players and learned to read music and mark time. But I longed to play the oboe.

The summer after sixth grade I enrolled in summer school. Mr. Burke was now the music teacher at East Avenue Junior High. He'd put on weight and didn't move so fast. When I told him I wanted to play the oboe, he didn't look up from his sheet music. "You play the flute."

Students swirled around us as they readied for practice. "You said I could learn in junior high."

He studied his stubby fingers. "If you switch you'll be two years behind."

Didn't he realize the oboe was superior? "That's why I'm here, to catch up."

He fiddled with his papers. "I don't think you can."

"But I waited two years." A whine had crept into my voice.

"The oboe's really difficult. It has an unbelievably tiny reed."

"I know. That's what makes it sound so special."

His shoulders slumped as he pulled himself up from the stool. "If you're determined to try, let's find you a loaner."

By the end of the day I was outfitted with the school's ancient plastic oboe. I also had an old cassette tape and the companion book, *So You Want to Play Oboe*. When Mom picked me up, I proudly displayed my new possessions.

I spent the summer teaching myself to play. The oboe's narrow double reed required more air pressure than the flute, so every day I blasted away until I grew too lightheaded to continue. I sat at the edge of my bed and blew until my head throbbed and my eyes bulged. The oboe screeched like a hundred cats in heat. My family huddled at the far end of the house. My sister said it was like sharing her bedroom with a psycho bagpiper. I barely registered the shrill whine and goose-like honk. All I heard was beautiful music.

By summer's end I could make it through the band pieces without passing out. I sounded better too. Not good, but better. Suddenly Mr. Burke was thrilled with the switch. He bragged that he directed the only band with an oboe.

I kept at it, and every month I played better than the last. By the time I reached high school, my parents were tired of repairing the ancient instrument. When I was asked to participate in the school's wind ensemble—an honor typically reserved for seniors and other talented musicians—I knew I was out of my league. Two years behind even the least gifted freshman, I shuddered when the conductor made it clear he wanted me to perform solos. The ancient loaner had to go.

On Christmas Eve I peeled shiny paper off a black case the size of a large jewelry box. Inside I discovered an oboe, its silver keys glistening against the ebony wood. I swallowed hard and pulled the two slender pieces from their red velvet bed. I twisted them together, interlocking the keys, and added the fluted bell at the bottom. I caressed the satiny finish, willing myself not to cry. My siblings already thought I was crazy for placing a musical instrument on my Christmas list.

With my new oboe in hand, Mom dropped me off for private lessons. Mrs. Traxler greeted me at the door. She wore a plaid skirt and sensible shoes, her thin frame held terrifyingly erect. Five minutes into my first lesson, she barked, "Who in God's name taught you to play that thing?"

When I said I taught myself, she frowned. I pulled out the cassette, and her mouth fell open. "Just a tape?"

"I had a book too."

She snapped her mouth shut and said to continue. Every few minutes she twisted the pearls at her neck and muttered. When I finished she said, "You have some bad habits, but you play pretty well, considering."

It was Mrs. Traxler who corrected my embouchure, improved my fingering, and taught me to make my own reeds. Because of her I finally learned to make my oboe sing.

As the only oboist in the region, I was in demand. I played in the orchestra, the band, and every high school musical. I worked hard to master the solos, but I never regretted my choice. I was doing what I loved. When I was only seven, I discovered my passion. Now I open the worn black case and think that if my heart had a voice, it would sing like an oboe.

~Cynthia Patton

55

Chicken Soup for the Soul

Big Gifts, Small Packages

Make the most of yourself, for that is all there is of you.
~Ralph Waldo Emerson

The day before I started junior high my mother took my older sister and me to a beauty school to let students cut our hair. We both hopped into salon chairs, long brown hair cascading down our backs. The stylist-in-training took one look at my sister and sighed, "Oh, look at this gorgeous, long hair!" She couldn't bring herself to do anything but trim it. Moments later, my beautiful sister bounced out of the chair, long hair intact, split ends on the floor. The student who got me rejoiced, "Oh, look at this long, gorgeous hair!" and proceeded to have the time of her life cutting it with a razor (which really tugged, pulled and hurt, by the way). I stepped down from the chair looking like a boy. Not a good way to begin junior high school.

To add insult to injury, later that year I was fitted with braces, joining the ranks of kids known as "metal mouths." But that's not all. Rubber bands were stretched from my top to bottom teeth so the inside of my mouth looked like a spider web when I yawned. I was also blessed with headgear. Metal bars started inside my mouth, came out, and then encircled my face to the back of my neck, inspiring kids to yell, "When's the monorail coming through?"

Did I mention that I was short for my age? Very short? Also, my name is really easy to mock. My siblings all have beautiful normal names that can readily be found on key chains or mini license plates. "Toby" is a more common moniker for dogs, horses and boys, so looking like a boy did not help matters. Looking back on it now, I wonder why I didn't fade into the background and hide until the braces came off, my hair grew, and I got taller.

My mother often said that "good things come in small packages" or whispered, "small but mighty" when kids made fun of me. Being a Girl Scout taught me that everyone is born with unique gifts. All we have to do is discover what those gifts are and utilize them. Girl Scouts also taught us to use our gifts for the betterment of others and the world at large. With all that seemed to be against me, I thought that philosophy was just a nice dream. I was anxious to discover my hidden talents, but what if I didn't have any? What if God or Nature accidentally short-changed me in that area as well?

I worked very hard in school. I just thought it was the right thing to do. I also loved to sing and had a powerful voice for a little kid. Audiences were surprised when this peanut of a girl, who looked like a boy, belted out a song with melodic accuracy and passion. Music became my life. I played in the orchestra and sang in choirs and ensembles. Then one day my mother took me to an audition for *The Sound of Music*. It was a huge casting call but I made it all the way to the final cuts. Standing on stage, seven brunettes and seven blonds, we awaited the decision. The call came two days later saying that the director was going with the blond cast.

"Such is life," my mother smiled. Still, *The Sound of Music* audition had made me feel comfortable onstage and opened up a whole new world. Back at school, auditions were held for the upcoming Charlie Brown Christmas show. I went for the part of Woodstock, Snoopy's little bird friend who doesn't say a word. I was cast as Lucy. No one was more surprised than I, except the bossy, popular girl who had expected the role. She was angry with me and I was crushed that I had been cast to play a mean character. Is that what the director thought of me?

Mr. Jacobs took me aside when I told him I didn't want the part. "You can do this," he said. "I know you're nothing like Lucy, but you can project, you've got a great voice and you're a good actor. It's not about being you on stage. Bring Lucy to life. It's because you are not like her that you will be able to do her so well." Clearly, he saw something in me that I did not.

He was right. It was fun to be bossy on stage and behave in a way I would never dream of in real life. People were shocked. I was shocked. "Small, but mighty," my mother whispered. The little girl who looked like a boy, with braces and short hair, had found a home on stage. In high school I went on to perform in every show and in the summer community theatre, then went on to earn my degree in theatre, studied in London and have been acting, singing, dancing and directing ever since.

Theatre can be so arbitrary. Things over which you have no control may determine whether or not you are cast: height, weight, hair color, vocal range, a "certain look." It's similar to what it's like being a teenager. So many things seem to be out of your control—everything from bad haircuts, zits, and homework, to bigger things like moving, or having a crush on someone who doesn't like you back. It's tempting to want to hide in the background until you grow out of it, but instead you can search for what really makes your soul soar. Getting taller was a dream that never quite came true for me. So I've hung onto my mom's old saying that good things come in small packages and made it my life's work to help children discover their gifts.

~Toby Abraham-Rhine

56

Chicken Soup for the Soul

The Dinosaur Wallpaper

Every child is an artist.
The problem is how to remain an artist once we grow up.
~Pablo Picasso

I don't know how she got the idea, but one day my teenage sister Karin unrolled eight feet of old wallpaper, spread it out on the living room floor backside up, and began a mural that would change my life.

With almost seven years between us, she always seemed so grown up and distant. We didn't have a lot in common, since she was in high school and I was a preteen. I suppose that's why I nearly exploded with joy while sitting across the rug from her, watching her concentrate, totally absorbed as her new world unfolded. First, she sketched the scene in pencil. I saw a tyrannosaurus take shape and attack a duckbill; a volcano in the distance spewed lava; lush plants seemed to move in an unseen wind while a pterodactyl floated on the same breath of air. A body of water shimmered in the distance with a brontosaurus eating nearby.

It didn't matter that these creatures didn't all belong in the same time period. What mattered was how dedicated Karin was to the vision—how each day and week she added more, and it came to life before my eyes.

Her hands skipped lightly as she added charcoal lines. The mural was mostly black and white, with red accents for lava, fruits, and the suggestion of a sunset. When it was complete, I beamed with pride for her as Mom hung it in our guestroom where it stayed for years.

I spent many hours gazing at the dinosaur wallpaper, lost in awe at the magical way she came up with thoughts and transformed them into something real with only her hands and some chalky sticks. I wanted nothing more than to do something like this amazing thing she'd accomplished, but I didn't have the natural talent she had. Still, my sister would look at my misshapen attempts and tell me they were good.

I didn't believe her, but hearing her say it was enough to keep me going. I only wanted the chance to sit on the same floor or at the same table with her while we both sketched.

Karin created many beautiful drawings that were added to the guestroom display. A few of my better attempts went up too, but I knew they paled in comparison to hers. "I couldn't draw that well when I was your age either," she'd comfort me. Her words kept me practicing feverishly in her company and later alone when she went on to college and then moved out on her own for good.

It was strange to be without my older sister, but I still had the love of art which she'd given me. Sometimes, I could imagine her sitting across the table working too. It was a comfort in the now emptier house. Over the years, I became more skilled. I still wasn't a natural, but my persistence was paying off. I looked forward to Karin's holiday visits so I could show her what I'd accomplished.

As Karin moved further into adulthood, her own art projects came fewer and farther between until new interests consumed her, and she left art behind. She still encouraged me, though. She sparked something inside me that remained for good. Now I paint, carve wood, sculpt marble, and use art when counseling children in schools. I sell some works and keep some, and offer others to family as gifts. It is my relaxation and my meditation. It's a safe space when everything else seems to be in turmoil.

Karin moved back to Vermont and bought a home where she displays my artwork in several rooms. We don't need art as a bond anymore; now well into adulthood, we have other shared experiences that provide much more in common than that. Seven years doesn't feel like such a big age difference now. Still, the art is one of the most precious gifts she gave me, and she beams with pride at my creations the same way I beamed with pride at the dinosaur wallpaper so many years ago.

~Tanya Sousa

57

Chicken Soup for the Soul

The Angels on the Artist's Way

My paintings are absolutely original. They are a power source.
A painting has power, and it can influence a person's whole life. When I paint,
beautiful things come to me. It comes from the Great Spirit.
~A. Kelly Pruitt

Growing up an only child was difficult, mostly because I had no one to talk to about how my parents treated me. Even at ten years old, I knew I was more adult, in many ways, than they were. Since I had no one to talk to about my problems at home, art became the way I expressed my frustration and sadness. I drew a lot in pencil and pen and ink, and painted on anything I could find, like white paper, construction paper and even flat rocks from the garden. Basically I drew and painted on whatever was handy.

I wanted to become a fashion illustrator when I grew up, but my parents discouraged me, saying there was no way I could earn an income as an artist. This made me sad, because I loved art more than anything and only felt happy when I was involved in drawing or painting. But my parents were strict, rarely praising me for my artwork. Even so, I kept drawing.

Thankfully, my middle school teachers were more enthusiastic about my art. In the eighth and ninth grades, they asked me to illustrate our school yearbook with cartoons of little blob characters I created. For instance, the sports section showed a little blob with a tennis racket and another with a basketball. I was thrilled that my art was recognized, although my parents cautioned me not to get too excited. "Artists have to have other real jobs in order to survive," they said. "So plan on becoming a teacher or a nurse, instead."

Because I read so many comic books on the long car trips my parents would take around the country and into Mexico, I knew that at least some artists found a way to make money. I wanted to grow up and draw comics and comic strips.

And so, even with my parents' disapproval, I made up my mind to do what my heart dictated and keep drawing, no matter what. In a way, I couldn't stop myself. I doodled all over my homework. I drew and painted greeting cards for my parents and my friends. My letters to friends and relatives always contained little illustrations.

One summer, when I was eleven or twelve, my parents decided to drive to Santa Fe and Taos, New Mexico from our home in Denver. This was the second trip we had taken to these beautiful places, where Native Americans sold their jewelry and pottery on the blankets spread out in the plazas. Also, at the time, there were many art galleries featuring the work of artists living in New Mexico. My parents and I went to many of these galleries, and I could see (despite what they'd cautioned) that some painters sold their works, often for high prices. These artists made a living painting.

One of the galleries featured the art of a man known as "the cowboy artist." Because my parents were from Colorado, his art struck a chord in them, and they wanted to own one of his paintings. So, they found out where his studio was—a short drive from Taos—and we took a side trip to see him and more of his art, which my parents hoped to buy.

As usual, I was the third wheel on this trip, tagging along on my parents' adventures. But I always liked the stark beauty of the New Mexican landscape, with its rolling green hills and random cactus trees, so I studied the stark setting and imagined myself living there as an artist.

After a while, we finally ended up at A. Kelly Pruitt's studio. We parked, got out and wandered around in the studio room where he worked and displayed his art. He came to greet us: a tall, lean man, with longish hair, wearing faded blue jeans and a Western shirt. His face was tan and weathered.

While my parents decided which of his paintings they wanted to buy, (their debate was loud; they often disagreed about money), Kelly motioned to me to follow him outside. He was holding a postcard showing one of his paintings in black and white on the front.

"I want to talk to you while your parents decide," he said. "And even though we've just met, I want to tell you I notice something special about you."

I must have seemed startled, but he continued. "Not many people I've met have the special quality that you have," he said. "And you should remember that you have it, especially when times are tough."

With that last word, he wrote something on the back of the postcard and then handed it to me. On the other side, he'd written, "Walk out into the light. Angels are near." and signed his name.

I thanked him, and he just winked and smiled. "Let's go see how your parents are doing," he said.

Eventually, they decided to buy an oil painting that showed four cowboys racing their galloping horses towards an unseen destination. Kelly carefully wrapped the painting for safe travel in our trunk on the way back to Denver.

I never showed my parents the postcard he gave me. I felt he meant it to be between us. But each time I looked at his painting hanging in our home, I remembered what he'd said, and it encouraged me to carry on—no matter what. His message helped me get through many arguments with my parents and the disappointments that followed in my lonely, chaotic life. Sometimes it seemed like there were more downs than ups, but I persevered, going towards the light, knowing something better awaited me.

I still have the postcard he gave me, which I keep in my book of treasured memories and souvenirs. I believed, as he had written, I had a special quality that would allow me to get past heartache and obstacles; the angels were close and would guide me, he said. And they did. And so did he.

~Sydney Kravetz

Riding Free

No hour of life is wasted that is spent in the saddle.
~Winston Churchill

verything went wrong the last few months just before seventh
grade came to a close. My mom was ill and she was getting
worse. And then I found out we were moving. I wouldn't be
able to start eighth grade in West L.A. with my friends. We were moving to Redondo Beach, which sounded fun, but I'd be alone. Could
life get any more depressing?

Relief came when my dad asked me if I wanted to go to summer
camp in Arizona. My best friend Ginnie was also going. Suddenly my
world held a small glimmer of hope. It would be a five-week camp
with horseback riding, trips to the Grand Canyon, swimming and
canoeing.

Even though I'd miss home, I was eager to escape from my sad
feelings about moving.

Camp turned out to be an adventure I'll remember forever.
Arizona was sunny and beautiful. Flagstaff has gorgeous mountains
as well as green meadows. I met new friends. Being from L.A., a lot of
celebrities sent their kids there as well. My cabin mates included the
daughter of a TV star as well as the daughters of the owner of a well
known Napa winery and a very famous child star.

The most exciting thing for me was being able to ride the horses.

On the day we were free to do whatever we wanted, my friend Pam and I strode over to the stables.

"Trust me, you'll love this," she said as we made our way down the trail to the barn that was on the other side of the campgrounds. "If you want to own a horse one day, you'll need to learn how to catch and saddle one."

They were beautiful. I could see about seven horses roaming around in a large ring. They were letting in two girls at a time to learn how to put on the tack—a harness over the horse's head—and, oh my gosh, real Western saddles! Each girl had a ranch hand to help her. We stood in line. When it was our turn, there were three horses left for us to choose from. There was a beautiful white horse, one black and white one, and a brown and white one at the far side of the ring. I couldn't see her face but she would occasionally look back, as if to say, "Don't bother me. I want nothing to do with any of you." As an only child and a loner, I knew how she felt.

All of a sudden my stomach knotted. I'd ridden a horse only a couple of other times in my life, and had absolutely no idea how to "break and saddle" a horse. These were no docile creatures. They avoided being captured and harnessed and wanted no part of being tamed by us girls.

One of the helpers walked up to me and handed me the harness. He quietly gave me some instructions on how to approach the animal and put the tack over its head and then secure it. He backed away. I was alone in the ring with all three horses.

"Choose the pretty white one, Kim," I heard Pam call out. I started toward the white horse, but she looked bored. The brown and white loner was the one I was drawn to.

I stopped walking and stood still. The brown and white horse watched me. She moved from the far side of the ring and began slowly walking toward me. I didn't know what to do so I just stood there. I heard the guy call out, "Go slow and easy. This one can be difficult." I looked at the horse and our eyes locked.

She seemed to challenge me to dare to put the harness on her. But, as we had been shown, I slowly lifted the reins and placed them easily over her head. I smiled at her. "Good girl," I said to both of us.

"Good work, Kim," the ranch hand called out. He slowly approached us, and then helped me saddle her up. I climbed on her back and he led us out of the ring.

"Off you go," the man said. I leaned down and whispered to her. "Let's get out of here." We started at a prance that quickly turned into a full gallop. Instead of being terrified I became exhilarated.

We took off through the meadows with the sun beaming down on us and the wind whipping through my hair. I held on tight. I looked around at the treeless meadow and watched as everything went by in a whoosh. As I let the horse have her stead, I blended into her. We were both racing to a better place, an exciting adventure where promises lay ahead and everything would be okay.

I'd never felt so free and alive.

I closed my eyes and completely let go of my fears. After a few seconds I realized I had tears running down my face. I felt so happy. I made a mental note to remember this moment for the rest of my life.

The horse seemed to know where she was going and we trotted back to the barn. I patted her and whispered, "We'll be okay, girl."

As camp progressed, I had the time of my life. It gave me happiness and a freedom I've cherished since that moment. I still had to begin eighth grade with strangers and my mom never did regain her health, but the time at camp was the happiest five-week period of my life.

~Kimberly Kimmel

59

Chicken Soup for the Soul

Softball and Self-Confidence

Whether you think you can or think you can't—you are right.
~Henry Ford

"**W**hat about the jersey?" I paused from placing clothes in a Goodwill bag and looked at my friend. She was holding up a small red and white jersey with the number twelve and the nickname "Runt" printed on back.

A smile tugged at my mouth as I snagged the tiny shirt out of her hands.

"I'll keep this one."

We were in the process of sorting which clothes were going to college with me and which ones were getting donated to Goodwill when my friend came across one of my fondest memories of junior high—my softball jersey.

I ran my hand over the soft cotton of the faded shirt and I was transported back to the softball field behind the school—the green grass was bare in places from gym class, dirt rose as one of my teammates slid home, and hot summer sun warmed my skin.

I was new to the school district the year I joined softball. I had made several friends, but being a self-described shy girl I was lacking confidence. I didn't raise my hand in class, I hung back in gym class and I wasn't participating in any after-school activities. So I surprised myself when one of my new friends asked me to join the softball team and I said yes.

We were the Dairy Queen Braziers. If we won a game we got a free ice cream cone from DQ. I don't recall us ever winning a game.

At our first practice we picked our numbers and the names we wanted on the back of our jerseys. I picked twelve because that was my age and my teammates picked "Runt" because at seventy-nine pounds I was the smallest seventh grader on the team.

As the coach started assigning positions, most of the girls jockeyed for first base and pitcher while I volunteered for right field. Hardly any balls came to right field and I wanted to be away from the action.

My first practice went well until it was time to bat. I was uneasy standing at the plate while everyone stared at me. It made me want to disappear. I swung at the first pitch and missed. Strike one. I swung at the second ball and hit a grounder right to the pitcher. I was out before I could even run to first base.

It turned out I was pretty bad at softball. When a ball did come to right field I was too afraid to really get under the ball to catch it, and when I batted, I either struck out or hit grounders that were easily caught. Despite this, I took practices seriously and enjoyed being part of a team.

I quickly became friends with the girls, and as they helped me adjust to the new school my confidence grew. I got better at the game. I started catching and occasionally covered third base. Although I never pitched, I learned I could throw the ball really far. I even hit a home run.

At school I started participating in class and in after-school activities, even performing in a musical. I was no longer the shy girl in gym class and was often selected to be a team captain.

Softball didn't make me popular, but being on a team gave me the confidence I needed to make friends, try new activities and succeed in school.

I folded the jersey and tucked it into a box that contained other items that would get packed away while I was at college. I'm still terrible with a bat, but I wanted to keep the jersey as a reminder that life is full of possibilities.

~Valerie D. Benko

60

Junior High Zoo

Metaphors have a way of holding the most truth in the least space.
~Orson Scott Card

I was sitting on the hard, plastic chair in my English classroom, fidgeting restlessly. It was the lower grades' recess, and I could hear them playing and laughing outside. I was green with envy. Don't get me wrong, I love English class. I hope to become a writer, and English class gives me lots of practice. It just gets harder and harder to focus when the minute hand on the clock is getting closer and closer to lunchtime.

Mrs. Chappell, my favorite teacher, started passing out an article for my class to read. It was about a writer who told some students to write about one of three different subjects: "The Strangest Person You Have Ever Met," "The Stupidest Thing You Have Ever Done," or "Advice for Junior High." When we finished reading the captivating article, Mrs. Chappell told us to write something about one of the three subjects. It was the last one that caught my eye. We had fifteen short minutes. I grabbed my notebook and started scribbling on my paper. When I finished it I looked at the clock.

"Whew, just in time," I muttered.

Mrs. Chappell then asked for a volunteer to read their paper. My hand instinctively shot up before I registered what she had said. Oops, I thought. Naturally, Mrs. Chappell called on me.

"I did my, um, paper on, um, advice for junior high," I stammered, and then began to read aloud:

"Junior high is a zoo! It's filled to the brim with a lot of naïve kids who all want to be top dog, but most of them are a completely different kind of animal. I consider myself a snake because I am hardly ever comfortable in my own skin. I have always been one of the quiet kids. When the spotlight is directed at me, I almost always say the wrong thing. Otherwise, I become like a parrot, simply echoing what the leaders of the flock say. Those leaders seem to be chameleons, because they change their appearance at just the right time to stay alive. There are also many mockingbirds in junior high, making fun of everything you say. But don't let those people get under your skin. My advice is this: Don't be a parrot, mockingbird, or snake. Be yourself, whatever animal you are, because that is the greatest gift you have."

My words were met with a long silence. My heart was pounding with anxiety. Would they like it? Mrs. Chappell just stared at me with something between a smile and a look of disbelief. Then, someone started to clap. Soon, the rest of the class joined in. My heart swelled with pride. They liked it! I was so relieved. Just then the lunch bell rang. Everybody stopped their clapping and got up to get their lunches. I joined in. On my way to get my lunch, many of the kids (chameleons, mockingbirds, and parrots alike) complimented me and patted me on the back, saying they completely agreed with me. I hadn't realized how universal those words might be to others until that very moment.

~Sara Hedberg

Homesick

Courage doesn't always roar. Sometimes courage is the little voice
at the end of the day that says I'll try again tomorrow.
~Mary Anne Radmacher

"Isn't this great?" Julie said, as the bus rumbled out of the parking lot. "Four whole weeks without our parents."

As Mom and Dad shrank into nothing, I swallowed hard to force the lump out of my throat. "Four weeks," I echoed. What had I done?

"Not to mention no more annoying brother," a girl in front of us turned around.

Another head appeared next to her with long black pigtails that whacked me in the face as the bus found every pothole. "Make that brothers. And Mom's new baby. Ugh."

Talk soon turned to camp. These girls, most of them around twelve like me, had been going to this camp for years. I had no idea what they were talking about and Julie, a girl I'd only met two months earlier, didn't explain. I just sat there, forgotten. How had I let this new friend talk me into a month at sleep-away camp? The frogs in my stomach were jumping so high, they were giving me a lump in my throat and pushing on my eyeballs.

Arriving at camp was no better. It was dry and dusty and smelled of horses. At least Julie and I were in the same A-frame cabin that we shared with five other girls and a counselor. She spent every day on a horse, smelling of horse, and covered in dust.

Sure, I'd ridden horses before, but one ride here was enough for me. The ground was so dry that riding meant being in a dust cloud. It took two days to get that taste out of my mouth, and the odor clung to me like a shadow.

I cried and wrote a sad letter home. First, I lightly sketched a picture of me crying. Then I wrote a letter over it. I'd been there more than a week by the time I got a reply: "We'll see you Parents' Weekend and talk about it then."

Desperate to get away from the heat and to cleanse myself of the acrid air, I went swimming every chance I got.

"Synchronized swimming today," a girl named April told me. I had no idea what that was, but if it meant being in the pool, I would try it. Soon I was part of her foursome, practicing a routine. We would perform it for Parents' Weekend.

Unfortunately, swimming couldn't last all day. I stared at the beckoning pool as I attempted to brush out my waist-length blond hair. "Well, come on," April yanked my arm. "Auditions are today. Finally."

"Auditions?" That did not sound like something to be excited about. Still, I tagged along with her through the dust.

"I've been waiting since I got here." She pulled a script from her bag. The edges were wet from her swimsuit. "*Li'l Abner.*"

"Huh?"

"That's the play they're doing this year."

"Play?" I stumbled. "Never heard of it."

"You're so short, you'd be great," she smiled. "Play one of the kids."

It turned out that girls all over camp had been practicing for the audition. There I was totally unprepared and not at all certain I wanted to be there.

"Just sing something," the counselor in charge of the play told me.

"Uh." My mouth was dry.

"How about 'Happy Birthday'?" She played it on the guitar and I stumbled through in my low voice.

When the parts were posted the next day, I had made it! I actually had two parts. One was playing this little salesman who shows up and tries drinking this concoction that Li'l Abner claims made him so big. After I drank it, I got to shake and moan and stuff. Then people crowded around me to hide me so this really tall girl could pretend to be me all bigger. The other part was to be a dancer, singing and dancing a funny song.

The days flew by and I was actually having fun. Suddenly it was Parents' Weekend. Our swimming routine went perfectly.

"Ready to go home now?" Mom asked.

I hesitated. The play was the last day of camp. That was two whole weeks away. Should I get relief from this horrible place and go home to my cozy bed and my mom's cooking? They could find someone for my small part. As for dancing, I hid myself in the back, so no one would miss me there. Still, I would be letting everyone down.

Then, April was there. "Just wait till you come back and see the play. It is going to be the best ever!"

Now that I had found my own way instead of following Julie around, it wasn't so bad. "Mom, I think I'll stick it out."

"I want you out in front," the play director ordered the following day. "So the others can follow you." Now the leader of the dancers, I hardly noticed the days passing.

That final day, with all the parents watching, I remembered all my lines and didn't trip or anything when we danced.

"The next time I go to camp," I told my mom on the ride home, "I'm picking it myself and going alone."

Mom hugged me. "Boy, you sure are growing up."

I smiled back at her. "Yeah," I whispered. "But it's good to be going home."

~D. B. Zane

The Write Feeling

Fill your paper with the breathings of your heart.
~William Wordsworth

A s a military brat, I moved a lot. I mostly went to school with other kids whose parents were also in the military, so I had an instant family. But when my dad retired from the Marines after twenty years of service, I found myself attending a civilian school with twelve-year-olds who did not understand about deployment, PX, commissary trips, and making friends instantly because we were all in the same boat. Suddenly, I was a new sixth grade student in a small town in Georgia, where we had settled in to help my mother's father.

I was a stranger in a strange land. Everyone in my class had grown up together, were cousins or other relations, and they had no room to spare for an outcast such as myself. I wore different clothes, had different thoughts, and spoke with an accent (so they said). I cried for the first few weeks of school. I had no friends, no activities, and no promise of a bright future.

To cope with it all, I began writing in my diary every day—stories of adventure, of old friends, of feelings that I could not speak. I wrote as if my life depended on it, as if the very next breath I took could not happen unless I wrote down words. I sat under trees at recess and wrote while other kids talked about me and played games, often pointing at me and laughing.

One day, my teacher, Mrs. Bush, came to me and asked what it was I did in that book. I didn't tell her about the adventures of my characters, all strong girls who roamed the world helping those in need. I didn't dare tell her about the pages that were wet from my tears. I hid the fact that sometimes I wrote about her students who made snide remarks to me and how it made me feel all alone in the world. But I did tell her I enjoyed writing and preferred writing to playing.

She smiled at me and walked away.

About three weeks later, Mrs. Bush gave us a writing assignment. It was connected to a history lesson somehow, but I can't remember how. All I know is that I was excited about it, thrilled that I could now participate in something I knew I excelled in.

That night I worked and worked on the essay. I wrote with great passion. It was my one chance to feel important and accepted by the class.

A few days after handing in my report, Mrs. Bush called me up to the front of the classroom.

I stood before thirty pairs of eyes looking at me, my long brown hair, my freckled face, my crooked teeth and I worried. Was I in trouble? Did I do something wrong?

Mrs. Bush gathered her stack of papers and told the class how much she appreciated all the work that went into the essays and that everyone had done a great job. But, she said, one student stood out as an excellent writer, one with imagination, creativity, and word mastery. That student was me!

The class clapped politely and Mrs. Bush handed me my paper, with the following remarks on it: "Malinda, you are an excellent writer. Please keep on writing and share your gift of writing with the world. I am proud of you and glad you are in my class."

Mrs. Bush helped me feel a sense of belonging, a place of purpose, and a way to survive a transition in life that was pivotal. She helped me gain confidence in myself that stayed with me well beyond sixth grade.

~Malinda Dunlap Fillingim

Chapter
8

Just for

Preteens

That Was Embarrassing

I am thankful for laughter, except when milk comes out of my nose.

~Woody Allen

63

Chicken Soup
for the Soul

A Hard Lesson in Humiliation

Perhaps I know best why it is man alone who laughs;
he alone suffers so deeply that he had to invent laughter.
~Friedrich Nietzsche

Has there ever been a time in your life when you were so humiliated that you wanted to either die or simply evaporate into oblivion? I have personally had my share of humiliating situations. And yes, I must admit, the thought has crossed my mind to skip town and simply disappear. But that was all it was, just a fleeting thought. I think fear and common sense keep us from ever seriously considering doing such a thing. Plus, as I've learned over time, placing geographical distance between yourself and your problems never really solves anything.

The worst day in Harold Fanning history began on a Monday morning when I was in the fifth grade. For some reason I had over-slept, and in my haste to get dressed I grabbed the first white shirt I could find. I hurriedly slipped it on and rushed out the back door heading for school. Unfortunately, my mistake didn't show itself until we were all on the baseball field during third period physical education class. Earlier I had spied a few of my classmates looking at me and talking among themselves. A few others were pointing and laughing but I didn't think it was directed at me and so I didn't give it much thought at the time. But as we were all standing around waiting to be chosen for a team, one of my friends finally informed me what all the commotion was about. I could hardly believe it! In my haste to get ready for school I had accidentally grabbed one of my sister's blouses. There I was, waiting to be chosen for a team, wearing the prettiest girly blouse known to man. It was complete with a rounded collar, cute little blue flowers, trimmed lace, and heart-shaped buttons down the front.

In my disgrace and desperation I realized I had to do something—this situation called for immediate action. Knowing that I couldn't leave school, I frantically searched the school closets, where I finally discovered an old leather jacket that someone had abandoned the previous winter. I immediately put it on to cover my shame and embarrassment. After school I walked almost three miles home enduring one-hundred-degree heat wearing my sister's blouse and a leather jacket! To add insult to injury, cars full of friends and neighbors passed me by, whistling and mockingly asking me if they could take me on a date and send me flowers.

So, what's the moral of this story? Here you are, reading this book, thinking that nobody has problems like yours. The moral is this—we all have those moments where we want to disappear from the face of the earth forever. But maybe now that you've read about my own humiliation, you'll realize that you're not alone, and it's not so bad after all.

~Harold D. Fanning

Bucky Beaver

Siblings are the people we practice on, the people who teach us about fairness and cooperation and kindness and caring—quite often the hard way.
~Pamela Dugdale

I f you were to look back at the pictures of my early years, you would be left with the impression that I was a happy child. Not that I wasn't, it's just that the evidence was, shall we say, obvious. The manifestation of my happiness was my large smile. You couldn't miss it. Unfortunately, you couldn't miss the extra large set of bucked teeth that went along with it.

It didn't help that one of the many nicknames my father gave me was Bucky Beaver. Nicknames used by my parents were always considered terms of endearment. To Dad, and to me, Bucky Beaver was an expression of love straight from the heart. Who cared that my teeth were the most prominent part of my profile? They were mine, and because my dad loved me, he also loved my teeth.

Unfortunately, my younger brother, John, didn't work under the same rules. John was a smart and articulate boy, with an uncanny ability to turn goodness into evildoing. And so it was with Bucky Beaver. What was once an expression of my father's fondness, my brother used to torture me.

"Hey, Bucky Beaver!" John would sneer as he rocketed past me and my friends on his bike. Occasionally, when we were old enough to walk to the corner ice cream store, which was where all the cool kids hung out, I would wait for my order at the walk-up window. Then I'd hear, "Order for Bucky Beaver!" and see my brother snickering off in the corner. My appetite gone, I would return home, defeated.

It's not like I could do anything to change the source of his teasing. Not like when he called me Smelly Kelley. To avoid any truth behind that name, all I had to do was routinely bathe. But the teeth—I could brush them all I wanted, but they still stuck out.

Even my mom, who was supposed to be my advocate, crossed the line. When she forwarded our school pictures to my grandparents in Seattle, Mom would call first to give the heads-up.

"I sent the kids' school pictures to you today," Mom would say with an almost apologetic tone. "Yes." she continued. "Kelley? Uh huh... well,"—nervous laugh—"we're hoping she'll grow into them." She wasn't talking about my feet.

To add to my indignity, when I was eight years old, three-quarters of my front left tooth got in the way of a school building while playing tag, and ended up in the dirt. I remember the shock of it all. Not so much that I had lost part of my tooth. To me, it was just one more in a line of many that had already fallen out, or were on their way. Losing a tooth up to that point had been a cause for celebration. It was a rite of passage, followed by money left under my pillow by the tooth fairy. This time was different. I got an entirely new reaction when I opened the door to my house after school that day.

"Hi Mom!" I yelled, smiling extra wide to show off my new look.

"Oh my God!" Mom shrieked. Her jaw dropped, and she began to slowly weave back and forth as she stood, pale faced, staring down at me.

"What? It'th jutht my tooth!" I lisped. It was then that I learned the significance of permanent teeth.

The next thing I remember I was reclining in the dentist chair with my mom and Dr. Roberts hovering over me. The good dentist announced there was no saving the tooth, particularly since what could have been saved was still lying somewhere in the dirt on the school playground.

Regardless, a crown was the way to go. A shiny silver half-crown covering what remained of my left center bucked tooth. A look that was memorialized in my next set of school pictures.

Things didn't improve when I graduated to a full-sized enamel colored crown. It didn't change the fact that my teeth were still... prominent. Which was all the permission my brother needed to continue on his quest to embarrass me.

My protests about my brother's relentless name calling, and ultimately about my teeth, fell on deaf ears until the summer before sixth grade. That's when my parents finally acknowledged my "condition" was not going to improve on its own. That's when the idea of braces was first introduced.

For weeks, my parents and I considered the evidence. There would be pain involved, and considerable expense. I would also have to sacrifice eating gum, gooey candy, and popcorn. On the other hand, straightening my teeth would severely weaken my brother's arsenal. How I welcomed that opportunity!

Finally, the big day arrived. Once again I found myself reclining in a chair, only this time I was in my new orthodontist's office. Dr. Ellis worked quickly to weld gleaming silver onto my smile. Pounding, pulling, gluing, twisting, the experience was unsettling. But I knew it would be worth it to finally be able to avoid my brother's persistent taunting.

Once I got home, I inspected Dr. Ellis' work more closely. I inched close to the large mirror hanging in the hallway and opened my mouth wide. Oh! I stepped back a bit, blinking, then began to stare. Each one of my teeth was individually wrapped in silver. A single horseshoe-shaped wire ran along each tooth on the upper jaw, and another on the lower jaw, to help rein in my wayward teeth.

At that moment my brother came bustling around the corner. He stopped abruptly, surprised to see me there. Silently, John eyed my transformation. He knew the days of Bucky Beaver were officially over. I caught a momentary flicker of defeat in his eyes, which made my insides feel warm and fuzzy.

But then his eyes slowly began to narrow, and the corner of his mouth curled up slightly. Squaring his shoulders, John turned and positioned himself for a quick getaway, as he yelled back over his shoulder, "Hey Brace Face!"

~Kelley Stimpel Martinez

Fighting Back

No one can make you feel inferior without your consent.
~Eleanor Roosevelt

I'm certain that psychologists have suggestions for dealing with bullies, but when I was in fifth grade, I hadn't heard any. I was just a quiet girl with astigmatism who had to wear glasses to read the board.

In our class there was one boy who had been held back a year. His nickname was "Red" since he had a carrot top and bright freckles. However, he was not very nice. He was taller and heavier than the other boys and girls in our class and would pick a fight at recess with anyone smaller than himself. We all avoided him as much as possible, which made him all the more hostile.

One day our teacher called on Red for an answer when he wasn't paying attention to her history lesson.

"That's a stupid question," Red responded in a surly tone of voice.

Our teacher ignored him and called on me for the answer. When I gave the correct response, there were snickers from some of the other boys. Red turned toward me, a person he'd ignored until now, his face flaming the color of his nickname.

"I'll get you for that," he threatened.

There were several gasps. I think one of them was from me.

That day, I didn't go out for recess. I went to the nurse's office instead. I told my teacher I had a sick stomach, and it wasn't a lie. I couldn't even eat my lunch. My stomach was much too nervous. I knew that Red would go after me. He'd beaten up boys much bigger and stronger than I was. He usually didn't bother with girls, but it appeared I was going to be the exception. I really didn't know what to do to protect myself from this vicious bully. I realized Red had problems, serious emotional and mental problems, but that didn't help me. And there was no appealing to his better side. Trying to talk to him wasn't going to work.

I waited a while to walk home from school that day, hoping Red would forget about me if he didn't see me. But fate was not that kind. Red knew where I lived, since he lived half a block away. I was nearly home when he sprang out of the shrubbery and ambushed me. He grabbed me by the jacket collar and I screamed. As he brought his fist up to punch me, I swung the book bag I always carried. It was full of heavy books. The bag connected with his head with a dull thumping sound. Red groaned and released me.

I ran the rest of the way home not even looking back to see if he was following me. I was crying and breathless when I came into the house. I was also shaking violently. My mother was there and asked for an explanation. Flustered, I told her as best I could about the incident with Red. She immediately wanted to call the school, but I begged her not to do it.

"All right," she said finally with some reluctance, "but if this boy ever bothers you again, I'm going to report the incident and ask your principal to take action."

I agreed with my mother. However, I couldn't help thinking that reporting Red would only make him angrier. I feared retaliation.

The next day, my mother insisted on taking me to school and I didn't refuse. I was grateful. But I knew that wouldn't solve the problem. I wasn't sure what would. When I got to class, several of the kids pointed at me and then at Red. I wasn't certain what that meant until I took a look at him. There he sat with the biggest black eye I'd ever seen.

Now I understood the buzz in our classroom.

Apparently, word had gotten around. It seemed another student had seen the attack Red had launched on me, and its aftermath. That student had spread the word. After our class settled down, our teacher turned to Red.

"That's quite a shiner you have there. I'd give up picking on smaller kids if I were you," she said to him. Then she turned to me with a pleased smile. "Some of them have the courage to stand up for themselves. You're giving bullies a bad name."

The entire class laughed and Red looked more than a little embarrassed. He was suddenly the object of scorn and ridicule. It was the best revenge anyone could have against a bully. He never bothered me again. In fact, his reign of terror had come to an abrupt end.

~Jacqueline Seewald

The Thing about Static Cling

Never say, "oops." Always say, "Ah, interesting."
~Author Unknown

S ome days are like an umbrella inverted by the wind—they just don't go the way they're supposed to. For me, one such day started with me sleeping through my alarm clock.

I had just a few minutes before I would have to leave if I was going to catch the school bus. I ran to our dryer and quickly grabbed some shorts and a shirt that I had washed the day before. I quickly pulled my clothes on and then grabbed my backpack as I raced out the door.

It was the last day of classes. I was relishing the fact that I would be giving my final science report in front of my class that day. The presentation would be my last assignment for the school year. Afterwards, I could finally relax and start my summer vacation.

My best friend, Charity, met me as I stepped off the bus. We instantly picked back up on the conversation we were having the previous day, which had only ended because we had to go home.

As we walked down the halls, I swore I saw some other kids look at me and then start whispering. Charity didn't seem to notice. A few steps later, a boy pointed right at me and he and his friends began laughing.

Once we were past them, I nervously asked, "What was that about?"

"Who knows," said Charity. "Boys are dumb."

Maybe it was nothing, just boys being dumb, but I still felt a little apprehensive.

There wasn't time to dwell on it though; the bell rang and it was time for my presentation.

"Good luck on your report," said Charity. "I'll find you after class." She continued down the hallway to her own class, as I walked into the science room.

When it was my turn to present, I grabbed my science binder and walked to the front of the room. I was just about to start reading what I had learned about DNA when I felt a small tickle on the back of my knee. I looked back to see what it was. And suddenly, I knew why the boys in the hallway were laughing.

To my horror, I discovered my little sister's underwear clinging to the back of my shorts by static. And it wasn't just any underwear either. No, this was special purple and pink princess character underwear.

I froze. Had my classmates seen it? I scanned their faces, but I couldn't tell. If they hadn't, they surely would when I walked back to my seat.

I made a rash decision. I reached back and grabbed the underwear as fast as I could. I flung the underwear into my science binder and slammed it shut. I could feel the burn of a blush spreading across my face as I heard the teacher. "Amanda, please share your report." Had they noticed? I checked their faces again. Some were smiling, but I wasn't sure if it was because of me. Perhaps no one had noticed. Perhaps I had moved so quickly, they didn't know. I sighed quietly and relaxed. The only thing I had to do was give my report and then I could sit down and let the nightmare be over.

But as I looked down to start reading my report, I realized my report was in my binder. The same binder holding my embarrassing secret. "Please, we're waiting," the teacher called.

Begrudgingly I opened the binder, holding it close to my body so no one could see what was inside. With their smiles morphing into wicked smirks, the princesses seemed to stare at me like a cat staring at a mouse. I couldn't see all of my report without moving the undergarment, so I read what I could and then clumsily recited the rest from memory. I wanted to disappear. Even if they hadn't seen the underwear, my unintelligible report was embarrassing enough.

When I finished, I sprinted back to my seat. Had they noticed? I'll never know. As soon as I sat down, I put my head on my desk and covered it with my arms.

The rest of the presentations dragged on. The bell finally rang and the rest of the class filed out. I waited until everyone had left and then shoved the binder holding my miserable surprise deep into my backpack. I staggered out of the room to find Charity waiting for me at the door.

"What happened?" she asked. "Did something go wrong with your report?"

"I can't say," I told her. "It's too embarrassing."

Charity finally coaxed me into telling her and when I did, she laughed. That made me even more embarrassed. It was a good thing it was the last day of school that year, because I wouldn't have gone back the next day.

I asked my parents what they thought about home schooling me. After all, I knew for certain the kids in the hallway saw the smiling princesses and I thought at least a few in my class probably did too. It would only be a matter of time before the entire school knew. And if my best friend would laugh at me, they would all laugh. They'd probably make up nicknames for me. I'd be known as Amanda Underpants for the rest of middle school. Maybe for all of high school too. My parents just smiled and said I would be fine.

The nice thing about summer vacation is it lasts a long time. Long enough to get bored. Long enough for kids to miss being in school. Long enough to realize everyone has embarrassing moments. That day it was my turn, tomorrow will be someone else's. Because that's the thing about static cling—it happens to us all. No one is immune from days like that; we all get a turn. The kids that laughed at me will spill chocolate pudding on their shirts or split their pants in P.E. or something like that. And when their day comes, I hope they don't get too upset. I hope they are just glad to have a funny story, the way I am now about the day princesses in pink and purple sabotaged my science report.

~Amanda Yardley Luzzader

Just Desserts

Whoso diggeth a pit shall fall therein.
~Proverb

It was a smaller version of a Ferris wheel, but instead of an open seat, it was an enclosed, cage-type thing designed for children, with two seats facing each other. A large lever between the seats could be pulled toward or away from the rider, causing the cage to rock back and forth. If you held the lever back long enough, the cage would go upside down and make a complete turnover.

The summer I was nine I was considered responsible enough to accompany my little brother, who was three, on various rides and my mother decided this one would be safe enough.

It was also the summer I not only learned a valuable lesson in physics, but also that what goes around actually does come around, and that one must live with the consequences of bad decisions.

We had gone around a couple of times when I decided to add a little variation to the ride by operating the lever. We began to rock as the cage went up and down in its big circle, and my brother began screaming for me to stop.

The more frightened he became, the more I enjoyed the ride. Finally I made the cage turn completely over, much to the terror of my little passenger. My mother was shouting from below for me to stop, but I was having so much fun I didn't hear her.

Then it happened. My brother was so terrified he had an accident.

I'm not talking a little water here, I'm talking heavy-duty stuff that escaped from his loose-fitting sun suit, and went flying every which way inside the enclosure.

The lever was stuck in the hold position so we kept turning over and over. I was so busy shielding my eyes, I couldn't free it. The stuff just kept ricocheting from side to side, top to bottom, around and around in the little cage. I wanted to scream for the operator to stop the ride, but I didn't dare open my mouth!

Finally it was over. The cage came to a standstill, and I had the option of remaining in it or facing my furious mother. But she decided that I had been sufficiently punished for the evil treatment of my brother, and all she said was, "It serves you right."

Then she said something about "just desserts"—but I sure didn't feel like eating anything.

~Jackie Fleming

A Simple Vow

I attended the sixth grade in an archaic, rural school in southern Ohio. With a red brick exterior, wooden plank floors, and a bell on the roof, it was straight out of an old-fashioned painting.

I was the new kid, having transferred into this particular elementary school from a Catholic school that had been forced to close. Being slight in stature, I barely weighed eighty-five pounds.

One day, my teacher was lecturing from the chalkboard at the front of the classroom, when he turned around and stated, "It's a bit stuffy in here." Then he looked directly at me, adding, "Master Scanlan, would you open the windows?"

"Yes, sir," I replied.

I arose from my desk and walked back to the first window in a series that lined the classroom's left wall. Using an underhand grip, I grasped the two metal handles, and lifted upward.

The window didn't budge.

Then I heard some girls giggle behind me.

So I exerted a little more effort—to the point of actually grunting.

The window still didn't move.

Now I could feel thirty pairs of eyes burning a hole into my back.

But then my teacher intervened, stating "Oh, never mind, Master Scanlan. You can return to your seat."

I trudged back to my desk, humiliated.

However, the teacher poured salt into the wound, adding, "Master Scanlan, a few years ago, the same thing happened to another young man."

You could've heard a pin drop.

"So I asked one of the girls to open the window," he continued, "and she did."

"Yes, sir," I mumbled.

The entire sixth grade erupted in laughter.

"But I will spare you the same embarrassment," the teacher added. After which, he returned to lecturing from the chalkboard.

That night, after dinner, I ducked into Mom and Dad's bedroom and locked the door. Then I stood in front of the huge mirror that graced their bureau. I removed my flannel shirt and stared at the body in the mirror. My chest was flat and smooth, with no pectoral muscle development. My shoulders were soft and frail.

I did a double biceps pose as if I were a body builder, examining what I perceived to be a lack of muscle in my upper arms. Then I lowered my arms and hung my head.

At that point, I made a vow to myself.

I stepped back from the bureau and found an open space in the carpet. Then I dropped my body down into a perfect push-up position.

"One... two... three," I began.

Seconds later, I finished counting with "...eighteen... uuuugh... nineteen... grrrr... twenty."

I plopped my body down upon the carpet. "Whew!"

I slowly rose, and then walked into the master bathroom, shaking out my arms.

There, I pulled open the shower curtain, and examined the structure before me. Mom and Dad's shower was an add-on to their bathroom and thus not your standard shower head mounted over a tub. Instead, their shower was a solid, rigid structure actually constructed out of some type of sheet metal.

I looked up at the metal rod that ran horizontally over the entrance to the shower. Then I jumped up and grabbed the rod, and momentarily hung there. "Good," I said, "It supports my weight."

After which, I struggled to pull my chin above that rod, again counting "One... two... three..."

Seconds later, I finished counting, with "grrrr... eight... nine... uuuugh... ten."

I released the rod and dropped my feet back down to the linoleum floor. My aching hands were still cupped like hooks in the same wretched position they had been in while grasping the rod. "Whew!"

Then I exited the bathroom and departed Mom and Dad's bedroom, shaking out my arms again.

From that date forward, I did push-ups in Mom and Dad's bedroom and pull-ups in Mom and Dad's bathroom every night. And just think—that never would've happened if only someone had told me there were latches on the windows in my sixth grade classroom.

~John Scanlan

69

Chicken Soup for the Soul

When Nature Calls

Laughter gives us distance.
It allows us to step back from an event, deal with it and then move on.
~Bob Newhart

Have you ever had the experience of being on the verge of panic because you couldn't find a restroom? I have, and one particular incident that comes to mind took place at my elementary school when I was in the fifth grade.

When school let out every day, the entire student body would spill out onto the playground, running, skipping, playing ball, and generally exhausting themselves until their parents came for them. I was no exception, but on occasion, my mother would be a bit late picking me up from school, as she had transportation duties in addition to her work as a classroom teacher. This day was one of those occasions.

It was getting late and most of the other children had already been picked up. Only a few stragglers, including me, were left on campus. It was at about this time, every day, when the school's student restrooms were locked for the evening. Of course, this was also the time when my bladder decided it needed to empty itself, immediately.

Having no place to answer nature's call, and exhausting every other possible option, including banging on the office door, I did what any self-respecting ten-year-old would do. I went in the garden.

Carefully avoiding the flowers and small shrubs, I found a little corner of dirt and breathed a sigh of relief. What I didn't realize, at the time, was that I was standing in front of a large tinted window that looked into the boardroom of the school's office, where a meeting of the board of directors was in full swing. You would think I could have, at least, turned away from the window, but nope... I was facing the window in all of my God given glory.

The principal was a very kind and understanding lady, and would have let the incident slide, except for the fact that the whole school board had borne witness to my indiscretion. She had no other choice but to suspend me for a day. My mother, not blaming me for the incident, never told me about the suspension and took me out for a day of Southern California fun instead. After all, my heart was in the right place, if not the rest of me.

As a result, I can imagine doing my own version of the famous commercial, "You've just dropped your pants and peed in front of the entire school board. What are you going to do now?"—"I'm going to Disneyland!"

~James Crowley

Chapter 9

Just for Preteens

Family Ties

To us, family means putting your arms around each other and being there.

~Barbara Bush

70

Sibling Rivalry

*Siblings — the definition that comprises
love, strife, competition and forever friends.*
~Byron Pulsifer

The day my parents brought me home from the hospital, my sister Patty started a rivalry between the two of us. As I slept she reached into the crib, grabbed the baby bottle and said, "My ba-ba."

The fight began at that moment and continued for many years. I weighed just under six pounds at birth and remained smaller than my sister for most of our growing up years. Bigger, tougher and far more aggressive than I, she artfully directed my actions like an Army staff sergeant. I dutifully obeyed her mostly from fear of retaliation, but as I grew, I developed my own personal methods of payback.

Mom worked long hours and during my elementary school years I got out of school before my sister. I walked home, usually to an empty place. One of the entrances to the kitchen was in the hallway. After a particularly difficult day, I waited patiently the whole afternoon. Just before she arrived, I hid beside the refrigerator and out of sight from anyone coming down the hall. Holding my breath and keeping completely still and quiet, I paused until a split second after she passed and then jumped behind her, grabbed her shoulder and said, "Boo!" She always jumped. Sometimes she hit me, but realized quickly that I'd get her back later if she did.

Patty had a strong fear of someone kidnapping her. The thought of a black-gloved man grabbing her from behind terrified her. On some occasions after we fought, she sat down to practice piano. One day, as she became more engrossed in notes, scales and her most recent songs, I tiptoed to Mom's bedroom and retrieved black leather gloves from the dresser drawer. I slipped them on my small hands, pushed the lock in on the bathroom door (leaving it opened of course) and returned to the living room with great stealth. At the peak of her practice time, I approached her back and threw my hands over her eyes. Her blood-curdling scream raced through the house as I jumped back in a fit of giggles, avoiding her fists. Before she recovered and stumbled from the piano bench, I ran to the bathroom and slammed the door behind me. What followed was a loud mixture of my cackling and her pounding fists on the door, but I stayed behind the locked door until I heard the piano again.

Eventually, I grew tired of the sibling rivalry. I really detested fighting with my sister. My fifth grade year arrived with turmoil at home and our parents' divorce. More than ever, I needed a big sister's love instead of an enemy. One day, I was helping the school counselor check some standardized tests, and we began to talk. She knew my family well.

I asked, "Why does my sister always pick fights with me?"

With a world of wisdom, she didn't answer my question. Instead, in a gentle voice, she said, "You know, it will hurt her more if you don't fight back. Try to just ignore it when she wants to argue."

The next time we started fighting, the counselor's words flitted around my mind. Why not try it? A little uncertain, but willing to try, I ignored Patty. She kept pushing. To make sure she got the point, I took it to the next level.

I said, "It's so quiet here by myself."

She muttered something insulting.

I retorted, "I hate being all alone in this big ole house." I made sure she got the point that I was ignoring her.

We kept going back and forth for a while, but I never broke

down. Sometimes I kept silent and at other times spoke only to myself. I directed nothing I said to her.

In sheer frustration, she begged, "You can hit me! Please just talk to me."

What do you know? It worked.

We repeated this process many more times until one day the fighting stopped. We began a friendship, and over the next two years became best friends. Although we still had occasional fights and sometimes intensely disliked each other, it no longer felt like a daily battle between us. We watched out for each other and shared secrets. Sometimes we spent hours telling each other our dreams. We passed the phone to each other when our grandmother called and talked for hours. We covered each other when someone cracked a glass table during a forbidden indoor game of blind man's bluff. Neither of us knew how in the world that table got broken, and neither admitted that we invited neighborhood kids inside that day. I removed her glasses at night when she fell asleep reading.

By the time we made it to junior high school, we genuinely liked each other.

I had a job working in the library during one of my class periods. One day, her English class came into the room. As I checked out her book, one of her classmates was shocked by the revelation that we were sisters. "You can't be sisters," they said. "You like each other too much." We both smiled.

Throughout the years, we watched most of our friends who had sisters fight like cats and dogs. Instead, I treasured my sister, who doubled as a best friend during some difficult years of my young life. The baby bottle incident became a family joke, and I learned that a sister could be a great friend.

She still is.

~Lisa Bell

Where I Belong

We should not be asking who this child belongs to,
but who belongs to this child.
~Jim Gritter

"Why didn't your parents want you? How does that make you feel?" "Is your real family dead?" "Will you have to go back someday?"

It wasn't easy being adopted—especially being a brown girl from Central America, with two white parents. Until seventh grade, it hadn't been too much of an issue for me. I'd gone to a small church school with the same people I pretty much saw seven days a week. We all knew each other as well as if we were related, and we'd grown up together from babyhood. Everyone knew I was adopted, and it was no big deal.

But when I was twelve, I left my safe cocoon for a bigger, public middle school. Like my elementary school, the new school was mostly white. I was used to that. What I wasn't used to were all the questions.

Now, I know—from the statistics—that there were probably as many as three or four other adopted kids in my class. But they were the same color as their parents, so nobody had to know their private business. I, on the other hand, couldn't hide.

It wasn't so bad when my mom came alone to help out at school or attend a meeting. When kids saw her, they just assumed I had a

Latino dad. There were other mixed-race students in my class and, just like I'd grown up with the same group of kids at my elementary school, these kids had all grown up together, too. They were used to mixed marriages.

At first, I didn't want anybody to know. I just hoped and prayed only one parent would show up to things. Then, for all anyone knew, I could just be another biracial kid. But, all too soon, people found out, and I had to start answering questions.

Of course, a lot of people didn't care either way. But when you're twelve and you feel very different, it really seems like everybody is staring and whispering—when in actuality, they aren't even paying any attention to you at all.

Some kids were just innocently curious. Others were downright mean about it. They were the kind of kids that tell their younger brother or sister, "You're adopted"—like it's a bad thing—even when they aren't.

At first, it felt as if I was defending myself. Maybe it was none of their business, but brushing them off would only have made things worse. I had to admit I was adopted. I had to explain why I was adopted, and what that meant.

It was frustrating a lot of the time. People just didn't get it. They couldn't understand why somebody wouldn't be living with their "real" parents. They couldn't imagine what it would be like, living with "strangers."

It drove me crazy. What did "real" mean, anyway? My adoptive parents were as real as anybody else's. I was their "real" kid. We sure weren't artificial. And after twelve years together, we were anything but strangers.

As time went by, I made true friends. They came over to our house and hung out. My mom or dad drove us to the mall or the movies. My friends were soon as comfortable with my family as the kids I'd grown up with.

But some of the other kids still didn't get it. It was as if they thought adoption was wrong or scary. I guess I could have kept trying to get through to them, but finally I realized they would probably never understand — and that was not my problem.

Adopted kids are just like any other kids. When we get in trouble, we get grounded. Our parents clean up our messes and stay with us when we're sick. They yell at us when they get mad. They're proud when we do well. Sometimes, they hurt our feelings or don't understand us, or they let us down. And sometimes they stand up for us, or they sit and listen when we are sad or worried. Adoptive families are forever, and we are just like anyone else.

It wasn't till I got a little older that I realized how lucky I really was, and that adoption was something that made our family even more special. I had friends with parents who were in jail or had just disappeared. One girl lived in a group foster home. Some kids were failing out or school or doing drugs, and their parents didn't even seem to care.

I am blessed to have a home and a family that cares about me. I know, too, that I'm blessed to have a birth family that loved me enough to let me be adopted when they weren't able to provide for me. A lot of people aren't so lucky. I am where I belong.

~Marcela Dario Fuentes

Lost and Found

A sister is a little bit of childhood that can never be lost.
~Marion C. Garretty

My sister Shannon and I have always had a unique relationship. My other friends and their sisters always fought and claimed they hated each other. But my sister and I were different. We always sought each other's guidance and help. Shannon didn't think of me as her bratty younger sister, and I didn't think of her as my annoying older sister. Sure, we had our fair share of fights, but we could never stay mad for long.

As we got older, my sister started hanging around with her friends more. It didn't bother me because I was only in second grade, and I didn't know any better. But as time wore on and I became older and wiser I began to notice my sister's change of behavior toward everyone, especially my parents. By the time I was in fourth grade and she was in eighth, I found that she started to do things behind my parents' backs that weren't necessarily bad, but I still didn't like it. I tried to convince her to change, but she refused. She told me to relax and not to freak out, that she wasn't doing anything wrong. I tried doing what she said but it didn't feel right, and soon I was back to nagging her to stop.

Then high school came for Shannon and everything changed — for her and for me. She started to think of me as her bratty younger sister, and I felt as if I had lost my connection with her. But instead of growing apart from her I was constantly trying to get back into her life, which irritated her even more.

One night I asked her if I could sleep in her room, something we used to do constantly. But this time she didn't use her repeated excuse of, "Not tonight but maybe some other time. I'm too tired tonight." Instead she responded, "Hailey no. Not for a while, okay?" Being the curious little sister I was, I asked, "Why not?"

And she said, "Because I said so, now just leave me alone!"

With that she stomped off to her room and slammed the door shut, leaving me sitting on the floor shocked. I came to the conclusion that I had lost my sister forever. I sulked and walked to my room. I quietly shut the door and fell asleep.

That night stayed with me through fifth grade into sixth. My parents told me I was being a drama queen, which made me even more angry and upset. They didn't know what it was like having a sister who used to care about me, but no longer did. I took everything very personally. Without my sister's support, I was falling apart. I couldn't have been more depressed.

Then something happened on my mother's birthday that changed everything.

My mom had picked me up from a friend's house to get ready for her birthday dinner. Everyone in our family was coming. As usual, while getting ready, my sister ignored me and I ignored her back. When we arrived at the restaurant, we got a pager that was going to beep when our table was ready. While we were waiting, I tried a couple of jokes. Both my parents laughed, but my sister just rolled her eyes. "Of course," I thought to myself. Finally, our beeper went off and our waitress seated us in a booth. I was forced to sit next to my sister.

The dinner went smoothly—some small conversation, but mostly eating. Then at the end of the meal, my sister said to my dad, "Hey Dad, can you do this?" She took her hands to her face and made a funny look. Then, after her hands covered her face and she reappeared, she was making a different face. "I can only do it with two hands though," she explained.

"No, I cannot do that, Shannon," said my dad, answering my sister's question.

Shannon's face fell. "Oh... well Hailey definitely can't do it with one hand! Show him, Hailey!" I felt everyone's eyes on me.

"Well... okay...." So I tried... and failed. Everyone started laughing which made me start to laugh. It felt good to laugh. So I did it again... and again... over and over. And just as I had hoped, everyone continued to laugh... even my sister. I felt as if a huge weight had been lifted off my shoulders, and I felt equal with my sister again. All the way home from the restaurant, my sister and I giggled together.

After years of searching for our lost friendship, it had finally been found. It took the most unexpected event in the most unexpected place to find Shannon, but in the end it didn't matter where we were. All that mattered was that we found each other and our bond again. My sister and I may lose that bond occasionally, but we will always find it. Sometimes all it takes is a funny face.

~H.M. Filippelli

73

Chicken Soup for the Soul

The Family Portrait

You don't choose your family. They are God's gift to you, as you are to them.
~Desmond Tutu

In my father's house, in my old bedroom, is a dresser. The dresser belonged to my older sister before she moved away. Then I inherited it. The smooth brown surface is free of scratches and marks. All the handles and knobs are still attached. It looks brand new, but this deceptive piece of furniture has been the silent guardian of my most precious treasure for twelve years.

Hidden behind the dresser and covered in more than a decade of dust is a family portrait of my mother and father, my older sister and brother, and me. It's a reminder of life before my parents divorced, when the five of us equaled a family.

I don't have to brush away the dust to see that I am the only one really smiling in the picture. A precocious toddler, I may have been the only one who didn't know at the time that my family was falling apart.

When I was four years old, my parents divorced. I didn't understand what that meant. All that my innocent mind understood was that mother didn't live with us anymore. The portrait remained on the living room wall and to me that signified that I still had a family. A few years later, to my dismay, my sister pulled the portrait down.

I spent the next several years struggling with the divorce. Our home became less and less like a "normal" home and I became envious of my friends who still had a mother and father who lived together. I sought the approval of my friends' parents, hoping to be adopted into their loving clans. I longed for family meals and family vacations. I wanted someone to rub my back when I wasn't feeling well.

My parents started dating other people and with each new woman my father brought home I felt utterly and hopelessly lost. Deep down inside I believed that my parents really did love each other and would get back together someday. I struggled to define what a family is. I felt like I was living with strangers because everyone was off doing their own thing and I was left alone. Home became a cold place where I didn't want to be.

I don't know where the portrait was stored, but when I was in seventh grade, my dad remarried and we moved into my stepmother's house. While unpacking boxes, I found it and quickly hid it behind the dresser. It was my treasure—my reminder of a time when I had a complete family. I was afraid if my stepmother found it she would throw it away and my family would be lost forever.

That first Thanksgiving in my new home was when I realized I had found exactly what I thought I had lost when my sister took the portrait down—a family. My stepmother cooked all day and the house was filled with mouth-watering smells of turkey, stuffing, biscuits and pumpkin pie. It was cold outside, but the house was warm and cozy. Seven of us gathered around the dining room table and our chattering voices filled the room. For the first time in a long time, I was happy.

I realized that day that a family doesn't have to live under the same roof. Even though my parents are divorced, they're still my family. They still love me and I love them. The great thing about a family is how it can grow to include stepparents and stepsiblings. There never was another family portrait, but I don't need a picture to remind me what a family is.

~Valerie D. Benko

Worth More than Money

All that I am or ever hope to be, I owe to my angel Mother.
~Abraham Lincoln

I slid my arms into my old gray coat and buttoned it as I looked at the wear around the sleeves. I hated that coat. Hated having hand-me-downs that neighbors had discarded as not good enough for themselves.

Biting my tongue, I forced a smile as Mom handed me my school lunch. "You could use a new coat," she said. "We'll have to see what we can do about that." She patted my shoulder as I hurried out the door, hoping she didn't see the tears in my eyes.

Seeing what she could do about it meant she'd find another old, used-up coat for me. I brushed the tears away and took a deep breath. The fall air was getting crisper. Soon winter would be upon us. I shivered, pulling my coat tightly around me. It did little good to wish that my parents had money like my friends' parents had. With six kids to feed, there was little cash left to spend on clothes and I couldn't remember when my mother had ever had a new coat. I told myself that I'd better get used to wearing castoffs. At least I had a coat, even if it wasn't fancy.

"Look what the neighbors sent over," Mom said, a few days later.

She was beaming as she caressed a soft, short-sleeved sweater. She handed it to me. "This will look lovely on you. The collar is so soft."

I ran my fingers over the white angora collar. It was the softest thing I'd ever felt and added a beautiful touch to the bright red of the sweater.

"And look at these," she continued, as she lay two skirts side-by-side on the sofa.

My jaw dropped. One skirt was pink and the other was light blue. My older sister and I could each have one.

There were other things too, but these were my favorites. I lay awake a long time that night, suddenly grateful that our neighbors grew tired of their clothes.

The next morning I put on my old gray coat. I buttoned it, kissed Mom goodbye and turned towards the door. She was smiling. "Yes," she said, almost to herself, "you definitely need a new coat."

Mom had a twinkle in her eye and a hum on her lips for the next few days. She was up to something, but what?

The weather suddenly turned cold. I put an extra sweater under my old coat and tied a scarf around my neck, but the wind chilled me to the bone, long before I ever reached school. I was still shivering when I went to bed that night, and Mom looked worried.

I had a fitful sleep. My room was upstairs and therefore usually quiet, but that night I thought I heard a sewing machine whirring all night. I pulled the covers up to my neck and put the pillow over my head. Finally, I dozed off.

Wind whistled, blowing snow into drifts. I groaned the next morning as I looked out the window. I had to go to school and I shivered at the thought of another cold walk in my threadbare coat.

Mom looked tired as she made us breakfast. But there was a twinkle in her eye and she was back to humming.

As usual, I was the last one to leave for school. As I sullenly slid into my gray coat and began buttoning it, Mom said, "Why don't you leave that old thing at home?" Then, before I could answer she slipped into the living room, returning with a beautiful green coat that sported a real fur collar. "Try this on," she said proudly.

It fit perfectly. I marveled at the softness of the green wool fabric, the heavy lining and the light-brown fur of the collar. "Where did you get it?" I was in awe.

She smiled. "It was in the box of clothes that we were given. I altered it to fit you."

"You mean, it was for a lady, and it would have fit you, Mom?"

"I suppose it might have," she nodded, reaching out to help me button the coat. "But you need a coat more than I do. And look how lovely it looks on you. Now hurry up, slowpoke, or you'll be late for school."

I wrapped my arms around my mother; my heart so filled will love for this woman who had always put her family's needs above her own. Who could ever ask for more than that? My friends' families might be better off financially than we were. But I had Mom, and she was worth far more than any amount of money.

~Chris Mikalson

Chicken Soup
for the Soul

Void in My Heart

To live in hearts we leave behind
Is not to die.
~Thomas Campbell

I had vivid dreams about my dad the night before my world came crashing down. He and my mother had divorced when I was eight years old, and I dreamed about being with him at least once per night, sometimes more. I would wake up in the morning warm and comfortable, wrapped up like a human burrito in my soft down blanket.

But this morning, strips of warm sunlight slipped through my blinds, projecting bright, perfectly straight white lines onto my yellow-painted walls. I was suddenly confused. Wasn't it Wednesday? I was wondering why it seemed so bright before it was even time to wake up for school. I rubbed the sleep out of my eyes, threw the covers off and glanced at the clock on my nightstand. It read 11:43 a.m.

I felt my heart do a back flip in my chest. I had made it all the way through the sixth grade without any absences or tardiness, a personal achievement that I was proud of. Mr. Stanley was surely planning to reward me at the end of the year for my perfect attendance record, and now it had been ruined.

I called for my mother as I angrily bolted down the stairs. "Mom? Mom! I'm so late!" I called, quickly peeking into her bedroom. She wasn't in there, and her bed was made. Where was she? "Mom! It's

Wednesday! Why didn't you wake me up for school?" I pulled my hair back into a messy ponytail and searched the rest of the house.

Finally, out of breath, I went into the kitchen, where my mother sat in a chair, staring like a zombie at the wall, her chin resting in her hands. Two boxes of tissues, one empty, sat on the table, and crumpled, used tissues littered the wooden tabletop.

My mom looked terrible. She was crying, and in that moment, she looked nearly ten years older than she had when I saw her the day before. My disappointment about spoiling my perfect attendance record turned into anxiety and dread that something far more serious had happened.

"Mom? What's wrong?" It came out in a whisper. "What—what happened?"

She looked up quickly; I had startled her. She gazed at me as I stood there in my pajamas, an unnerving look of anguish in her eyes. She opened and closed her mouth a few times, but was clearly unable to find the right words. Finally, she rubbed her eyes and found her voice.

"Cassie," she began, speaking slowly, "I have something very important to tell you. Please sit down."

My heart pounded so hard that I could hear it in my ears and feel the blood pumping through my body. I took a seat across from her. She took my hands and held them in hers. I felt her shaking, and began trembling myself. The anticipation nearly killed me.

"Cassie, your father became very sick last night, out of nowhere..." she began. "He didn't make it, Cass. The doctors at the hospital tried so hard to save him. They tried so, so hard, but..."

That was all I needed to hear before I lost it. I couldn't see straight or think clearly. I jumped out of my chair and flipped it over. The heavy wood made a loud sound when it hit the tile floor. I kicked the wall and cried out in pain. I screamed, fell to my knees and sobbed in disbelief. Random questions that had no answers flooded my brain.

What about our weekends together?

What about the museum trip we had planned for this Saturday?

What about our ginormous rubber band ball, or our fake air guitar band, or our road trips together?

What about father-daughter day in gym class?

I looked at my mother and tried to compose myself. A few minutes later, when she felt I was calm enough to listen, she explained that he had a heart attack in the night. I thought about how I had never seen him come down with more than a head cold. I thought about how life could change in an instant.

The weeks that followed passed in a blur of anguish and tears. The funeral came and went, our relatives visited and left, we ate all of the food that our neighbors and friends graciously brought us when we didn't have time or energy to cook. Eventually it was time for me to go back to school, where my teachers and friends were kind and thoughtful, and did their best to comfort me during the most difficult time of my life.

Growing up and being a kid without a father was at first impossible. After a few years it was difficult, but I learned to manage. By high school, I adjusted. My mom took me to the museum one day, and I added to our rubber band ball for years, until it was nearly as big as my head.

I am older now, and while the void has remained, it is getting better. My questions have changed with time. What about my wedding: who will walk me down the aisle? What about my children getting to know their grandfather? How would my life be different if he were still here? There are no answers, but one thing is for sure: Dad is with me every single day in my heart and thoughts, and I will love him for as long as I live.

I will always miss my daddy, but it is easier now to feel grateful for the short time I was given with him, rather than dwelling on the fact that he is gone.

~Cassie Goldberg

Daddy

I love my father as the stars —
he's a bright shining example and a happy twinkling in my heart.
~Terri Guillemets

I don't remember clearly
all the times you held my hand
while crossing a busy street,
risking your life
for mine.
I do know
that each time I climbed a tree,
you stood at the bottom,
arms open,
in case I fell.
Faintly I recall,
like a hazy photograph,
you cheering me on
as you held my training wheel-less bike
And I pedaled away.
I never saw the look on your face
as I went off
to my first day of kindergarten,
but I know it must have been
happy for me,

sad for you
that I was growing up,
and maybe even a bit scared.
I don't clearly recollect
much of when I was really young,
but I do recall your loving me
All the time
and how much I loved you back.
And that's one thing I know
I'll never forget.

~Jennifer Lynn Clay

77

Chicken Soup for the Soul

Every Precious Minute

When someone you love becomes a memory, the memory becomes a treasure.
~Author Unknown

No one said it out loud, but I knew Grandpa was dying. He had been sick since I was four years old. By the time I was nine, I was used to the routine. I became a pro at waiting in doctors' offices when Grandma or Mom took him to appointments. I had favorite magazines in each lobby and would read them again week after week. Words like "blood transfusion," "valley fever," and "myelofibrosis" seemed commonplace.

But when Mom would talk about such things, it was at a whisper. "What did the doctor say? He needs to go again next week? What time?"

Even more, I saw the changes in Grandpa every time I visited. His tall, lean body stooped in weariness. The already deep-tan skin of his forearms sprouted big, dark blotches and scabs. He loved his garden on the back patio, but some days he was too tired to walk five feet out the door to tend to his plants. Sometimes, he couldn't even stand up to give me a farewell hug.

He was dying. I knew it. That knowledge terrified me. From overhearing Mom and Grandma, I learned that Grandpa was supposed to have lived only six months from the time he had been diagnosed. Years had passed, yet he was still alive. How much more time did he have?

I wanted to do something. Anything. I daydreamed about finding a cure, something that would make Grandpa well and everyone else happy again. But deep down, I knew I didn't have that sort of power.

Other friends and family reacted in a different way. They were polite to Grandpa and Grandma, but would walk away quickly, whispering as if they were scared of him. I didn't want to be like that. I wanted Grandpa to know that I loved him and that I was there for him.

During my summer break, I would reach for the phone. "Grandpa, can I come over?" I would ask. If he said yes, I ran for my bike. I rode the mile to my grandparents' house.

"What can I do today?" I asked him.

"Well, you can water the plants," he said.

I watered the plants on the patio. I brought him books off the shelf. I handed him the phone. If he felt up to it, he leaned against the kitchen counter and cooked me a hot dog on the stove. On really good days, we would take a bag of stale bread and walk a few blocks to the pond to feed the ducks. He always taught me to look for the slow duck. "Be sure to get some bread to that duck in back," he would call. "Or the others will get fat while he starves."

One day I biked over and found one of my uncles visiting as well. Uncle Tim didn't seem too pleased at my arrival. He and Grandpa were looking over an ink drawing of a broken-down homestead with cracked windows, holes in the roof, and a ramshackle porch.

I peered over their shoulders. "I can draw that, too," I said.

Uncle Tim opened his mouth, his face looking strange and almost angry.

Grandpa placed a hand on Tim's arm. "It's okay," Grandpa said. "I want to see your drawing, Beth."

Fifteen minutes later I presented my drawing to him. He praised it and told me to put it on the fridge where Grandma could see it when she arrived home. My chest puffed with pride. I thought my drawing was much better than the one Tim brought.

Months passed. Another school year came and went. Grandpa

slowed down. Every other day contained a doctor's appointment or blood test. When he was home, he stretched out in bed and dozed with the TV on. Finally, he couldn't walk by himself at all.

"I want to push Grandpa's wheelchair," I said.

Mom's expression was doubtful. "You have to be careful."

Grandpa smiled at me. "Can you go really fast?"

"Sure!" I said, and grabbed the handles. He dubbed me his official chauffeur. We raced down the sidewalks as I made vroom-vroom noises and harsh squeals for the brakes. Grandpa laughed and added some engine sounds of his own.

A few weeks later, I came home from school. Mom seemed dazed and pale. "Grandpa's in the hospital," she said. "We'll go see him in an hour."

He returned home a few days later and died at peace in his own bed. Even though I had known it was coming, nothing can describe the hollowness that filled my chest. Grandpa was gone.

At his funeral, I took my seat in the front row. Memorial booklets were passed to us. I glanced down and gasped. There on the cover was the ink drawing of an old house, the same one that Grandpa and Uncle Tim had talked about almost two years before. Oh no. I treated it like an art competition, while all along they had been working on the preparations for Grandpa's funeral. No wonder my uncle had been upset.

They should have told me when I butted in. I knew what was going on with Grandpa's health. I wasn't stupid.

I rubbed my fingers against the coarse paper of the booklet. No, it wasn't about being smart or stupid. Grandpa knew that I knew. He wanted me there with him. He did protect me, but only to a degree. He just didn't want me to be sad yet.

I stared at the shiny wood of the casket. I thought about how Grandpa would answer the phone without his dentures in and make me giggle. I remembered his love for his sweet basil plant, and how he would ask me to bring it close so he could smell the fragrant herb. All those days he probably felt so sick and awful he could barely move, but he still let me come over.

Those afternoons together—that was our time to water plants, watch TV, and brown hot dogs until they burst. We both knew he was ill. We both knew he was dying. When we were together, that didn't matter. We were too busy making memories.

When it was time, my family stood up and filed alongside the closed casket. I blinked back tears. There were so many things I wanted to say to Grandpa if I could talk to him again, but only two words echoed in my mind: "Thank you."

~Beth Cato

78

Sisterly Love

Sisters are different flowers from the same garden.
~Author Unknown

ince the time we were young children, my sister and I have never gotten along. She was born two years, three months, and thirteen days after me. I've always been the good daughter, and she has always been the one in trouble.

My sister isn't like other sisters. She has had a lot of problems since birth and has always been hard to handle. She had to have a gastronomy tube to eat, she had seizures, and she required a lot of attention from our single parent mom. We were constantly making trips to the children's hospital to see doctors, the dentist, and other specialists.

But that wasn't the half of it. As she got older, my sister was diagnosed with ADHD, ADD, bipolar disorder, and eventually with pervasive developmental disorder, which falls somewhere on the autism spectrum. She doesn't show her emotions, doesn't talk about things, and is very angry and self-focused. I can't hold a conversation with her, show my feelings toward her, or do anything normal with her. I walk on eggshells when I'm around her, because I never know what will set her off.

When we were younger, we would play with Barbies together. She would always throw a fit when I wanted to clean up and go do something else. It was hard being her sister. We always fought and

I would usually lose. I became her punching bag somewhere in our growing up years. She would hit me, leaving red handprints, sometimes drawing blood with her fingernails. I also became her verbal target. I'd hear things like, "I wish you were dead!" "I hate you!" and "There's no excuse for you."

I don't know how many times she left me in tears after one of her rages. There were times I would hide in my room because I was so afraid of her anger. Everyone around me kept saying, "Oh, it's just sisterly love. She'll grow out of it." I really grew to hate that saying. It wasn't sisterly love, and she wasn't going to grow out of it. I kept waiting for her to, but she never did.

I was put into counseling when I was in middle school, and the focus quickly went from what I was in there for to what was going on at home. My "relationship" with my sister was one of our main focuses in counseling. It was always frustrating for me, because it seemed no one was on my side. My sister got away with so much. In counseling, my counselor would call me the instigator, saying that I spurred her on. I was so angry with my counselor, I began lying to her when she asked about how things were going with my sister. I was tired of having it blamed on me. It just wasn't fair.

Right before I went away to college, all I kept hearing was, "I can't wait until you leave! I hate you, and I hope you never come back." I know she said it in anger, but it still hurt. I was relieved when I left for school. Home was once my refuge from the torments at school, but my sister took that refuge away. On breaks from school, I would go home and things with my sister were the same. We still didn't get along, and I was still scared of her when she was in a rage.

I've always observed other sisters and have been jealous of their relationships. I want to be able to joke and tease with my sister and not make her angry. I want to hug her, cuddle with her, and show her my love for her. I want to be able to sit and have talks with her. I want to hear about what is going on in her life. But I know these things aren't possible.

So, I'm doing the best I can with what I have. I send her text messages that let her know I am proud of her and that I love her. I leave her notes that tell her she can talk to me about anything, and I promise her that I won't tell Mom. She never takes me up on these notes, nor responds to my text messages. I've come to realize that she doesn't really hate me. She's probably just as frustrated as I am in dealing with all that is going on with her.

I've always wished that I could be in her shoes for one day so I could try to understand how she thinks and feels. While this is impossible, and I still don't understand her, I am beginning to understand a few things. I understand that if I refuse to argue with her, things don't get loud and explosive. If I watch, I can tell when she is getting aggravated and will stop whatever I'm doing that is causing her aggravation. I've learned that I can have a good time with my sister if I'm careful.

I wish I could understand more. I wish I could understand her disorders so I know how to interact with her. But I know things are not my fault. I've had to accept and love her for who she is, and I've stopped wishing she could be someone else because, while things are tough sometimes, she is still my sister.

~Mandilyn T. Criline

79

Chicken Soup for the Soul

My Daughter the Cat

Little children, headache; big children, heartache.
~Italian Proverb

My knees grazed the bottom of my fourth grade daughter's desk. I stretched and shifted my legs so that I could occupy the space that would be hers for the next nine months. I looked around self-consciously, relieved to see other parents wiggling, maneuvering and just plain giving up trying to fit into their children's desks.

My daughter Amy, giggling with several friends in the back of the classroom, saw that I'd found her desk and came prancing over to join me. I scooted over to make room for her and soon both of us were balanced on the honey-colored wood and metal schoolroom chair. Just as she was about to show me the contents of her desk, a man in the front of the room cleared his voice, and everyone perked up and sat at attention.

"Welcome to 'Back to School Night' everyone. For those of you who don't know me, I'm Mr. Jones. I'd like to tell you a little bit about myself and why I love to teach fourth grade."

Mr. Jones was a friendly-looking man, with a balding head and kind eyes that looked out through round wire-rimmed glasses. He wasn't very tall; in fact some of the taller students could nearly look him in the eye if they stood on tiptoe. He wore a plaid shirt, khaki pants and a cable knit sweater vest. His enthusiasm was contagious, and I almost wished I were back in school again.

"The reason I like to teach fourth grade," he continued, "is because fourth graders are like dogs. Think about it—they love to see you when you come home, and then follow you around like a shadow, thinking you are wonderful. They want to be with you every second, whether you're sitting and reading a book or outside weeding the garden. They love to go for walks with you or ride in the car and will give you their unconditional adoration on a daily basis. Every day is new and exciting and they meet it with enthusiasm and joy."

There was a blanket of murmurs that fell over the classroom full of parents and children, and it seemed that everyone else was as confused as I was. Where was he going with this?

"And then around fifth or sixth grade," he said, shaking his head sadly, "something happens. Almost overnight, they turn into cats. Instead of running to greet you at the door, they barely look at you from their cushion on the couch."

There were subdued bursts of laughter and a few knowing "uh huhs" floating amongst the audience, which was now being very dog-like, hanging on his every word.

"Yes," Mr. Jones went on, "suddenly instead of coming when you call them, they might stroll by and grace you with their presence, if they feel like it. They no longer want to be on the same planet with you, let alone the same room. Gone are the days when they'd sit by your feet in front of the fire. Now they disappear to their rooms and only come out for food, and then turn up their nose at what you are serving. They don't want to be seen on the street with you anymore, so no more of those walks after dinner. It's a sad, sad thing. But don't worry, because this phase doesn't last forever. Sometime during the high school years, things change again and they slowly turn back into dogs! You just have to be patient, and know that this too shall pass."

Everyone applauded at the end of the teacher's presentation, laughing and nodding in agreement. My daughter leaned over, her eyes wide in amazement and whispered in my ear, "Mom! Lindsey's a cat!" She was referring to her older sister, a seventh grader, who had been exhibiting more and more feline qualities every day. We finally understood! I stifled a laugh, and had to agree; she was right.

Several years later, Amy came home from school like a tornado, jacket, shoes, and a backpack flying everywhere. She was in a prickly mood, and she ignored my cheery greeting: "Hi! How was school?" She retreated to her room and slammed the door behind her.

I tiptoed down the hall and knocked gently on her door. "Amy?"

"What?" she hissed from behind the closed door. It was decorated with a sign that said: "KEEP OUT! Only enter if you are NOT a parent or my sister!"

"Can I come in?"

"I don't care," she growled.

I opened the door a crack and peeked inside. Sprawled on the bed was my beautiful, gangly twelve-year-old daughter. Her head was buried in her bunched up pillow, and I had to strain to hear her muffled sobs. Sitting down on the edge of the comforter that resembled Monet's water lilies, I placed a gentle hand on her back, hoping to give some comfort.

"What's wrong with me?" she sobbed. "I'm always crabby and I can't help it no matter what I do! I hate it! What's wrong with me, Mom?"

I hesitated a moment, and then softly said," Honey, I think you're turning into a cat."

A tear-stained face turned to look at me. Tugging at the corners of her mouth was a small smile. The glint of the afternoon sunlight on her braces made her look like a cartoon princess, as her smile covered her face. In that moment, I knew that she remembered her beloved fourth grade teacher's story and my heart filled with gratitude. Not only did his story help me understand her frantic adolescent moods, but most of all, it helped Amy make sense of it herself. We were both able to breathe a sigh of relief and understanding that afternoon as we sat on her bed, me with my daughter the cat.

~Nancy Roth Manther

80

Chicken Soup for the Soul

Staying by His Side

A grandfather is someone with silver in his hair and gold in his heart.
~Author Unknown

We all have a best friend when we're young. The friend you remember when you think of playing video games, walking through the mall, and staying up late, doing nothing in particular.

For me, that companion was my grandpa.

The little bit of gray in his full head of hair was the only clue that he was over seventy years old. When he climbed on the roof to fix our TV antenna, it was my dad who almost had a heart attack. Grandpa was a man who spent his time doing what he wanted to do, and that included a lot of road trips with me. From Cape Canaveral to Disney World to Space Camp, Grandpa drove everywhere, and we did everything. As any kid would, I took it for granted that all of our days would be filled with action-packed amusement—until one of them wasn't.

One time when I had a day off from school, Grandpa drove me to Busch Gardens in Tampa. We were immediately focused on the main attractions, so we hopped on the gondola skyride and a few roller coasters. We checked out the dolphin show, and stopped for lunch... a few times. I had a hot dog, a pizza slice, a slushie... and a funnel cake. Finally, we stopped at the Marrakesh Theater to investigate a slide show about animals. I was eleven—I wanted to see action, ride roller coasters, get splashed by dolphins, and dry off while I rode another roller coaster. If I wanted to watch a slide show, I'd have asked my dad to show me pictures of Christmas, 1975.

To make it worse, the theater was warm. Very warm. The air conditioner wasn't really working, but after walking all morning, it was nice to sit and watch. There was a freeze-frame of a Tanzanian sunrise. A freeze-frame of a gorilla family. A freeze-frame of a lioness pouncing on a gazelle. That reminded me: I was hungry again. Then I heard a sliding sound from my left and was brought out of the virtual safari back into reality. The man in the seat next to me had slumped over, slid out of his seat and collapsed on the floor. It took a second for this to register. This was a day full of fun and games and roller coasters and funnel cakes. Grandpa's collapsing on the floor wasn't part of the script.

I heard murmuring and gasps. Everything became a terrifying blur. The paramedics came and put Grandpa in a wheelchair. His eyes were open. "Grandpa? Grandpa?" I said. He didn't answer. I followed the wheelchair to a golf cart with a big red cross on it. The paramedics let me sit next to him in the back. He looked at me and said one word that made the terror subside: "Marc?" Just then, it was the only word he could say, but it was enough.

Then, we went for a ride most people don't experience in Busch Gardens or Disney World—or anywhere else. We drove through the employees-only back roads of the park. I held Grandpa's hand the whole time, but my eyes were mostly on the road during the golf-cart safari. I knew we wouldn't see any lions, hippos or giraffes on this safari, though. We stopped at the infirmary. Grandpa was talking a little as I helped the paramedics get him into a wheelchair. Inside, they took his pulse and blood pressure and listened to his heart with a stethoscope. He finally started talking in full sentences: "It was so hot in there," he said. "I remember feeling dizzy and having trouble breathing. Then it was like I just fell asleep. Next thing I remember is seeing my grandson when you were helping me onto the golf cart."

"How do you feel now, Grandpa?" I felt a little awkward talking with him like that in front of all the medical people, but it seemed like the right thing to do.

"Much better, but I'm a little dizzy," he replied.

"Lie down on one of the infirmary beds for a few minutes, Mr. Kruza," the nurse said. "We'll check your vitals again soon. They're fine, we just want to make sure they stay that way."

"Is he okay?" I asked.

"Yes, son. He just needs to rest."

"Isn't the arcade close by? Can I go over there for a little while?" It never occurred to me that it wasn't the best time to ask.

"It is," the nurse affirmed with a knowing smile.

"Marc," Grandpa interjected in a weak voice, "Please stay right here. It won't be long." His face looked as desperate as his voice sounded.

"Okay," I said. I felt guilty for wanting to leave, but I hadn't thought there was anything I could do by staying. Suddenly, I wanted to help, and that meant staying with Grandpa. It didn't seem like much to ask. I could stay in the one place he wanted me to be after all the times he had gone anywhere and everywhere to please me.

So began the best thing I ever did for my grandpa. The next ninety minutes were a marathon of pacing, since I was a nervous kid even under normal circumstances. I stared at Grandpa, the ceiling, the floor, Grandpa again, then the ceiling again. After the nurse checked on him a few more times, he asked if he was okay to drive.

"As long as you can walk, it's okay."

"Marc," Grandpa said, "I really want to go home. Is that okay with you?"

"Yeah," I said without hesitation. The nurse had Grandpa walk around the room a few times. We crowded into the golf cart, and the safari went all the way to Grandpa's car. I repeatedly asked how he felt on the way home, and he repeatedly thanked me for being there for him.

Seeing Grandpa's vulnerability slowed me down long enough to grow up a little bit. Before that trip, I thought that our adventures would last forever. But I realized that staying by my grandpa's side that day didn't cost me my innocence—it helped me gain a true best friend.

~Marc S. Kruza

Auntie Cathy

Remember, we all stumble, every one of us. That's why it's a comfort to go hand in hand.

~Emily Kimbrough

rowing up, I thought the world was as safe and sound as it was in the sitcoms I watched. Then, as hopscotch and Barbies gave way to trainer bras and braces, followed by a dash of sassy attitude, our family went in another direction. My parents saw this change in me and tightened their rules.

I lived in a do-as-I-say-not-as-I-do household and I was not allowed to show any negative emotion. Back then, keeping my emotions in check was becoming less and less controllable as the end of my twelfth year neared.

I was just coming off a weekend grounding for (are you ready for this heinous defiant act of preteen behavior?) stomping my foot at my father. He refused to let me go to a friend's coed party, and I instinctively stomped. So while I was stuck in my room, everyone else was not only having fun, but was sure to tell me all about it when the weekend was over.

By Monday morning anger and frustration still had a grip on me. I wanted to stomp my foot again! I wanted to give him a real piece of my mind. I wanted nothing to do with that mean tyrant. I wanted freedom. My dad was driving me to school that morning and was criticizing my new hairdo. It was none of his business (although many years later I would come to realize he had a point). When I purposely slammed the car door I knew I was risking another grounding, but it felt worth it.

About twenty minutes later, I was standing in the multi-purpose room in my P.E. clothes after fainting. I was sent to the nurse's office and soon was told that no one could come get me because there had been a death in the family. I'm mortified to say that the feisty, naïve, preteen girl I was stupidly and flippantly answered, "Well, I hope it was my father."

Many hours later when our neighbor came to the nurse's office, my heart pounded in panic. Why would Vivian be picking me up?

"Marilyn honey, I'm so sad to have to tell you this, but your dad died this morning." She was crying. "He had a heart attack. He died instantly." As best as I could tell, I had fainted in P.E. at the exact time my father had his heart attack.

I stared at her... past her. No tears. No way. Tears meant it was true. No way could this be real.

I thought I heard Vivian tell me that it was all right to cry. But who could hear anything over the screaming in my head?

She took me home and I made my way through all the sobbing people to my bedroom. I sat on the bed and stared at nothing. I stared at an empty future. I stared at the earthquake that had just changed my world forever.

Did I do this? Hadn't I wished him dead?

I couldn't breathe.

My Auntie Cathy walked in. She sat down next to me and put a soft arm around my shoulders. I continued to stare.

"Honey, I know this is devastating, but I promise you will get through this horrible loss."

"No, I won't."

"I promise."

She could promise nothing. She said the words that adults say to children when something bad happens and no one can do anything about it except sprinkle their pity with a little false hope. I wanted her to leave my room so I could begin my punishment.

We sat in silence for a long time and then she wept. "Your dad and I were in a fight. I never got to make it right."

Tears were washing her face and making little pools in the creases of her neck. I put an arm on her quivering shoulder. She was so upset.

"It's not your fault," I comforted.

It was my fault, I thought.

"No one knew this was going to happen, Auntie Cathy. Who knows, maybe tomorrow you would have fixed it."

Who knows, maybe tomorrow I would have fixed it, I thought.

"You're pretty smart for a twelve-year-old, you know?" She blew into her already saturated hanky and sighed a long one. "You are so right, little one. People don't have heart attacks because of arguments. They have them because their heart—the organ, not the soul—is defective. If his heart had gone out next week I might have already called him and made up. I was thinking about doing that. I love... loved... no, love... my brother, and he knew it. The fight was so stupid." With that she began to cry again.

You want to talk about a stupid fight? How about fighting about my hair? That was really stupid, I thought to myself.

Hot tears finally began to come. We cried forever. We cried and laughed and cried again. We did this for days. And slowly—sometimes with years in between—we began to heal.

I hated myself for slamming that car door. I will always regret it. But that devastating day could have been so much worse for me growing up if hadn't been for my aunt's own guilt. In trying to make her feel better I was unable to ignore the logic of my own advice.

~Marilyn Kentz

82

Chicken Soup for the Soul

You're Going to Wear That?

One should either be a work of art, or wear a work of art.
~Oscar Wilde

I pulled the bleach from the cabinet, set up the plastic bowl in the sink, and grabbed my jeans from the hamper. My mom, folding laundry next to me, shot over her famous "What are you up to?" glare. I knew I would have to explain, again.

I should have waited and snuck downstairs when she wasn't there, but I didn't have time. The next day, my friends and I were going to the movies, and I wanted to wear these pants.

Wondering when the third degree would start, I bunched up part of my dark blue jeans—the part above my right knee—and dipped it into the bleach and water combination before my mother could stop me. The spots were supposed to be cotton white. I didn't really know how to get the spots that white. It smelled pretty bad, so I guessed I had added enough bleach.

"What are you doing?" my mother shrieked. Horror filled her eyes, like she had just seen a ghost or something.

"I told you the other day. I'm bleaching my jeans." A few of my friends had done the same thing—spotted their dark jeans white, reverse snow leopard style—and then slashed the fabric to get that fringy thread look. They were cool.

"Are those your new jeans? The ones we bought a few weeks ago?" My mom couldn't get her head around why anyone would destroy perfectly good clothes in what she considered such a barbaric manner. It was beyond her understanding.

"Uh, yeah," I said.

"And you're going to wear those? Outside? Like that?"

"Duh, yes." I shook my head and kept dipping away, sporadically fading the color from patches of cloth around my butt, hips, calves, and thighs. She didn't get it. She was still wearing sweaters from three years ago.

"It's not like I'm dying my hair blue or anything. They're just jeans," I insisted. She was always nagging me about stuff. You'd think just once she would like my suggestions. "This is art, Mom. Fashion. You know? No, you probably don't know." I clucked my tongue, and waved my hand, dismissing her lack of fashion sense.

She gave me that glare again. Oh, great. Here it comes, I thought. Another long-winded rant about my strange tastes and how ridiculous she thinks I'd look wearing a clown suit. But, then she shocked me.

"Do what you want. They're your clothes," my mom sighed, rolling her eyes. In the bigger scheme of things, white spotted jeans must have seemed more logical to her than blue hair. Last week, when I mentioned that maybe I would add a few blue streaks through my blond hair, she went nuts, thought it was the most absurd thing she had ever heard. I couldn't convince her. She didn't buy the line that blue hair would match my eyes. Well, it was only an idea. I wasn't really going to do it anyway.

"There's a lot of bleach in there. You should use gloves. Here, take these." She handed me the yellow rubber dish gloves on her side of the sink, and slid the pile of clean towels closer to her. "But, please, don't get bleach on anything else. I'm sure the rest of us would rather not look like zebras."

"Leopards, Mom. Zebras have stripes," I corrected. Unbelievable. How could she not know the difference between zoo animals?

We stood side by side a few minutes longer, concentrating in silence on our individual tasks. When I finished speckling my pants, I rinsed them quickly in the sink and hung them on the clothesline we had in the basement. My mom told me to put them in the dryer. I didn't want them to shrink. Jeans never fit right when they come out of the dryer.

"With the amount of bleach you used, you won't have to worry about them shrinking. You'll have to worry about them falling apart." She picked up the laundry basket and headed upstairs.

"Whatever," I mumbled, blowing off her commentary. What did she know?

I stepped back and admired my work, mentally deciding where I should cut the fabric in the morning. "Not bad," I muttered. "I think the girls will like it."

And, they did. The next day on our way to the movie theater, we swapped bleach-spotting techniques and decided dark jeans worked better than light ones. And, man, did we laugh when people at the mall did a double take as we walked by. The looks on their faces — priceless! Maybe, famous fashion designers would hear about us and want to copy our look. We pretended to be models prancing down the catwalk, loving the attention we drew.

But, my mom was right. I had used too much bleach. In places where I double-dipped or dipped too long, the bleach spots turned into threadbare holes. After wearing them a few times, the threads vanished completely, and my jeans resembled a slab of Swiss cheese. I didn't mind much. By then, the leopard look was so yesterday. My friends and I had moved on to our jackets, using hundreds of safety pins to make complicated designs. Oh, and then we started painting our boots fire engine red and fuchsia.

My mom often would look over my shoulder, and roll her eyes when she saw me slicing or shading my next work of art. Once in a while, she would complain about the mess I was making, and I'd have to come up with a good excuse so she would let me finish what I was doing. Sometimes, though, she had really great ideas. Like when she showed me how to fasten safety pins so they wouldn't leave big marks in my denim jacket. Or, when she joked about adding yellow swirls to my freshly dyed boots. Hmm…maybe there was hope for her yet, old sweaters and all.

~Jennifer Baljko

Chapter 10

Just for Preteens

Bullies and Bully Payback

For every minute you are angry, you lose sixty seconds of happiness.

~Author Unknown

83

Chicken Soup for the Soul

The Bully and the Braid

Kindness is in our power, even when fondness is not.
~Samuel Johnson

"**S**omebody's gonna get beat up," announced May Jordan while casually leaning against the monkey bars. Frozen by fear, the group of students surrounding May silently hoped that her latest victim wasn't among them, but they knew full well that there was always a chance. "We'll see after school," she said before flexing her large muscles for effect. Meanwhile, I hugged my Cabbage Patch Kid on a nearby bench, trying desperately to ignore the lump in my throat; it now felt the size of a small tangerine. I couldn't wait for recess to end.

I loved school, I really did. But since May had transferred in, Elliott Elementary had become an uncomfortable place. At approximately five feet eight inches, May was the tallest kid in our fifth grade class, and, in fact had already sprung well above every student in the school. Although her height was intimidating, it wasn't a problem—her attitude was. No part of the student population was beyond the reach of May's menacing taunts: She routinely hurled insults at innocent third graders who were too afraid to defend themselves; she blatantly bullied boys during gym class; she even threatened to snatch the patches off the sashes of Girl Scouts.

After carefully looking over their shoulders so as to ensure that May wasn't within earshot, many students contended that she was all bark and no bite. But I wasn't so sure. I had managed to fly under May's radar—and I wanted to keep it that way. But all that changed when I showed up for school one morning with a new (albeit unoriginal) hairstyle. Apparently, by wearing my hair in a French braid, I had managed to change my fate.

It all started when my best friend, Jaime, said my hair looked nice. I noticed May's piercing glare—and it made me uncomfortable—but I remained focused on my math worksheet. Then came May's daunting proclamation as she passed me in the cafeteria: "Nice braid. Somebody might cut it off."

I was scared. But what really sent me into a tailspin was when May, who was now clear across the room, moved her fingers to imitate a pair of scissors in motion. My stomach dropped to my knees, and I immediately came up with a plan, which involved hiding out in the bathroom at the end of the school day so as to avoid running into May on the walk home.

I awoke the next morning with a start and scurried to the bathroom to watch my mother get ready for work. Although my watching her had become routine, she knew something was up.

"What's wrong, Courtney?" my mother said, while sweeping the apples of her cheeks with blush.

"Nothing," I replied.

"You're lying. Tell me the truth," she persisted.

"May Jordan wants to cut off my braid," I sputtered with a mouth thick with saliva; tears began to fall.

"She's a bully," my mother said earnestly while taking my chin in her hand. "She thrives on making others scared, that's all. Don't be afraid of her, Courtney. If she can see that you're not afraid, she will stop. I'll bet she's like everybody else—she just wants to fit in and make friends. Perhaps she just doesn't know how."

I rolled my mother's words around in my head. She did have a valid point. May wasn't so great at making friends. Maybe—just maybe—underneath all that toughness was a regular fifth grader who simply wanted to be liked. Did I have what it would take to befriend May? I wasn't sure, but I wanted to find out.

Later that morning, I told Jaime that I had made the tentative decision to talk to May.

"You're crazy," she said. "Do you know what she could do?"

"Maybe not," I replied. I didn't quite believe my own words, but I realized that, for the first time, my curiosity outweighed my fear.

After lunch, I approached May at the pencil sharpener and went for broke: I invited her to come to my house after school. "We could walk home together, if you'd like. Maybe watch the Nickelodeon Channel?" I offered. (I'd be lying if I didn't admit that I was somewhat pacified by the idea that I'd be on home turf, under the watchful eye of my parents, where little could go wrong.) Still, I was proud that I had extended the invitation.

Then, something unprecedented happened. Something that I would not have believed had I not seen it with my own eyes. May smiled. And then she said yes.

I don't remember what we watched on television, or what my mother prepared for our after-school snack. But I do know that I went from ruing the day I wore a French braid to school to realizing that it had become the catalyst for a new friendship.

May Jordan never bullied me again, and, in fact, we became pretty good friends. After spending countless afternoons at my house, I quickly realized that, yes, underneath the tall girl's armor was an insecure fifth grader who wanted nothing more than to be accepted.

I've since learned that the old adage, you can't judge a book by its cover, certainly rings true, and that someone who looks different on the outside can really be just like you.

~Courtney Conover

Finding Cool

The reputation of a thousand years may be determined
by the conduct of one hour.
~Japanese Proverb

In junior high, being cool is everything. I was not cool. Luckily, I had Sarah. Although she wasn't a member of the popular crowd, she was definitely one of the coolest people I'd ever met. She was a slender and graceful blonde who seemed to float everywhere she went.

I admired a lot about Sarah—her thin frame, her hair, her confidence—because I felt I had a lot less to offer. Not only was I not as skinny and not at all blond, I had the grace of a rhino—or maybe, I should say, a kangaroo. I had a bouncy, on-my-toes kind of walk that was embarrassing. I looked as if I were eternally about to plunge into something. My mom used to say that every time I walked down the hall to or from my bedroom, it sounded like a herd of elephants thundering into the house. Because my walk so desperately needed fixing, Sarah took me on as a project.

In the mornings before our first period classes began, Sarah and I would roam the halls of our school. Sauntering around the building wasn't just to pass the time, it was my homework: to practice being graceful. I had to come down off my toes, begin each step with my heels, and try leaning backward instead of perpetually forward. I had to relax. It seemed impossible.

"You're on your toes again," Sarah would warn each time I slipped back into my natural walk. I'd focus my efforts and try again. We'd pass through the halls, occasionally stopping to talk to friends. While Sarah was relaxed and natural, I was often lost in concentration, fervently practicing walking like a girl instead of a marsupial.

When we weren't practicing my walk, we were usually hanging out at a nearby mall or at Sarah's house. I loved to sit on her bed and admire all her beauty products, usually strewn around her room as if they just spontaneously sprouted there. Sarah's room was a glorious garden of cheap, drugstore make-up, the kind affordable to girls like us, too young to have real jobs. Her nail polish collection was especially impressive, featuring a rainbow of bright colors. Whether she was having a hot pink kind of day or a glitter-filled burgundy evening, she owned a bottle to fit her mood.

At first things were fine. She was helping me improve myself, edging me closer to cool, I thought. Gradually, though, the imbalance in our relationship grew. She seemed to be treating me with contempt more often, and telling me what to do even when it had nothing to do with self-improvement. I didn't like her bossiness, but I didn't have much confidence, either, so I just shrugged my shoulders and did what she wanted. After all, she was the cool one, right?

I never expected to confront her, but one day in art class our relationship reached a turning point. We were doing large-scale painting projects that required the class to move into the halls to get enough space to work. I was in the middle of my project, surrounded by supplies and covered in paint, when Sarah called to me from across the hall, where she was sitting near another group of students.

"Go get me more red paint," she ordered.

I crinkled my eyebrows, annoyed. Couldn't she see I was busy? Should I put down my stuff, get up, and go back into the classroom to get her the paint anyway?

"C'mon," she prodded. "Get me the paint."

"Can't you get it yourself?" I asked quietly.

"No, you get it."

I paused, then answered. "I'm in the middle of this," I protested weakly. "I can't."

"If you don't get for me, I'm not going to be friends with you anymore," Sarah announced.

I looked at her, stunned. Was she serious? She'd dump our whole friendship just because I wouldn't fetch her the paint? Maybe my instincts were right; this wasn't much of a friendship after all.

My heart was racing. Other students were looking at us, judging, waiting. Sarah just sat there, appearing as confident as ever. I hated confrontations, but I couldn't bring myself to be her slave anymore. I gave her an answer that I doubt she expected to hear.

"I'm not getting it." I turned back to my project.

Sarah was smug. "You'll come running back to me," she said with self-assurance. "They always do," she added, perhaps for the benefit of the crowd that surrounded her.

She didn't realize it, but saying those final words sealed our fate. Any doubt I'd had about taking a stand was chipped away like a single coat of cheap nail polish. I was never going back. I may not have had much in the confidence department, but I had more than enough stubbornness to stick to my decision.

Sarah and I never spoke again.

It was strange going through life without Sarah after I'd gotten so used to our relationship, but I didn't regret my decision. Standing up for myself was a skill that would take me many years to master; I struggled with it in high school and again in college. I had been raised to be helpful, polite, and pleasing, and most of all, to never talk back to the people in charge. It made me an obedient daughter, but it also made me a social doormat.

Realizing that sometimes I had to put myself first, even if it was going to make other people unhappy, was a long learning process—but that day in art class, I took my first big step. Standing up for myself was something to be proud of, and even better, it was the cool thing to do.

~Alaina Smith

Chicken Soup
for the Soul

Flowers of Forgiveness

Forgiveness is the fragrance that the violet sheds
on the heel that has crushed it.
~Mark Twain

The Children's Theater was actually an old mill building with cement walls, twisting passages and big staircases. Everything smelled of mothballs, metal, and old grease. Static crackled in the air and every footstep echoed eerily.

One afternoon, my eight-year-old sister Brittany and I were with the drama group rehearsing *A Little Princess*, a children's play based on a book by Frances Hodgson Burnett.

"Break a leg!" I whispered as Brittany adjusted her boarding school costume.

"Take your places for act one, please. Everyone, places for act one!" called the director, a woman with spiky blond hair and rings on every finger.

The lights went out and the rehearsal began. Halfway through the first act, Brittany finished her part and went backstage. She grabbed her script from the make-up table and read along with the rehearsal that was still at full swing in front of the curtain. A small group of fellow actors joined her, and started practicing lines. Suddenly, something wet exploded on the back of Brittany's head! Spinning around, she saw a tall girl with a bottle of Febreze in her hand. She aimed it at Brittany's ear, grinning widely. Splat! Gooey blue liquid slid down

Brittany's face. The older girl guffawed and looked to the other girls for a reaction. Brittany glanced at them, expecting them to speak up and defend her. Instead, they shrieked with laughter and pointed mocking fingers at Brittany, who ran out of the make-up room in dismay.

Ten minutes later, Brittany met me backstage. "A big girl just sprayed me with this stuff and laughed at me," she said, trying to wipe the chemical out of her curly hair. "All the other girls laughed, too."

I didn't even know the girl's name, and she was bullying my sister!

When we got home, we looked at the cast list and found that the girl's name was Jessica. Our mom e-mailed the director, who said she would talk to Jessica and arrange time for an apology right before the next rehearsal. Nobody really expected a heartfelt apology from Jessica, but Brittany was prepared to forgive her.

Next rehearsal, the director met Brittany at the door and announced that we had a problem on our hands. "Jessica swears that she was never even near you yesterday."

But Brittany knew the truth. As she glanced across the room full of young actors, she glimpsed Jessica slouching defiantly in a metal folding chair. For a split second, their eyes met. Jessica quickly whirled away to stare in the opposite direction. For weeks afterwards, no matter how hard Brittany tried to talk to her, Jessica refused to look her way.

It was very difficult for Brittany to work with Jessica every rehearsal, for three hours each week. But finally, we were ready to perform. There would be three performances over the course of the next weekend. Brittany and I were glad that the ordeal was almost over.

After the first show, Brittany and I each got a beautiful bouquet from our church's pastor and his wife. Jessica didn't get a single flower.

The second night, we received flowers from our grandparents. Again, Jessica received nothing.

On the way home, Brittany spoke up.

"Mommy," she said quietly from the back seat of the car, "I've been thinking, and I decided I want to buy some flowers for Jessica."

Mom smiled in surprise. "That would be very nice."

Before the last performance, Brittany met Jessica on the way into the theater. She handed the older girl a big bunch of yellow roses, bought with her own savings. "Great job with the show last night, Jessica. These are for you."

Jessica's eyes popped in astonishment. "For me?" she faltered, squinting incredulously at Brittany's warm smile. "These flowers are for me? Are you sure?"

"Yes, I want you to have them!" Brittany skipped towards the dressing room, leaving Jessica staring after her with a bewildered look on her face and a bouquet of beautiful flowers in her arms.

That night, Jessica finally received some flowers from her dad. She pulled out a sprig of carnations and smiled shyly as she gave them to Brittany.

Maybe Jessica will never apologize to Brittany. Maybe she won't ever even admit her wrongdoing. But she is just beginning to realize what wonderful things God's love does in people like Brittany.

~Caitlin Brown

Luck Be a Day-of-the-Week Panty

The only sure thing about luck is that it will change.
~Wilson Mizner

On my eleventh birthday, I received a package of day-of-the-week panties. Each of the seven white undergarments had a different trim color with matching thread that spelled out a day of the week—Sunday through Saturday. These panties became my barometer for good fortune.

When I dressed before beginning my day in sixth grade, I opened my dresser drawer, closed my eyes and reached in. If I blindly chose the panty embroidered with the correct day of the week, I believed that I would have good luck for twenty-four hours. If I failed to choose the correct day-of-the-week panty for the day I was about to start, I feared the worst.

Any interaction with Margaret was bound to be on a wrong-panty day. I met Margaret when I moved to town in fourth grade. At recess on my first day as the new kid, Margaret walked up to me on the blacktop where kids played hopscotch. I smiled, thinking we were about to strike up a friendship. That's when Margaret punched me in the stomach.

Her punch carried experience. It was obvious by Margaret's form she had punched before. It was the only time I have had the wind intentionally knocked out of me by another human being.

By sixth grade, I was relying heavily on my day-of-the-week panties to predict if it was to be a Margaret kind of day. She hadn't socked me again in the two years since the playground punch, but she taunted me. The day she pulled my elastic headband down over my eyes, I was wearing the Monday panty on Thursday.

Luckily, I had enough correct-panty days to get by.

Like the day we were square dancing in gym class. Square dancing in and of itself made a day unlucky with its embarrassment of holding a boy's sweaty hand and the agony of do-si-do-ing and promenading. However, for me, the day the teachers selected dance partners amongst the students, the aura of square dancing turned on a dime. My teacher scanned the bevy of girls. He walked up to me, bent down, extended his hand and said, "Would you like to dance?" I blushed, took my handsome teacher's hand, and floated to the middle of the gym floor where other teachers and their student-partners gathered. The record player spun, and we danced the Virginia reel.

From among all of the sixth-grade girls, my teacher picked me as his dance partner. I smiled. I was wearing my pink-trimmed Wednesday panty, and it was Wednesday.

Time marched on, and I outgrew my day-of-the-week panties and my need for a good-luck accessory. I began to learn that it takes a higher power to define my days.

Then, on a summer afternoon when I was seventeen, I was riding my bicycle. A Doberman began chasing at my wheels. Someone called the dog from across the street. I looked over and saw Margaret. She was wearily pushing her baby and toddler in a stroller. Margaret looked like life had punched her in the stomach.

As I pedaled away from the snapping dog, I realized that Margaret was proof that no object—not even a day-of-the-week panty—can bring us luck. Each of us is responsible for making our own.

~Angie Klink

A Bully's Tale

If you judge people, you have no time to love them.
~Mother Teresa

My family moved a lot when I was a kid. I was always just a little overweight and we were poor, so my clothes were not the nicest. I was often tormented by bullies. I survived the bullying and went on to live a rewarding life. Eventually, I understood that bullies are usually unhappy kids from troubled families. This helped me to forgive them and let go of my resentment. That's what this poem is about.

> I am a big bad bully
> As mean as I can be,
> I like to beat up little kids
> And steal their lunch money.
>
> I guess you think I'm different
> Than you could ever be,
> But it is really not my fault
> It's just my family.
>
> My mother isn't very nice
> She often hits me once or twice.
> My father is the village drunk

Our house looks like the city dump.

They never taught me to be nice,
Or how to get along.
They never read me storybooks
Or sang me silly songs.

They taught me life is scary
And to win you must be tough.
So I am loud and nasty
And I handle people rough.

But if you turned me inside out,
A sad young boy you'd see.
I'm lonely and I'm frightened,
Confused as I can be.

I long for hugs and kisses,
And for an "I love you."
Instead of feeling safe and loved
My life is cold and cruel.

So please try not to hate me.
Just stay out of my way,
And pray I someday get some help
To learn a better way.

~Cynthia Baker

Rites of Passage

You can out-distance that which is running after you,
but not what is running inside you.
~Rwandan Proverb

My best friend Michelle and I decided it would be a good day for a swim. Checking the schedule of the local public pool, we found a public swim at 3:00 p.m. My father said he would drive us if my brother and a friend of his could go too. I agreed. It wasn't a sacrifice to take my brother along.

Dad dropped us off at the pool and said he would be back later to pick us up. We shouted our thanks and ran off to the huge cement building, the scent of chlorine getting stronger as we got closer to the pool.

Before long, we had enjoyed all the pool had to offer. I found my brother and gave him the signal that it was time for us to be finished, while Michelle and I packed up our stuff and took a seat on one of the concrete benches to wait for my dad.

I don't know how long we were there before the group of kids came up to us. There had to be at least twelve of them, all punked out and dressed in black. Lips and eyes black as night. They surrounded us, and the girl who looked to be the leader of the group came forward. The others formed a loose semicircle around us, smiling. The girl in front did not look happy with Michelle. She was huge. Not so much tall as she was stocky, she reminded me of a bull, all muscle under her clothes. It was the first time I had seen a girl with a Mohawk, and by the way she was staring at Michelle I was sure this wasn't going to end well for either of us.

"What the heck are you staring at?" she asked Michelle.

"I am not staring at anything," Michelle replied.

"I think you are. I think you're staring at my hair." She gave Michelle a push on the shoulder.

Michelle didn't say anything, just looked back at her. Michelle was a tall girl for thirteen. She was strong too, and athletic, but I knew she would not raise a fist to this girl. That wouldn't stop me from coming to Michelle's rescue though.

"So what if she was?" I said, surprising myself.

"I wasn't talking to you. It's her I have a beef with."

I almost laughed at the beef comment, because I had just thought of her as a bull only moments before.

"She's not going to fight you. She's a PK kid," I went on, my courage growing with every spoken word.

"What the heck is a PK kid?"

"A 'Pastor's Kid,' so she won't fight you. Michelle sometimes just stares out into space; I'm sure she wasn't staring at your hair." I thought a clear concise explanation would do the trick and everything would blow over. The punked out girl was not amused by the way things were going. From what I could see it didn't look as though she was going to back down. Where the heck was my father?

"Well then, I guess you are going to have to do." She leaned closer to me, so close that I could smell her breath. Her friends started to cheer her on.

Up until this time I had never been in a fight, and the thought of being in one had never even crossed my mind. Now, faced with the possibility, my heart pounded in my ears, and adrenaline coursed through my veins. What was I going to do now? This girl towered over me and would beat me to a pulp in no time. I was dead for sure. With her friends penning us in there was no easy escape either. I didn't see any other option. I took the duffel bag I had, full of my brother and his friends' flippers and masks, and threw it at her head.

I thought this would give me enough time for some sort of escape. I was right. When I threw the bag, the semicircle of friends gasped at my audacity and they were caught off guard. I ran and broke through the circle at one end. I could hear the pounding of their footsteps chasing after me.

I soon realized that I had made a crucial error in judgment when I took off. Instead of going towards the pool and the adults inside I had run out into an empty parking lot. There was no one to help me out here, only Michelle yelling for help. I had a good lead on them since I was pretty quick, but suddenly something in me snapped. I no longer wanted to run. I felt like if I didn't stop running right now, in this situation, I would spend my entire life running. I wasn't sure I wanted to do that.

She was like an advancing tank, her face a storm of rage. I was out of luck and options. It didn't matter; I had to take a stand. I mustered all the courage I could and faced her. Everything around me slowed as she came forward, her arm and hand drawn back; I could see, close up, her thick fingers and protruding knuckles. BAM, her mammoth fist hit me square in the nose and mouth. It's true what they depict in cartoons—I did see stars when my head snapped back. My hands went to my mouth to comfort the sudden pain there. I watched as she drew back and prepared to hit me again. Suddenly I heard honking; it was my dad coming to the rescue. The girl and her friends scattered to the wind. He came to me, asking if I was all right, tilting my head this way and that, trying to see through the blood. I told him I was and Michelle ran up and offered her towel to clean up my face.

I learned a lot that day. Mostly, I learned to stand up to my fears and meet problems head on instead of running. I vowed to myself that I would always try to stay strong, brave, and capable of anything.

Time went on and the years marched by. I was in my second year of junior high when I saw a poster saying peer counselors were needed, so I applied. I grew with the position, listening to kids and their problems and helping where I could, until one day when I was paired with an unexpected visitor. It was her—the same girl from all those years ago. She no longer wore the Mohawk, and the black make-up was gone, but it was her all the same, there could be no mistake about it. I was shocked. I almost didn't know what to say. I waited for her to recognize me from the fight we had, but she never did.

I listened to her problems like I did all the others, and to my amazement I actually could feel compassion for her and her situation even after what she had done. After all, despite the pain, she had given me a gift. A chance to take what life offered, learn from it, and most importantly, grow from my experience.

~Tracie Skarbo

Armored and Dangerous

Courage is being afraid but going on anyhow.
~Dan Rather

A dolescent idiopathic scoliosis. When I was twelve, that sounded like "idiot-something," which is what I knew I was going to feel like when I realized how the scoliosis would be treated. I sat in the doctor's office while he explained to me this horrendous contraption I'd be wearing to straighten my curved spine. Every day, all day long, for the next two years. A metal and plastic brace would cover my entire torso. I would have to eat in it, sleep in it... go to school in it. The tears came, fast and heavy.

I'd always been shy and awkward. A head taller than the rest of my class, I was all legs and lanky arms. The other kids teased me with a sarcastic, "How's the weather up there?" People often asked, "Do you play basketball?" I'm sure they meant it as a compliment, but to me it was only a reminder of my lack of physical coordination. I wanted to be petite, or at least normal. Anything but tall and gawky.

And now, my early growth spurt had earned me a sentence in a suit of armor.

The fitting was best described as "mortifying." A plaster mold was taken of my torso, which meant wearing nothing but my underwear and a set of nearly transparent fabric tubes while a cast was set around me from armpit to lower hip. It couldn't have been worse.

Then came the day I met the beast. Thick, ugly, white plastic in a wide band molded to my hips. Another, narrower band curved around my upper chest and under my armpits. Metal bars connected the two plastic sections—complete with bolts and screws. I was going to be a real-life Frankenstein.

The brace was uncomfortable at first, but that was not the worst of things. The doctor had told me it wouldn't be noticeable under my clothes.

He lied.

Maybe he'd meant that it wouldn't be noticeable under my clothes, because I wouldn't be wearing it under my clothes. No, I would be wearing it under all new, bigger clothes because the thing was so bulky my clothes would never fit over it!

I was thankful, at least, for the fact that the brace didn't extend up to my neck, as some back braces do. I told only my closest friends. And with the help of a loose-fitting jacket, no one else seemed to notice. It took time, but eventually, I got used to getting into the brace and wearing it to school. But I never liked it.

Although there was one day I was really glad to have the beast.... On that day, my friend Carla and I had stepped into the girls' bathroom. Another girl emerged from a stall, cigarette in hand. My heart nearly stopped. It was Tanya—a girl in my art class who happened to be friends with the biggest bully in the school, Mandy.

Even with my unusual height, Mandy towered over me. And I was tall and skinny, but Mandy was tall and thick. Panic set in.

"Carla, let's go," I whispered, and dragged her out of the bathroom. Tanya glared after us, until the door shut. As I pulled Carla down the hall, she began to protest.

"I'm turning her in!" she said as she yanked free and crossed her arms.

"No, you can't... she's friends with Mandy Anderson." I continued to beg and plead, desperately hoping my words would take hold. As she stalked off, though, I knew they hadn't.

The following day, Tanya confronted me in art class.

"Mandy's going to beat the crap out of you. Tomorrow, on the P.E. field."

I tried to explain to her that I was not the one who turned her in, that it was a friend of mine. She wanted the friend's name, but I refused to give it. Carla had done nothing wrong. Something stupid... but not technically wrong. I wouldn't make things worse by telling on her.

"Well, if you don't tell us who she is, then you take her beating. Tomorrow." She smiled cruelly, right in my face, and went back to her seat.

That night, I called another friend of mine. Jen and I had been friends for a couple of years despite our totally opposite personalities. Where I was shy, introverted and intellectual, she was outgoing, extroverted, and street-smart. She was shorter than me, but stronger. She knew how to fight. I told her what happened.

"Mandy Anderson?" she asked.

"Yeah, what do I do?"

"Pray she gets hit by a bus before school tomorrow, I guess. Otherwise, nice knowin' ya."

I hung up the phone, fighting tears. If Jen couldn't help me, I was doomed.

The following day, Mandy approached me. She questioned me, and she threatened me. I fully understood the saying "shaking in my boots" at that moment. I tried not to cry as words flew out of my mouth. I didn't even realize most of what I was saying. I wanted to turn and run, but she would have come after me. So I talked, and then a light dawned.

I knew something she didn't.

Mandy had no idea I wore a back brace. She didn't know about the heavy plastic and metal bars under my clothes. My heart slowed to normal and my confidence rose. I tried not to smile as I talked my way out of the fight. I really didn't have much to worry about. I only had to protect my face—if she landed a punch anywhere lower,

Mandy would have broken her hand. Then who would feel like an "idiot-something?"

The following year, I was allowed to wear my suit of armor part-time and go to school without it. And eventually, the day came when I didn't need it at all. For months after that, it sat in my closet. For some reason I had a hard time letting it go. How could I just throw it out? The beast had saved my life.

~Kat Heckenbach

Ugly

Everything has beauty, but not everyone sees it.
~Confucius

It was the last day of school before winter vacation. Gray clouds drifted across the darkening sky; icy winds whipped outside my sixth grade math class, and despite the fact that I normally paid very close attention in class, I found myself slipping into a reverie. After all, how could one focus when Christmas and all its joy were just a few days away?

The bell rang and students darted out of classrooms. I joined the crowds, in a daze as backpack after backpack thumped against my body and voices roared over my head.

I made my way out of the school, and smiled as I saw my twin sister Meli and our good friend Peter chatting near a frozen tree. I raced towards them, and I found Meli wearing an odd, almost breezy smile. Peter's eyes glowed with the promise of juicy gossip.

"Hey," I said, glancing towards our temporarily immobile school bus waiting a good distance away. I didn't want to miss my ride home, after all.

"Aaron called us ugly," my sister said. "Peter sits with them in math class and he told me. Sam said you did a weird licking thing with your tongue whenever you talk, too," she added.

For a moment I was stunned, confused, and sad. In an instant, those emotions melted together into humiliation and shame.

Meli seemed oblivious to my hurt feelings. "I don't even know who Aaron is," she admitted and Peter laughed. I thought for a moment. It was our first few months in the new middle school. Both boys were from the elementary school on the other side of town, and I knew Sam from numerous classes we had together. I only vaguely recalled Aaron. He was a jock with a petite girlfriend.

My eyes began to tear up. "Thanks a lot, Peter," I managed to spit out before racing away from the people who I couldn't wait to talk to moments before.

I rushed towards the bus, burrowing into the corner of a two-seater. My breath fogged up the cold window I leaned my cheek against. I fought the lump in my throat, the tears behind my eyes. As if things couldn't get any worse, a girl I was slightly friendly with sat next to me. We had played softball together for the last few years on the recreational team and lived near one another. I turned my face away from her as the first hot tear rolled down my cheek. She said a few things to me, nothing I can remember. It took her a moment to realize I was crying, I believe, and she stopped talking. I silently thanked her.

All my insecurities had transformed into sharp knives, and each one was stabbing me over and over again, a relentless force.

My hair was too frizzy. My eyes too brown. I had uncool clothes. I was fat. I was ugly.

Ugly.

After what seemed like a million years, the bus rolled to a stop in front of my house. Hunching forward, I stepped out, my sister walking quickly several feet in front of me.

I was eager to tell my mom about my horrible day, but my sister sprinted upstairs first, and I couldn't bear to face both of them at once.

I took a few minutes to wash my puffy face, trying to hide the tears I'd shed. My mother would make it better, I knew. Well, I hoped. At this point, it was the only thing I had left to hold onto.

When I heard my sister heading into the kitchen, I trudged

upstairs. My mom was typing away on her laptop, her glasses propped on the straight bone of her nose. She looked up when I entered.

"A boy at school called me ugly," I said, my voice drained of any pride, my pulled-together demeanor crumbling.

Mom nodded. "He called Meli ugly, also."

My eyes stung as that awful lump swelled again in my throat. "Well, a different boy said I did a weird thing with my tongue, too!"

My mother switched gears from college professor to concerned mother. "Come here," she soothed, and I fell onto her bed, as my repressed tears sprung forward.

"Meli said she didn't care. She didn't know the boy," Mom said matter-of-factly.

"He's in my advisory!" I spit out. This wasn't working out as I'd planned; my mother simply didn't understand the pain I was feeling.

She looked at me with wide green eyes. "Do you care?"

I jumped off the bed, wiping away my tears and yelled, "You don't get it!" I slammed her door and stormed to our bottom floor, past my older brother Matt and into our overheated laundry room, where my sister and I shared a computer.

My heart ached and anger surged through every one of my limbs.

How dare they destroy my vacation, I thought bitterly, cursing Sam and especially Aaron.

The fury was overwhelming and it took up so much space in my body it cast away everything else: my good grades, my loyal friends, any confidence I had in myself. I was a mess, and all because of one little word. A few minutes later, my mom quietly entered the room and sat next to me. "Al," she said and I looked at her. "I don't want you to be upset. He's just a boy. One boy might think licking your lips or whatever is weird; another might think it's beautiful." She went on. "And so what if one person thinks you're ugly? You're not ugly. Not everyone will think you're great looking, but no one will think you're ugly because you're not. Even Matt said he's just some stupid boy."

I looked at her and nodded. My anger towards her melted away easily, as it always did. We embraced and I felt slightly better.

Everything she said made sense. Considering she was my mother, her compliments weren't the biggest confidence booster, but I could feel my spirits lift a little bit.

Two and a half years later, my life has moved on from the words of two boys I had barely ever spoken to. Still, there have been days when I've gone back to that horrible moment in time, and felt myself shrink back to sixth grade. I've used it as an excuse to cry, to pity myself. But, I've realized over the years that if I render those two boys and their words powerless, then I am the one in power, and I choose when and why I don't feel good about myself. I am superior.

No one, I think, ever forgets the first person who calls them ugly. But, I'm lucky enough to realize that I don't need to forget what happened to understand that other people's words—no matter how cruel—are as important as I make them. In this case, they're meaningless.

~Ali Lauro

91

Chicken Soup
for the
Soul

The Ultimate Revenge

Sin makes its own hell, and goodness its own heaven.
~Mary Baker Eddy

I sat in my chair in seventh grade homeroom staring cross-eyed into the taut rubber band stretched in front of my left glasses lens, the only thing separating my eye from the sting of the snapping elastic. "I'm gonna snap your lens out!" the boy sitting in front of me said, much the same as he did every day. My blond, blue-eyed torturer's name fell in the alphabet so close to mine that I had no hope of ever escaping him; whenever we shared a class, he sat in front of me.

Being the "new kid" in seventh grade left me feeling like an alien. My parents had just divorced; my mom got my brother and me and a cramped apartment on the other side of a set of abandoned railroad tracks. After only a few weeks in the brand new school, I still felt alone and sad, missing my friends and my old comfy bedroom. At half the size, my new bedroom felt as cramped and dark as I did inside.

My homeroom torturer only added to what I already felt was the start of a miserable, lonely, painful year.

Every day the boy turned in his seat and stretched that rubber band in front of my eyes, I stared at his improvised weapon and tried not to show any fear. I'd never been bullied before, and I didn't really have any game plan to deal with the threats. I woke up in the morning, dreading the homeroom class and the forty-five minutes of wondering and worrying when he'd turn around in his seat and taunt me again.

Most bullies are very careful to hide their actions from the teachers, and this boy was no different. I was so embarrassed when he'd pick on me and other kids sitting near would laugh into their hands. It was so unfair! I wasn't the one acting out and breaking the rules, but it seemed like everyone was on his side and against me. I kept quiet, because I knew it would only get worse if I told on him. I had let him pick on me without a word for weeks.

That day, though, something inside me changed. I got angry. I was so mad I wanted to push him or shove him down on the hallway floor in front of everyone so they would all laugh at the boy who got beat up by a girl. I wanted him to feel as embarrassed and outcast as I felt! But I also knew my thoughts were really only stupid fantasies and that I would never actually hit him or do anything violent.

I just knew I didn't want to take his malicious teasing anymore! I stared past the rubber band, looked him in the eye, took a deep breath, and calmly said, "If you hurt me, you will get into trouble." He frowned just a little bit, and he pulled his hand back, slightly. "So you might as well stop. You don't scare me." He rolled his eyes and called me a chicken, or a baby, or some other stupid name. But he turned around and left me alone the rest of the class.

You know how you feel when you master a complicated move in a video game, or you learn a new chord on your guitar or you play your piano recital piece all the way through with no mistakes? Like you want to do an end zone dance? I felt that way in that moment. I stood up for myself and didn't back down to a bully! And I did it without any kind of physical violence. I felt great!

That wasn't the end of the story, though. I made a good start, but I only won the first battle. He picked on me throughout junior high every time we shared a class. I never again took his teasing quietly, though, and always stood my ground. He may not have quit, but he never actually hurt me, either. Plus, I made lots of good friends who respected me for standing up for myself.

Seems like a pretty lame ending to the story, doesn't it? I mean, in our fantasies, the bullies go on to meet their match, get beaten up and never pick on anyone smaller than them again, right? Sometimes, real life can bring an even better ending.

As luck would have it, I didn't have to share any classes with my bully in ninth grade, so I didn't give him a second thought. Until tenth grade. There he was, sitting a couple of seats in front of me. Even though he'd grown taller and was no longer the scruffy little boy from junior high, I recognized him immediately. I groaned inwardly, thinking about the trial I would have to go through all over again. Finally, we were paired in a group assignment and I noticed him looking at me an awful lot. Uh-oh, he's recognized me, I thought, and braced myself for more teasing.

Almost as anxious as those days in seventh grade, I waited and waited for him to humiliate me in front of our classmates. Several days after the group assignment, he approached me in the hall. Here it comes, I thought.

"Hey, um," he stammered and seemed a little embarrassed. "Uh, did you catch the last page of the homework assignment?" he finally asked.

I stared at him in disbelief a moment until I caught myself and answered, "Um, yeah, it's page fifty-eight." Where was the teasing? What was he going to do? These thoughts ran through my head, while he fidgeted and looked around the hall, everywhere but at me.

Finally, he swallowed hard and said, real fast, "So, are you going out with anyone?"

I blinked slowly and then said, "Um... what?"

He scratched his right ankle with the toe of his left foot, his face reddening and said, "Uh, you know... are you, uh, 'with' anyone, like, um dating?" He took a deep breath and added, "You know?"

I couldn't help it; my mouth fell open and I started to laugh a little. Was my junior high torturer really asking me out? Then it dawned on me. As much as he'd changed, I had changed too! "You don't know who I am, do you?"

He looked at me weirdly, so I pulled a rubber band out of my bag, stretched it like he used to and said, "Maybe this will remind you!"

I plopped the rubber band in his hand and walked away feeling that "end zone dance" feeling. My torturer wanted to be my boyfriend, and I got to tell him no!

~Julia D. Alexander

Chapter
11

Just for Preteens

Friendships
to Last a Lifetime

Friendship is a sheltering tree.

~Samuel Taylor Coleridge

92

The Lunchtablers

A friend is one of the nicest things you can have,
and one of the best things you can be.
~Douglas Pagels

Life's best and worst moments happen when you least expect them. When I was in sixth grade, finding a good lunch table was difficult. I didn't have any classes with my fifth grade friends, and I hadn't had time to make new friends yet. I remember sitting at different lunch tables every day the first two weeks of school, trying to find a group I fit in with. It took me about three weeks to get it right.

Even today, I'm not quite sure how I found the seven girls who became my best friends. I used to think it was some mixture of fate and coincidence that brought us together, but later I came to realize that it must have been God's will. Like me, they had been separated from their elementary school friends, and somehow we all ended up at the same lunch table.

We never really discussed it. We just sat together every day at lunch. Before long, we started inviting each other to our birthday parties and getting together on weekends. I always wanted a best friend, and somehow I was blessed enough to find seven. As a group, we decided to call ourselves the only name that seemed appropriate: "The Lunchtablers."

There was no other name that could describe us because,

although we were friends, the only thing we had in common was we ate lunch together. Honestly, we were an odd group. Christy was a studious soccer player, Lauren was a shy golfer with an infectious laugh, Hayden was a tomboy on the swim team, Meghan was a dancer who loved shopping, Kim was practically a hippie who only shopped for necessities, Laura was a dramatic cheerleader, and Sara Parker, whom we affectionately nicknamed "Sparker," was a religious new girl in town. I was a cheerleader, but first and foremost, I was a writer.

It was writing that brought me to a particular winter night. Sparker and I were in the same newspaper class, and we were co-reporters for a basketball game. We had covered games together before. As a cheerleader, I had a good view of the court, so Sparker would sit in the front row, and we would write the story play by play. However, an hour before the game, Sparker called me and told me she wouldn't be able to come. Her mom had to go to the hospital. She said it wasn't anything serious, so I didn't give it much thought. After all, everyone knew that Sparker's mom suffered from a rare form of cancer, but it had been in remission for years now. She seemed fine.

The next week we found out what was really going on. Apparently, Mrs. Parker's cancer had metastasized, and there wasn't much hope of a recovery. Sparker wasn't at school the next day, and during the final class period, a voice came over the school intercom, calling all of the Lunchtablers into the front office. When we got there, Christy's mom said she was taking us to the hospital to keep Sparker company during this difficult time.

We went with Sparker to one of the hospital's waiting rooms. At first we asked about her mom's condition. Before long the conversation diverted to school and other middle school concerns. At the end of our hour-long visit, we hugged Sparker and said goodbye so she could spend time with her family.

About a half hour after we left the hospital, we got the call. Sparker's mom had died. I'll never forget when my mom came into my room and told me the devastating news. I didn't know Mrs. Parker very well, but I did know that she was a wonderful, Christian woman.

Sparker said throughout her mom's life and even on her deathbed, she always said, "God is in control."

The day after her mom's death, Sparker came back to school. All of the Lunchtablers rallied around her, and on the day of her mom's funeral, we sat in the pew behind her for support. After a few weeks had gone by, Sparker told us more about her mom's life and even about her final moments. She said that before her mom died, their family minister prayed aloud for Mrs. Parker, ending his prayer by saying, "God, please welcome this beautiful woman into heaven." Then, as soon as the preacher said "Amen," her heart monitor flatlined, and she passed away.

When Sparker told me that story, I was sure without a shadow of a doubt that God was, indeed, in control. I became convinced that even when life seems impossible to understand, He is working behind the scenes in unexpected ways, and He never abandons us.

To commemorate Mrs. Parker, the Lunchtablers dedicated a plaque in her honor at our high school, so she could be with us throughout the next four years of our friendship. Sparker followed in her mother's faithful footsteps, starting a weekly Bible study for us to attend, and the Lunchtablers have stayed together ever since. Although we all attend different colleges now, we have annual sleepovers to share what is going on in our new lives and reflect on our past.

Adolescent life is full of changes. Some of them are good changes, like meeting a lifelong group of friends, and some of them are difficult changes, like dealing with an unexpected loss. Through my middle school experiences, I learned the necessity of trusting God in small and large matters. Whenever my life changes or my future seems daunting, I think about the Lunchtablers, and I am reminded that God is always in control.

~Kara Marie Hackett

93

Fourteen Angels

We are each of us angels with only one wing,
and we can only fly by embracing one another.
~Luciano de Crescenzo

My grandma was diagnosed with lung cancer when I was only ten, but I didn't really understand her illness until three years later, when I was thirteen and thought I had it rough. Between big crushes, massive amounts of homework, and arguments with my parents, I felt like I might just explode. I knew Grandma was sick, but it was merely a small thought in the back of my mind. At thirteen, I had enough to keep me occupied.

I'd been playing hockey since I was nine years old, and I loved it. When I was thirteen I played my first year of Bantam hockey. From the very beginning of the season in December, my team and I wanted nothing more than to win the championship, which would mean getting a banner hung up in the rink with our team name on it. We would become a part of hockey history in our small town. That's what we worked for all year, and why we went out every game and played until we gave everything we had.

Finally, at the end of our season, we were close to winning it all. I was pumped for this game; we were playing the team that had been first in our league all year. We'd won our first playoff game against them, and if we won one more game, we'd win the banner. We'd be the top dogs. I was grabbing my equipment and my team jacket when I heard a familiar voice from the other room.

"What's wrong with Mom?" I heard my mother ask. I walked down the steps to see my teary-eyed mother on the phone. As soon as I saw her in that state, I knew something was wrong. My mom's been in the military her whole life, so trust me—she learned how to mask her emotions early on and she doesn't show them easily.

"Rachael! Time to go!" Dad called to me and I scurried up the stairs, grabbing my hockey bag and sticks and heading out the door.

On our way to the rink, I asked what exactly was wrong with Grandma, since I figured that's who Mom was talking about. He seemed reluctant to tell me, but I weaseled it out of him. Grandma was in the hospital, coughing up blood and having a hard time breathing. I wanted to be told that everything would be fine, that Grandma would be okay. When I asked if she'd come out of the hospital, my dad said what I didn't want to hear: "I don't think so."

I knew I needed to focus, but after waving halfheartedly at the few girls who were already at the rink, I found an empty hallway and sat down on the ground. I tucked my knees up to my chest and soaked the knees of my jeans with tears. "God I hope she's okay," I prayed out loud in that hallway by myself. Somewhere inside of me, I didn't think that my grandma was coming out of the hospital. Somehow I thought this was the last time she'd go in.

My legs were starting to cramp up from being curled into such a little ball in the hallway. I stood, and three of my teammates saw me and ran over to where I was. They asked in worried voices what was wrong, and I realized I needed someone to talk to.

I let my sorrow flow over as I told them how scared and worried I was. Part of me figured they'd probably just turn away; they needed to focus on the hockey game, not my personal misery. These girls weren't my absolute best friends—we didn't have sleepovers every Saturday. They were teammates, girls who knew me because we had similar skill levels at a sport we all enjoyed. I finished my story. I expected them to say they felt sorry for me, but I didn't expect what was coming next.

Our team captain, with whom I'd had a number of spats, pulled me into a comforting hug. "I'm sorry," she whispered. I have no idea how long it was, but each of those three girls helped to comfort me, gave me hugs, and surprised me with their warmth. We went to meet up with the rest of the team for the warm-up.

Even though I knew that I needed to focus on my game, I was still acting melancholy as we walked into the dressing room to change into our equipment. Apparently, my feelings were obvious because a lot of girls asked me what was wrong. Our team captain asked me if I felt comfortable telling the team what had happened. When I agreed to do so, she turned off the music and I stood in the middle of the room, all eyes on me.

"You all may have noticed that I'm... not quite myself," I began. "Just before this game, I found out that my grandma's in the hospital. She probably won't be coming out." Tears welled up in my eyes and rolled down my cheeks. I recalled a conversation I'd had with my grandmother over the phone a few weeks ago. "She told me she couldn't wait to hear that we'd won the banner." I was crying quite heavily now. The reality of the situation hadn't hit me until that moment.

Every single girl hugged me. Lots of them were in tears as well, some because of their own experiences with cancer, some simply from compassion.

"We're going to win this for your grandma," the team captain said, and all the girls nodded in agreement. I was bawling. Their caring touched me more than anything else had.

When we started the game, I saw girls who were killing themselves trying to get the puck, and perfectly controlled shots hitting the back of the net. I saw girls who normally worked hard working even harder. I saw the numbers on the scoreboard for us go up. Even I felt the difference—when I felt too tired, or didn't think I had the energy, I thought of my grandma and how every breath was a struggle for her. I found extra strength.

The buzzer sounded at the end of the third period and I basically tackled my goalie. Tears were streaming down my face. "We won for her," I cried. "We won for her." My teammates cheered with me.

"Your grandma is the most proud grandmother in the world," one of my teary-eyed teammates said as she hugged me. I was the first girl to bring home the banner and I sent a picture of it to my grandmother.

My grandma died the day after we won the banner. From what I hear, it was only seconds after she received my picture that God took her away. My mom was with her and told her the story of what I'd done with my hockey team. She said she was proud of me.

After that day, I believe that love and friendship can help you accomplish anything. My teammates' compassion and love for my grandma and me was the most amazing thing I've ever experienced. That day, God sent me angels in the form of fourteen Bantam hockey players.

~Rachael Robitaille

Heart to Heart

A single rose can be my garden... a single friend, my world.
~Leo Buscaglia

We're arm in arm when we're strolling down the sidewalk
Laughter fills the phone line every time that we talk
Smiles and tears alike we share
Sunshine seems to follow us everywhere
When we're together, hearts seem so light
But when they are broken
You make it all right

I've never had a friend like you
So easy to get so close to
Distance cannot separate us
We love and understand each other too much
To let time or change break us apart
We're not just hand in hand
We're heart to heart.

Now time has come between us
Change and troubles too
But you have not forgotten me
And I will never forget you
It's true some friends do come and go

They are the people you think you know
It's true some friends break you apart
And hand you the pieces of your own broken heart.

There are some things that are made to last
Some things are forever, while others will pass
But I am sure as the sky is blue
That one thing I will have forever
Is you.

~Rae Starr

95

The Beholder's Eye

Strangers are just friends waiting to happen.
~Rod McKuen

I was about to enter seventh grade, and I had no social life. Well, that's not entirely true. I had a social life, but it was choking to death.

Did I have friends? Well... yes. In one sense of the word. The girls I hung with throughout sixth grade were of a few categories: old friends from elementary school I was drifting away from, friends who were more like parasites, clingy and annoying, and friends of friends of friends—how we even ended up on the same cafeteria bench, I couldn't tell you.

So there I would sit every lunch hour, halfheartedly gnawing my carrots and casting forlorn glances in the direction of other tables. Those girls looked like they were all having a good time. They couldn't stop laughing. I could. They grinned at each other as often as they made eye contact. All my smiles lately had been consciously summoned. I was not where I wanted to be. Friendships are supposed to bring joy, right? So here I was, a lonely piece of driftwood lost in the swirling rapids of junior high, and I wasn't expecting the seventh grade to be any different from the sixth. Little did I know.

On the first day of school, I spotted a couple of new girls, obviously identical twins. This in itself interested me, as I am an identical triplet. I observed them from a safe distance. To begin with, they were short. Extremely so. The entire seventh grade dwarfed them, and their height was sizing up to be their best feature. They both had stark white skin, thin faces, hair that was neither curly nor straight (except the bangs, which went absolutely haywire with curls), and a decided scrawniness. Bulky watches on their left wrists only emphasized this last attribute. Hmm, I thought offhandedly, they won't be getting any friendship offers soon. Except mine, I told myself, resignedly.

After third hour, I spotted one of them in the hall and fell into stride with her.

"Hi," I began awkwardly, glancing at her sideways. "What's your name?" She responded in a voice so quiet I had to lean in to hear it.

"Taylauw." Taylor. Great. At least one of them could not pronounce her R's and spoke in barely audible tones.

"Well, hi, I'm Alex... you're a twin, right?"

"Yeah."

"Uh-huh, I saw you guys together earlier today, and I thought it was kind of cool since I'm actually a triplet." I paused. Taylor gave a hint of a smile. I was struggling to keep the conversation afloat. "So, what's your sister's name?" I asked brightly.

"Lauwwee."

"What?"

"Lauuwey."

"WHAT?"

"LAAUW-EE!" No matter how I twisted the syllables as I replayed them in my head, I could not form a recognizable name through the distorted R. I would have to work it out later. Meanwhile, now was looking like a great time to end the conversation.

"Well, I'll have to meet... her... later, guess I gotta get to class, see ya!" I faltered clumsily, and, with a little wave, strode away down the hall.

"See you," said Taylor softly. She looked a little happier.

I would have been happy ending the acquaintance right there—nothing more than the occasional smile in class, the few exchanged words in the hall. But this was yet another case in which I was reminded that events rarely play out according to my plans.

Not long after our first encounter, Taylor and Laurie (I'd finally thought to look her up in the school directory) plopped down next to me and my group at lunch.

"Mind if we sit here?"

"No, not at all!" I made a few introductions, after which the entire table promptly resumed ignoring the newcomers, leaving my sisters and me to initiate any and all conversation with them.

And so it began. Lunch hour after lunch hour, we filled awkward silence with icebreaker questions: Where'd you move from? What's it like there? How do you like it here? What're your hobbies? Any siblings? We told family stories. School stories. Church stories. Any stories.

We discovered we were born sixteen days apart, had younger siblings approximately the same age, and shared the many joys and woes of being multiples. We all loved music—I learned that Taylor was amazing on a drum set, and Laurie had a beautiful voice. We were each from very conservative families that were uncommon in our society, so we had connections on another level that others could not be part of, such as being the only kids in class who didn't shop at Abercrombie or Hollister or American Eagle.

We whittled away time with small talk, dumb jokes, and a handy little device we dubbed the Awkward Turtle. And all the while we were slowly, inevitably growing closer and closer. Avoiding silence stopped requiring effort. I was having the best conversations I'd had since fourth grade! When I talked to Laurie or Taylor, I didn't talk like a character outside of myself, editing my initial thought before making a well-planned comment. I simply said what came to mind. And they simply accepted it. I came to the realization that my longing for true friends was being satisfied.

Seventh grade finished. Eighth rolled in. Our friendship had long since extended beyond lunchroom chats. We visited outside of school. Hung out in jazz band. Talked during classes and in between. We even ran track together, which meant at least an hour or so together after school. We saw each other all the time, yet never saw enough of each other.

As eighth grade drew to a close, I thought back to when we'd first met. The twins' mispronounced R's had been difficult to comprehend and their voices so faint I was constantly leaning over, asking, "WHAT?" Now, they spoke confidently, and their awkward R's were barely noticeable. I didn't notice their lack of height so much these days—were they a bit taller than before? And surely less scrawny. Their wild bangs seemed tamer, but I still grinned whenever Taylor smashed her cymbals together with such force that her hair flew out of her face. And I had to laugh every time Laurie checked that trademark watch, permanently attached to her wrist, to pronounce the also-trademark line that went with it: "We now have twenty seconds to get to class!" At the cross-country camp we'd attended together, my sister and I had actually convinced the two of them to sit in the sun with us for an hour to tan: an activity, Laurie said, which had been a foreign concept to them prior to their move, which explained the pale complexion. It had been uncomfortable to talk to them at first. Now... they were my best friends.

Yes, I thought, they've certainly changed. But then I considered the old saying, "Beauty is in the eye of the beholder." Now that they were my best friends, they were definitely more beautiful to me. So maybe it wasn't Taylor and Laurie who had changed. Maybe I was the one who was different.

~Alexandra Berends

96

Chicken Soup for the Soul

Mountaintop Mindset

Nobody can go back and start a new beginning,
but anyone can start today and make a new ending.
~Maria Robinson

Change, to me, has always been like a cold swimming pool. At first it seems chilling, but once you get used to it, it's not nearly as bad as you thought it would be. Sometimes it's surprisingly refreshing.

As a seventh grader in Indiana, I thought I had life figured out. I was a cheerleader and a straight-A student, yet I struggled to find my place in the middle school social scene. I did my best to dress the right way, act the right way, and hang out with the right kind of people.

For a while it worked. I was comfortable, and life seemed satisfying. I didn't feel the need to attend church every Sunday, and participating in youth choir seemed pointless. I only had one real friend at church. Her name was Sara, and she was my sole motivation for trudging through those dreaded double doors for Wednesday evening choir practice.

Every week of the school year, choir was the same: suffer through song after song, repeat the choreography halfheartedly, and escape as soon as possible. The other people in choir were nothing like me. There was a quiet girl who only wore black, an obnoxious boy who wore girls' pants, a few sixth graders who seemed too terrified to talk, and a small group of kids in my grade whom I thought I knew too well to befriend suddenly after all this time. Not exactly the ideal crowd.

Halfway through the year, I begged my mom to let me quit choir. After some consideration, she said if I finished out the school year, she would let me decide whether or not I wanted to continue with the program. At my second to last choir practice, our music director made a special announcement. She told us about the unprecedented opportunity we would have as middle school students to take part in the high school choir's West Virginia trip that summer.

The idea was somewhat intriguing. I had never been to West Virginia, yet I didn't have much of a desire to go until Sara told me she was going. She assured me there would be lots of free time, and we would even get to do some hiking in the mountains, so I agreed to go. There was something inside me, I wasn't sure what, that made me want to go for reasons even I didn't understand.

When I left for West Virginia on that humid June morning, I was uncomfortable. The long van ride was hot and sticky. I didn't know anyone in my assigned van. I hardly knew anyone at church, let alone in choir, so I closed my eyes and tried to sleep. At one point, I remember crying and thinking, "This was a huge mistake."

That night we arrived at our host church. After everything was unpacked and arranged, we began playing games as a large group. There were about twenty-five of us in grades six through twelve, but everyone was so friendly that the age gap didn't matter. I noticed how the high school students were close friends. They were always hugging each other and laughing. For the first time, I wanted to be a part of the community they shared, so I began reaching out to the middle school students in my choir I had long overlooked.

I found out that the quiet girl's name was Suzie and she was an excellent hairstylist. She even helped me curl my hair before our performance. When I talked to the obnoxious boy, I found out that his name was Alex. He had an incredible sense of humor. Even the sixth graders turned out to be wonderful people.

As for the other kids in my grade, they have since become some of my closest friends. Although I originally thought I knew who they were, after I took time to talk to them, I was surprised to see how much we had in common, and, more importantly, how much we could learn from each other.

At the end of the first evening, our choir director instructed us to form a prayer circle.

"When we pray, we hold hands interlocking our fingers," she said. "This represents that we are filling each other's weaknesses with our strengths."

We all had differences, but when we prayed, we were united, and our differences made us stronger. It was a strength I had never known.

As the trip progressed, our choir grew even closer. On our last day in West Virginia, we embarked on that promised hiking trip in the mountains. We drove to a site called Bald Knob, and spent most of our morning struggling along the wooded path to reach the clearing at the mountain's peak.

The view from the top of Bald Knob was breathtaking. Blue hills rose like waves across the horizon, bending in perfect harmony with the green trees rooted on their backs. Rivers wove through valleys, winding into reservoirs, and tiny houses squatted on sparse patches of flatland in between. It was like looking through God's eyes and seeing everything as it truly was—small in comparison to Him and His incredible love.

On the ground level, I could only see what was right before my eyes—a limited portion of all that existed. However, hoisted above the trees and towns, I got a clear vision of the whole picture. I finally saw my peers for who they were rather than what I had labeled them.

I thought of all the people around me, people I hadn't known this time last week and perhaps would never have known had I not come on this trip. I loved them now even though they were different from me. Their differences made them wonderful.

When I came home, I began to see the people around me from a new perspective. I decided to stay in youth choir until the end of my senior year of high school, and I became a leader in my youth group. Before I left for college, my youth pastor told me I should consider a calling in the ministry.

At some point, we all need "mountaintop" experiences. For me, it just happened to take place on an actual mountain. However, what matters most is not the experience itself, but rather maintaining that mountaintop mindset throughout the peaks and valleys of everyday life.

~Kara Marie Hackett

97

Chicken Soup for the Soul

What Are Friends For?

A true friend is one who thinks you are a good egg
even if you are half-cracked.
~Author Unknown

eing Ted's best friend is not something I would have wished for! Somehow, I ended up being best friend to the meanest bully in sixth grade. Not only that, I found myself standing up for him when he was accused of doing something I knew he didn't do.

Surviving sixth grade was a matter of keeping your head low and pretending that you didn't exist. But you couldn't be invisible all the time, like when the teacher called on you in class, or when you somehow ended up alone in the hallway with one other person: the biggest bully in sixth grade.

Ted was a loner, but that was because other kids just naturally got out of his way. Everybody dispersed when they saw Ted shamble out of his math class. I had my head stuck inside my locker and didn't hear the sudden scuffling of sneakers that signaled a mass migration away from Ted. By the time I looked up, he was standing right over me.

Ted's eyes were blue, and when he glared at me, I felt like I was about to be tossed overboard into a stormy sea that was going to pound me. He grabbed the scruff of my shirt and hauled me to my feet.

"You're in my way, flyweight."

I looked up and down the hallway. It was deserted. I looked back at Ted and swallowed something hard. "S-sorry. I didn't hear you coming."

"Well, here I am," he said, shaking me. "What're you gonna do about it?"

"F-faint dead away?" I stuttered.

Then Ted did something I'd never seen him do before. He laughed. His face twisted into an expression that didn't look normal for him and he let out a loud, long laugh. He set me back down on the floor.

"Man, you beat everything, flyweight. Faint dead away?" He laughed again and swaggered down the hallway into his next class.

The next day I decided I wasn't going to take any chances. At lunchtime I ate under my table. In class I hid behind a tower of books. When it was time to go home I beat everyone else out the door. I felt like I was home free.

Then I ran smack into Ted. I'd taken a shortcut through the edge of the woods to get to my house and didn't see him squatting down in the tall grass. He reached out and grabbed hold of my arm. I thought he was going to twist it and make me beg for mercy, but instead he pointed to a spot in the grass. I looked and saw a baby deer with its tiny legs curled around it.

"Don't move, flyweight," Ted whispered. "You'll scare it off." He watched the deer. "I figure its mom is somewhere close by."

I saw the fawn flick its ears. I looked at Ted, and the expression on his face was different. He wasn't mad, and he wasn't angry. He had a soft expression in his eyes. That softness turned to stone when he saw me watching him.

"You say anything to anyone and I'll pound you into hamburger," he snarled.

I should have just nodded, but something made me say what I never should have said. "It's cool, Ted. I like to watch deer and raccoons and stuff, too."

He looked at me, and the stoniness left his eyes. He pointed at the fawn. "This one's a girl. She was born in the early spring. Her mom moves her a lot."

"What does a fawn eat?" I asked.

Ted's whole face brightened up. I sat and listened while he told me all about baby deer, and what the birds around us were called, and lots of other stuff. I sat with my mouth open while he talked and grew excited about a dozen things. Finally he stopped talking and looked at me.

"You're a good listener, flyweight." Then he crawled away from me through the grass, being careful not to scare the deer.

Over the next few weeks we ran into each other once in a while. Ted was still a bully, but whenever there was no one else around, he'd tell me about some animal or bird he'd seen out in the woods. It was strange being friends with him. I didn't know I was going to have to make one of the hardest decisions of my life because of that friendship.

Monday morning I was on my way to school when I heard a noise come from the back of the feed and grain store. The next moment I saw Ted rush out with a sack of feed. He saw me but kept running, and I stood there wondering what I should do. Since I was late, I continued on my way to school, hoping I could figure things out.

Later that day I was out in the field running laps past the bleachers. Ted was hanging out in a corner of the school building when all of a sudden the principal and a couple of policemen came out and walked over to where Ted was standing. I ran up to the gathering crowd to see what was up.

"Come on, Ted," the principal was saying. "You know you stole those trophies from the gym this morning. Someone said they saw you in there around eight o'clock."

Ted scowled at both him and the cops. "I didn't do nothing."

One policeman reached out to take hold of Ted when I remembered what happened that morning. I stepped up to the principal and said, "I saw Ted taking a sack of grain from the feed store around eight this morning. He couldn't have taken the trophies."

One of the policemen turned to Ted. "Is that true?"

Ted never lost his scowl, but he finally said, "Yeah, I took it. I needed the grain for a fawn that lost its mother to a hunter. I'm trying to raise it. I didn't have enough money, but I left what I had in the grain room."

The police talked a while and finally let Ted go. The principal shook his head and told Ted to talk to the feed store owner after school. Later we learned that it was a student who was sore about being cut from the football team who took the trophies. After the police left, Ted let out a long sigh.

"You ratted me out, flyweight," he said, his eyes unreadable.

I nodded. "I'm sorry. I didn't want you go to jail for something you didn't do."

He scratched his head. "No one's ever done that for me before."

"You're my friend," I told him.

Ted didn't say anything for a long time. When he finally did speak again, he said, "I have to fix things with the feed store owner, but after that, flyweight, you want to give me a hand trying to take care of a wild fawn?"

I smiled. "What are friends for?"

~John P. Buentello

98

Chicken Soup
for the Soul

Invisible Girl Finds Her Spotlight

A friend is someone who understands your past, believes in your future,
and accepts you just the way you are.
~Author Unknown

I never felt like I fit in at school, in my family, or in life in general. As the middle child, I felt like I was invisible. Not the oldest or the precious baby, but a fifth wheel in an otherwise perfect family of four. I grew up in the shadow of a perfectionist who set swimming records, designed the school mascot for our middle school and got straight A's. I was always known as her little sister. Being much taller, with a stockier build and mousy brown hair, I lacked the long blond hair and body she had that the boys liked. A good way to describe me was a fly on the wall—an observer rather than a participant, except when I was being picked on or bullied.

I met Mike when I was in fifth grade and we became best friends. His mother was deaf and his father was an alcoholic who could be very mean. Mike was also a middle child with older and younger sisters; he had his own tough stuff to deal with. Finding a best friend who understood me and with whom I could identify was pretty cool. He saw my strengths and I saw his—the things we couldn't see in ourselves.

"You're a great friend Mike," I would say to him. "You really hold your family together. I'm not sure I could live with your dad."

"Well, your dad is no peach either. He always makes you be quiet," he responded.

"I hate families. My sister always calls me fat and tells me my feet are as big as battleships."

"Well as tall as you are, you'd look pretty dumb with tiny feet," Mike said. "You're a good swimmer, artist, and great in drama, so stop trying to be your sister—just be yourself."

Unfortunately, I couldn't seem to figure out who that was. I felt like an alien and a freak with other people. My sister and her friends would tease me. My mom even bribed me to lose weight and said she'd buy me new clothes if I did. I couldn't understand what everyone thought was so wrong with me.

Mike and I used to walk to the airport to hang out and sit in silence with the red and green lights flashing around us. I loved those lights and could watch them for hours—nobody else understood that, except Mike. It always made me feel better. Why couldn't I live at the airport?

At lunch I sat with a few other nerds, since Mike had a different lunch period than I had. One day, I decided to try out for the school play, so I sat immersed in my lines for the audition. Drama, I realized, was so much fun for me. Since I was given lines to memorize, talking to others wasn't such a puzzle.

I ran up to Mike as soon as I got the news.

"Mike, I got a leading part—an old lady who is a killer."

"Cool, I knew you'd get it!"

"And some of her victims are those jerks from student council."

"Sweet."

I smiled and said, "I think I'll enjoy this play."

I managed to survive school, one year at a time and one play after another. It wasn't until I grew up and had children of my own that I understood that I was not the only one who felt like an alien or fly on the wall. I discovered there was a name for what I experienced growing up—Asperger syndrome, a form of autism. When my own son was diagnosed with Asperger syndrome I found that it takes continuous positive reinforcement to help young children with Asperger's—exactly what I had missed growing up. I needed to be praised when I showed good manners or positive communication in order to be more comfortable being out in public. I still fight feelings of wanting to be alone, of avoiding social interactions, but Asperger syndrome will not defeat me; it is just a part of what makes me a unique individual.

What I've learned from all this is that if you ever see anyone dealing with tough stuff at school, try reaching out to them. You just might make a new friend, or find someone else who feels just as alien as you.

~Jan Beaver

99

Chicken Soup for the Soul

Through Renee's Eyes

Today, give a stranger one of your smiles.
It might be the only sunshine he sees all day.
~Quoted in P.S. I Love You,
compiled by H. Jackson Brown, Jr.

At my Catholic school, which went from first through eighth grade, boys and girls sat together until the seventh grade. Then, just when they were starting to notice each other, they were separated: boys at one table, girls at another. Instead of eliminating any budding attractions, the separate tables seemed to heighten awareness of the opposite sex. No, there wasn't any handholding or stolen kisses... instead, there were food fights and an excess of goofy pranks, mostly started by the boys to get the girls' attention.

Unfortunately, the attention they got was frequently from the principal, and it was always negative. The short nun we referred to as "Mother" shouted at the upperclassmen daily. "Keep it down!" "Stop wasting food!" she'd yell. If that didn't calm the wild beasts, the entire class would have to stay in the cafeteria until the lunch period ended.

That summer before seventh grade, my friend Cathy and I imagined how cool it would be to sit at an upper class table. We'd romanticized every thrown banana or cookie to be an offering equivalent to a rose bouquet. We even picked the boys we'd like to have teasing us:

Gary and Rich, two members of the Cabana Club Swim Team. They were super tan and super cute!

On the first day of school, Cathy and I raced to the cafeteria. We wanted seats closest to the boys' table. Just as we entered the cafeteria doors, Mother called us to her. Exchanging alarmed glances, we thought we must be in trouble. The only question was: for what?

A rare smile formed on her lips, shocking us even more. She motioned to a corner where no one would hear our conversation. "You girls are such nice friends. I picked you to sit with the new girl, Renee. Make her feel welcome."

"Renee? Sure, we'll save her a seat," I agreed more anxious than ever to get to the good table.

Mother shook her head indicating that we didn't understand something. That negative nod allowed a flood of dread to enter my thoughts. Renee was on crutches and her legs were encased in metal braces. It struck me that she'd have a hard time making it to the far side of the cafeteria where our beloved table beckoned us.

"No, you girls will join Renee at this end of the third grade table since it's closest to the door. She can't walk any farther."

Cathy and I exchanged pained glances. This was a disaster!

We were afraid to say no and more afraid to ask how long we had to do this. Our silence pleased Mother and she urged us to be friendly and get Renee whatever she needed from the snack bar.

No longer hurrying, we meandered to the third grade table and introduced ourselves to Renee. Her blue eyes lit up as we sat on either side of her. This only made me feel bad about still longing to sit at the cool table.

It was funny the way she opened up to us. In class, she hadn't said a word, but here she had a list of questions about our school, our teacher, and especially about us. I was surprised by how quickly that lunch period passed.

We walked her back to our classroom, keeping pace with her instead of skipping or trotting as we liked to do. When she went into the room, Cathy and I dashed to the bathroom. Paula and Barbara were laughing as they faced the mirror, combing their hair. Barbara seemed to be bragging about something Rich told her. When they noticed us, Barbara made a mean comment about our new babysitting service.

We continued sitting at the third grade table with Renee and noticed her transformation. She giggled and laughed as much as we did and even seemed more outgoing in class. She had worn her dark blond hair pulled away from the front and clipped with a big plastic barrette. What seemed wrong was the pastel-colored plastic barrette. It looked like something a little girl might wear. In contrast, Cathy wore a plaid or checkered headband to hold back her thick black hair and I wore a satin ribbon to separate my bangs from the rest of my light brown hair. Though we'd never mentioned the difference between our hair accessories and hers, Renee suddenly lost the barrettes and sported satin ribbons like mine. We complimented her profusely on her new look.

Daily drama continued to erupt from the upper level tables, but our reactions had changed. Cathy and I were no longer yearning to have grapes thrown at our heads. Instead we found ourselves fascinated by Renee's extensive travels and broad interests. We began to realize that she was opening doors to us that we would never have known existed had we become a part of the lunchtime shenanigans.

My eyes were also opened to the social plight of handicapped people. When Renee shared that she often felt invisible or ignored, I was ashamed because I would never have thought to forfeit my upperclassman seating status if Mother hadn't made it an edict.

Right before Christmas vacation, Renee gave each of us an embroidered silk coin purse. They looked like they were from San Francisco's Chinatown and we loved them. We were embarrassed for not bringing her a gift but she insisted our friendship was the best gift of all.

I admit that Cathy and I had at first hoped to be relieved of our daily duty by other classmates taking turns at the third grade table. By December, however, we were more than content with our seating arrangement. Talking with Renee made us feel grown up and in touch with a world outside our neighborhood.

Rich and Gary noticed us too, probably more than if we'd been sitting across from them every day. At any rate, they never teased us the way they teased the other girls. They acknowledged us with a newfound respect that I think we earned by seeing things through Renee's eyes.

~Marsha Porter

100

Chicken Soup for the Soul

The Empty Chair

Fear makes strangers of people who would be friends.
~Shirley MacLaine

"**L**ook what my mom bought me for the first day of school!"
I watched my new best friend, Stacy, emerge from her closet like a super model, and twirl around in her black and yellow striped pants.

"Cute. When can I borrow them?"

Stacy and I liked the same clothes, purses, hairstyles—everything. That's why we became best friends over the summer break.

Stacy stopped twirling and flopped down on the bedroom floor next to me.

"I have to warn you about the first day of school," she said. "Paige will be looking for you."

"I know," I sighed. Paige was my best friend last year.

"When she finds out that you're my best friend now, she's going to freak."

Sometimes having a best friend is a pain, I thought. I knew I should just give it up and hang out with a larger group of girls, but the others were so silly and immature. Stacy and I called them "The Strange Girls"—or "Strangies." We, of course, were different. We acted our age.

When the first day of school arrived, Paige ran up to me with a big smile.

"Hi! I love your zipper top. It's almost like mine. Look!" She spun around.

"Uh... yeah." I smiled briefly and glanced at Stacy who stood a few feet away with a frown on her face. This was going to be hard.

As we entered our classroom, Mrs. Hall told us we could push the desks together to form groups of two, three or four.

One of the "Strangies" stood up and called out to me.

"Hey Sharon! Come sit over here with us."

Pretending I didn't hear, I headed toward Stacy, who was pushing two desks together near the back corner of the room. We neatly stacked our books and placed our backpacks side by side on the top.

Over the next few days, Paige continued to be friendly. She smiled at me in the middle of a spelling test and waved at me during P.E. Deep inside, I felt myself wishing we were good friends again, while Stacy rolled her eyes and made fun of her.

A couple of weeks later, Page invited me over to her house for an overnight. We crunched on popcorn, watched funny movies and talked about boys. Before the weekend was over, Paige and I were best friends again.

At school on Monday, I wondered how I would break the news to Stacy. When Mrs. Hall switched off the lights and put on a film about the Revolutionary War, it gave me a chance to slide Stacy a note explaining what had happened. She was pretty upset. When the film ended she pulled her books out of the desk, made her thoughts crystal clear and marched across the room to find another place to sit.

"Hey, Stacy. Come sit with us."

The "Strangies" pushed four desks together and gestured for Stacy to join them. Stacy desperately looked around for another option. With nothing else available, she reluctantly plodded over and dropped her books on the fourth desk.

Days turned into weeks, and my renewed friendship with Paige grew strong. November was just around the corner, and I caught the flu and had to stay home for several days. One evening, as I lay on the couch with a bad headache, the phone rang.

"Hi Sharon. This is Stacy."

"Oh, hi." My head pounded. Why in the world would Stacy be calling me? Wasn't she still mad at me? It turned out she had called to see how I was feeling. Her cheerful banter soothed my spirit. She made me laugh when she mimicked one of the "Strangies," and I was so happy when she told me I was much more fun to be with.

Toward the end of our conversation Stacy commented, "You've got to get away from Paige. She's sooo juvenile."

As I fell asleep that night, confusing thoughts tangled in my head. I wondered if I should take up with Stacy again. Paige had been getting on my nerves—always flirting with the boys at lunchtime. Should I end the friendship?

By the time I returned to school the next week, I had made my decision. I approached Paige before the first bell rang and told her our friendship wasn't working out.

"You've got to be kidding. You want to go back to her?" she said, slapping the desk with her Phonics book. "It will be the biggest mistake of your life."

Later, when Paige was sitting alone, one of the "Strangies" called quietly to her. "You can come over here with us if you like." Another "Strangie" helped Paige carry her books. She slipped into the fourth desk.

Over the next few months my feelings about both girls moved up and down like a roller coaster. When I was with Stacy, I wanted to be with Paige. When I was with Paige, I missed Stacy. Little did I know the roller coaster was heading for disaster.

On a morning I'll never forget, I walked into our classroom and got the biggest shock of my sixth grade year. Stacy and Paige were sitting together. Their books and backpacks were side by side, and my stuff had been moved to the back counter. They whispered and glanced in my direction. I wanted to disappear.

Trying to hide my tears, I gathered my books and searched for a desk... one that would be away from everyone. Deep down, I knew I deserved this treatment. After learning about the Revolutionary War, I couldn't help but feel like Benedict Arnold, the traitor, standing in the middle of the room—all alone—in my stiff red coat.

I spotted a small desk on the side of the room and began to move my things. One of the "Strangies" softly stepped to my side and whispered, "Would you like to sit with us? We have an extra desk."

I hesitated.

Another "Strangie" came over. "It's okay. We've got room."

I slowly walked over and sat down. They didn't embarrass me or ask questions. They just smiled and opened their science books. Their kindness felt like a warm blanket tucked around my heart. It wasn't long before one of them giggled. Another girl made a funny face when her pencil dropped to the floor. The girls laughed. I smiled. Maybe it wasn't so bad being "strange."

From that day forward I made some changes. I no longer judged the other girls in my class. Instead of being exclusive, I was friendly to everyone—even to Stacy and Paige.

Today I am blessed with many good friends. And although time has passed since my sixth grade year, I still benefit from that painful experience. I've learned to treasure all the friends that God has given me, and appreciate their differences. To this day, I still get together with those wonderful "Strange Girls." We meet at a restaurant for dinner on each of our birthdays. And on those special evenings, as I head toward the table, I'm grateful that a fourth chair is always available.

~Sharon Pearson

The Future Is Now

How wonderful it is that nobody need wait a single moment
before starting to improve the world.
~Anne Frank

I was a floater in junior high. I had no real clique or group, but I was friends with just about everyone. I was in band and choir, did theatre and played sports. I was happy just as often as I was sad; in short, I was your average American preteen.

Out of all of my hobbies, my favorite thing to do was make people laugh. I was very quick-witted and always had a quick reply for anything. While in junior high, I heard or read somewhere a phrase that I found quite amusing: "Don't worry about the future, it's already tomorrow in Australia." The cleverness of this phrase attracted me, and I quickly added it to my repertoire of favorite sayings and quotes. Naturally, this phrase made its appearance in my daily life at school, as I wanted to share it with all of my friends, so that they too could enjoy it with me.

Gradually, however, new phrases came and took the place of this particular one in my daily life. It survived only as a vague memory that popped up occasionally when I thought of the future.

The summer before eighth grade, I was spending the night at my friend Veronica's house. Veronica was one of my best and closest friends, though I had only known her a year. We ate pizza, watched a movie, and generally just hung out in her room. We stayed up late listening to music and talking. We even gave each other temporary tattoos by drawing on each other with permanent markers.

As the night went on, our conversations became more serious. We opened up to each other like only close friends will do. Veronica got out a journal that she occasionally wrote in, and offered to read some of it out loud to me. I felt honored that she trusted me. Veronica shared some of her deepest secrets, hurts, and dreams with me. I began to understand her more. I was surprised when she came to a new passage and laughed lightheartedly, as much of the journal was serious. She looked up from her reading and looked me in the eyes. "You're in this entry," she said with a playful glint in her deep brown eyes. I wasn't sure what to think. It could either be really good or really bad. Noticing my apprehension, she resumed her reading.

Her story recounted a regular afternoon in choir. Before the bell rang and class started, she and I were talking. She had been frustrated with homework, teachers, and the drama in her life. She had come to me for advice about what to do. I had given her some to the best of my ability, and as the bell rang, I said, to lighten her mood a bit, "Besides, you don't need to worry about the future, it's already tomorrow in Australia." She laughed and hugged me, like I had hoped, and we went to our seats.

I was smiling while I heard my dear friend read, but I still didn't understand why she had recorded this particular day in her journal. It didn't seem to me to be anything out of the ordinary or even worth writing down. She read on to explain. That day, in passing and without much thought, I had changed her world. That simple phrase about the future struck a chord with her. She told me that at that moment, I had given her one of her life mottos. "It changed me," Veronica said. From that day forward, she made it a priority to worry less about the little things that came up in her life; she became a more positive, optimistic person.

Junior high ended and Veronica and I went to different high schools. We drifted apart slowly and eventually it got to the point where we hardly ever spoke to each other. She made new friends, and so did I. I bumped into her at the mall one day, three or four years later. We talked excitedly for several minutes about what was new in our lives, where we were hoping to go to college, and everything else we could think of at the moment.

As we were about to part and go about our shopping, she once again looked me in the eyes and told me that I had changed her life. My friendship and advice had made her into the young woman who stood before me now. Even though I was very young, I had made a difference. "The power of words is amazing," she said, "and age doesn't mean anything. It does not matter how old or young a person is, he or she could very well change the world as we know it." I smiled when I thought about how young I still was, and how many more words I had left to say.

~Sarah Sawicki

Just for

Preteens

Meet Our Contributors
Meet Our Authors
Thank You
About Chicken Soup

Meet Our Contributors

Brianna Abbott is a normal teenager who likes to laugh and run in the rain. She loves her family and her friends with all her heart and plans to continue writing for the rest of her life.

Toby Abraham-Rhine is a performing artist, high school counselor, wife and mother of three. She has traveled the world on a shoestring budget with her husband and children. That adventure is chronicled in their book, *A Brilliant Teacher*.

Julia K. Agresto is a Communications and Marketing Specialist for a renowned medical center in Massachusetts, as well as a freelance writer/journalist. She graduated from the University of New Hampshire in 2009 with a degree in English/Journalism and Sociology.

Mallory Albeck is a senior at the University of Florida. She plans to pursue teaching after graduation. Mallory has been a member of the University of Florida marching band, and loves music, traveling, and working with preteens and teens. E-mail her at mallory.albeck@gmail.com.

Julia Alexander attended enough college to get her BFA but alas, an unfortunate Algebra requirement kept her from acquiring her

Bachelor's. She is a wife and mother and "closet" writer. Literally. Her office is in her closet. She writes young adult fiction. E-mail her at julia5764@gmail.com.

Cynthia Baker has a B.S. in Education from Millersville University in Pennsylvania. She sells real estate in San Diego, CA. Her interests include literature, psychology, and philosophy. She is currently working on short stories and a collection of poetry. E-mail her at cynthia.baker22@sbcglobal.net.

Jennifer Baljko specializes in business, technology, and travel writing. She is an avid traveler, and is currently based in Barcelona. To find out more about what Jennifer is working on, visit www.jenniferbaljko.com, or e-mail her at jenn@jenniferbaljko.com.

Garrett Bauman has published several pieces in *Chicken Soup for the Soul* books as well as in *Yankee*, *Sierra*, *The New York Times* and many other publications. A retired professor of English from Monroe Community College, he is the author of a popular college writing textbook. He and his wife, Carol, live one mile from the nearest road in rural New York State.

Jan Beaver received her B.S. and M.S. degrees from the University of Central Arkansas. She has autism/Asperger syndrome and is author of *Why Don't They Come With Instructions?*—a book about raising special needs children. She lives with her husband, children and dog aboard a boat in Washington. Learn more at www.jbeaverbooks.com.

Lisa Bell received her B.S. in Business Management, with honors, from the University of Phoenix in 2005. She is a freelance writer and lives in Texas. Lisa enjoys anything outdoors, volunteers with local organizations and writes both fiction and nonfiction. Learn more at www.bylisabell.com or e-mail her at LisaBell@bylisabell.com.

Valerie D. Benko is a freelance writer from western Pennsylvania. Her stories have appeared in four *Chicken Soup for the Soul* anthologies as well as *Patchwork Path* editions including *Christmas Stocking*, *Treasure Box* and the soon to be released *Mother's Life*. Learn more at valeriebenko.weebly.com.

Alexandra Berends is a high school student. She enjoys her writing classes and plans to further her writing experience in college.

Lil Blosfield is the Chief Financial Officer for Child & Adolescent Behavioral Health in Canton, OH. She has been writing poems and stories pretty much since she learned to write many, many years ago. She loves being with her family and friends, and always makes time for a good laugh! E-mail her at LBlosfield40@msn.com.

Caitlin Brown, a sixteen-year-old homeschooled student, enjoys reading, playing paintball, baking, producing movies featuring her three younger siblings and writing children's stories and novels. She works yearlong with www.OperationChristmasChild.org filling shoeboxes with gifts for needy children overseas. E-mail Caitlin at shoeboxgirl@comcast.net.

Leigh Ann Bryant is a wife and mother of three sons. She received her BSN from the University of Texas at Arlington. She loves the Lord and is very active with the youth at her church. She loves to write, travel, and watch her sons do gymnastics. E-mail her at bryant_leighann@msn.com.

John P. Buentello has published fiction, nonfiction, and poetry for both adults and children. He is currently at work on a short story collection. E-mail him at jakkhakk@yahoo.com.

Sandy Bull's dream of being a writer was put on hold for many years. In 2006, she relocated to central Florida and earned a diploma in Freelance Writing. She loves to swim and enjoys the beaches of Florida, which give her the inspiration to write. E-mail her at sandybull2006@yahoo.com.

Barbara Canale is a freelance writer and columnist for *The Catholic Sun* in Syracuse, NY. She has been published in several *Chicken Soup for the Soul* books. She is the author of *Our Labor of Love; A Romanian Adoption Chronicle.* She enjoys biking, skiing and gardening.

Beth Cato's true life stories have been featured in *The Ultimate Cat Lover* and four previous *Chicken Soup for the Soul* titles. She's also an associate member of the Science Fiction & Fantasy Writers of America. Learn more at www.bethcato.com.

Jennifer Lynn Clay, 21, has been published over eighty times in national and international magazines and in several worldwide-distributed books including *House Blessings* and *Forever in Love*. Her work has appeared in five other *Chicken Soup for the Soul* books. She has written several young adult novels, two of which are under consideration by publishers.

Courtney Conover is a freelance writer and yoga practitioner who resides in Michigan with her husband, Scott. The couple eagerly awaits the birth of their first child this fall. This is Courtney's fourth contribution to the *Chicken Soup for the Soul* series. Learn more at www.courtneyconover.com.

Harriet Cooper is a freelance humorist, essayist and instructor living in Toronto, Canada. Her humor, essays, articles, short stories and poetry have appeared in newspapers, magazines, websites, newsletters, anthologies and radio. She specializes in writing about family, relationships, cats, psychology, and health. E-mail her at shewrites@live.ca.

Mandilyn T. Criline holds a B.A. in professional writing. She enjoys reading, art, music, and being outdoors. E-mail her at writingtobreathe88@gmail.com.

James Crowley is a singer and an author of children's literature. To date, he has written three novels. He lives in Phoenix, AZ with his Border Collie, who happily herds him to and from his computer every day. E-mail him at read@maginarius.com.

Dani d'Spirit lives with her moms, brother and two sisters in rural southern Delaware. She loves reading, outdoors, cultures, history, science and world peace. Right now she is looking at a career as a cultural liaison for the U.S. State Department. E-mail her at daniwoodsprite@earthlink.net.

Rachel Davison has enjoyed writing ever since she was in first grade. Since then, it's been one of her favorite pastimes, along with drama, watching movies, and hanging out with her friends. She hopes to one day have a novel published.

Alena Dillon received her B.A. with honors from the University of Connecticut. She will receive her Master's in Fine Arts from Fairfield University. Alena enjoys traveling, cooking, reading and writing. She is currently completing her memoir and two screenplays. E-mail her at alena.dillon@yahoo.com.

Stephanie Downing is a teenager who enjoys dancing, shopping, playing tennis, and going to the beach. She hopes that her story will inspire kids to help those in need.

Sara Drimmie loves to hang out at the mall with her friends, go swimming, play her guitar and cello, and love her pets. Sara is a member of the local Air Cadets squadron. She hopes one day to become a fashion designer and share her love of designs and clothes with as many people as she can. Unita is still greatly missed, and her other cats are doing fine.

Mariah Eastman goes to a public integrated arts high school. She loves to dance and aims to become a professional dancer. In her spare time, Mariah likes to write and do photography.

Although blind, **Janet Perez Eckles** thrives as a Spanish interpreter, international speaker, writer and author of *Trials of Today, Treasures for Tomorrow — Overcoming Adversities in Life*. From her home in Florida, she enjoys working on church ministries and taking Caribbean cruises with her husband Gene. She imparts inspiration at www. janetperezeckles.com.

Shawnelle Eliasen and her husband Lonny reside in Illinois. They raise their family in an old Victorian on the Mississippi River. Shawnelle home teaches her youngest boys. Her blog, My Five Sons, can be found at Shawnellewrites.blogspot.com.

Harold Fanning holds B.A, M.A., and D.M. degrees. Dr. Fanning has served several churches as senior pastor and currently is a hospice chaplain. He is also the author of three books available on www.amazon.com and is a regular conference speaker. E-mail him at haroldfanning@yahoo.com.

H.M. Filippelli loves to play soccer, play the trumpet and write. She hopes to someday be an actor or author. H.M. is currently a seventh grader. She likes to sing and loves other singers like Justin Bieber and Usher and hopes to meet them.

Malinda Fillingim loves writing and has journals marking the highs and lows of her fifty-two years. She enjoys going to churches and sharing stories of faith. Her daughters still roll their eyes when she writes about them and her husband still hopes she includes stories about his cowboy music. Her dog, however, only wants her to rub his belly. E-mail her at fillingim@comcast.net.

Jill Fisher received a Master of Arts in education from the University of Iowa in 2004. She taught elementary school for seven years in Lone Tree, IA, before returning home to raise her two children. She pursues a lifelong love of writing during naptime. E-mail her at yellowsmoke1010@hotmail.com.

Jackie Fleming, a native Californian, raised three boys on a little island in the California Delta. Her hobbies are traveling the world by freighter, Yoga, reading and writing. For six years she wrote for two weekly newspapers. She now lives in Reno, NV. E-mail her at Jaxaco@aol.com.

Marcela Dario Fuentes was adopted from Honduras. She is a professional musician and performance resident in bassoon at Carnegie Mellon University, and her stories have appeared in several previous *Chicken Soup for the Soul* books. She enjoys hearing from her readers at wereallwright@gmail.com.

Cassie Goldberg earned her B.A. in Public Relations from Hofstra University in 2007. She now works as Field Communications Manager at the National Kidney Foundation. Her interests include reading, writing and spending time with her friends, family and boyfriend. E-mail her at cassie.goldberg@gmail.com.

Sharon Grumbein received her Associate of Arts summa cum laude from Craven Community College in New Bern, NC, in 1986. She homeschooled her six children, and now has two grandsons. She writes inspirational nonfiction stories, and has been published in several magazines. She's currently working on her first novel. E-mail her at misssharon@embarqmail.com.

Kara Hackett is a twenty-year-old professional writing major at Taylor University. Her freelance articles have appeared in *Christian Communicator*, *Grief Digest*, *The Aboite Independent*, *Christian Book Previews*, *Church Libraries* and her campus newspaper *The Echo*. She lives in Fort Wayne, IN. E-mail her at karahackett@gmail.com.

Julie Havener lives in Lincoln, NE, where she works as a counselor in an agency serving battered women and their children. She loves writing and was previously published in *Chicken Soup for the Soul: Think Positive*. E-mail her at jdhavener5@aol.com.

Kat Heckenbach graduated with honors from The University of Tampa and now homeschools her two children. She has more than forty short fiction and nonfiction stories published, and is the author of the someday-will-be-published middle grade fantasy, *Finding Angel*. Learn more at www.kat-findingangel.blogspot.com.

Sara Hedberg is in the eighth grade. She enjoys reading, writing, fencing, music and video games. She plays the flute and piano, and absolutely loves The Beatles, Queen and the Decemberists. She encourages you to always work hard, and never give up!

Hilary Heskett holds a Bachelor's degree in Business from San José State University. She is currently a Marketing Director for a software provider as well as CFO to a small production company. In her down-time, she also writes paranormal romance, science fiction and young adult fiction. Learn more at www.hilaryheskett.com.

Amelia Hollingsworth discovered she liked to write when she was a preteen living in Brazil. Now she has a family of her own and still likes to write. Amelia is an aspiring scientist, novelist, violinist, and domestic goddess. She lives in Mississippi with her husband and daughter.

Claire Illies is currently a senior in high school. She wrote this piece as a junior for a composition class. She is unaware of where her life will take her next year, but is very excited about the future. She loves all bodies of water, hockey, soccer, her family and friends, traveling and writing stories. E-mail her at c.illies@live.com.

Carley Jackson was born in Florida. Writing was never a passion of hers as a kid. But when she began going through a hard time in her life, writing seemed like the only thing that kept her sane. Carley likes writing short stories because they are your own stories and also interesting. Her goal is for other kids to start writing and find a passion for telling their own stories.

Ruth Jones lives in Cookeville, TN, with her husband Terry and a very bad cat named Annabel.

Stacie Joslin grew up in Wasco, CA, with a love for reading and writing. She is an administrative assistant in her hometown. Stacie is married with four children and she enjoys traveling, writing and spending time with her family. Stacie is currently working on writing novels. E-mail her at stacielopez@att.net.

In the 90s **Marilyn Kentz** and her next door neighbor surprisingly landed an NBC sitcom called *The Mommies*, followed by a Showtime Special, and the ABC talk show, *Caryl & Marilyn*. Since then, Kentz has co-written three books: *The Motherload*, *Not Your Mother's Midlife*, and *Fearless Women*. E-mail her at marilynkentz@aol.com.

Kimberly Kimmel, a journalist, writing instructor and former editor for a music/fashion magazine, has sold numerous articles and short stories. She has interviewed dozens of celebrities, mostly for the teen market. Kimberly has two grown children and is from Los Angeles. E-mail her at kimberlybkimmel@hotmail.com.

Sarah L.M. Klauda lives in Baltimore with her husband. She aspires to be a successful author and open an educational rescue center for animals. In her spare time, Sarah studies linguistics and astronomy, and volunteers for animal rescues. She loves swimming, cooking, hiking, and reading. E-mail her at sklauda1@gmail.com.

Angie Klink authored *Divided Paths, Common Ground* about two dynamic women of Purdue University, the children's books *Purdue*

Pete Finds His Hammer and *I Found U*. She is published in *Chicken Soup for the Soul: The Gift of Christmas*, *Chicken Soup for the Sister's Soul 2* and *Republican's Soul*.

Tom Krause is one of the most quoted author/poets today. His work has appeared in many books in the *Chicken Soup for the Soul* series. Tom grew up in Boonville, MO. He is also a very popular motivational speaker. Contact him at www.coachkrause.com.

Sydney Kravetz has a Bachelor of Journalism from the University of Missouri. A former political reporter and freelance magazine writer, Sydney collects and sells rare books and vintage clothing. She authors two blogs—one about mystical experiences and one about the history of food. E-mail her at Sydney@psiwonder23@aol.com.

Marc Kruza is an aspiring novelist. He is currently writing a young adult piece, *Out of My Head*, about a boy who escapes the everyday through graphic novels and comic books he creates. It documents his adventures and misadventures navigating the bizarre parallel universe of freshman year in high school.

Margaret Lang is a published nonfiction short-story author and a grandma of three little girls. She leads Good News Clubs in elementary schools and Aglow Lighthouse meetings in homes. She loves to get away in a Rocky Mountain cabin by a lake in a fragrant piney woods.

Ali Lauro is a fifteen-year-old high school student. She has enjoyed writing and reading from an early age and aspires to work someday in this field. She lives with her parents, twin sister, brother, and two dogs.

Pearl Lee received her B.A. in Literature from the University of California, San Diego. When she's not reading or writing, she loves to cook, bake and spend time with family and friends. E-mail her at inanoyster@gmail.com.

Kathy Linker received her B.A. in Psychology from The University of Western Ontario, a graduate degree in Clinical Art Therapy and her Master in Education from the University of Victoria. She has traveled the globe extensively and is writing inspirational stories about her adventures. E-mail her at kathylinker@hotmail.com.

Amanda Yardley Luzzader left the financial industry to devote her time and attention to her two delightful sons. They enjoy jumping in puddles, homemade root beer, and cloud watching. She also enjoys photography, writing stories, reading, and spending time with her charming husband.

Elizabeth M. is twelve years old. She currently attends middle school in the 7th grade. Elizabeth loves reading *Chicken Soup for the Soul* books and is very athletic and has played soccer since she was five but recently found a new interest in basketball.

Steven Manchester is the published author of *Pressed Pennies, The Unexpected Storm: The Gulf War Legacy* and *Jacob Evans*. His first full-length feature film, *Gooseberry Island*, was released in 2011. When not writing, Steven is spending time with his children and beautiful wife, Paula. Learn more at www.StevenManchester.com.

Shawn Marie Mann is a geographer and freelance writer living with her husband and three children in Central Pennsylvania. She enjoys writing, reading, gardening, quilting and visiting amusement parks. Please contact her through her website www.shawnmariemann.com.

Nancy Manther received her B.A. in Child Psychology from the University of Minnesota in 1978. She enjoys writing, reading, cooking, traveling and spending time with family and friends. Nancy is currently writing her first novel.

Melanie Marks has had over fifty stories published in magazines such as *Highlights*, *Woman's World* and *Teen Magazine*. She's had four children's books published, and numerous teen novels including: *Stranger Inside*; *The Dating Deal*; *A Demon's Kiss*; and *Paranormal Punch*. Visit her at byMelanieMarks.com or e-mail her at melanie@ byMelanieMarks.com

Kelley Stimpel Martinez has a college degree and gradutate degree in law. But none of that matters because what gives her the greatest pleasure has nothing to do with work or money. It has to do with finding the humor in life's adventures, one quirky step at a time.

Chris Mikalson is a retired bookkeeper, who is now enjoying camping with her husband, as well as pursuing the creative "loves of her life"—writing and painting. Chris is a Reiki Master and finds great joy in helping others heal with the aid of this beautiful energy. E-mail her at chris_mikalson@yahoo.ca.

Mary Neil keeps busy in retirement teaching six Jazzercise fitness classes a week in Gastonia, NC, were she lives. Hobbies include writing a weekly Health and Fitness column for the *Gaston Gazette*, reading and working her champion Paso Fino horse, Flamenco. E-mail her at maryeneil@earthlink.net.

Sylvia Ney received her B.S. in Mass Communication from Lamar University in 2000. She lives in Texas with her husband and two children. She enjoys reading, writing, traveling and spending time with family and friends. She writes in a variety of genres. You can visit her blog at http://writinginwonderland.blogspot.com.

Cynthia Patton has worked as an environmental attorney, scientific editor, nonprofit advocate, and consultant. The California native writes poetry and nonfiction and lives with a rowdy dog, even rowdier cat, and her seven-year-old daughter. Cynthia's work has appeared in magazines, anthologies, and books. She's revising a memoir. E-mail her at cynthiapatton@att.net.

Kyra Payne is a hopeless romantic and falls in love at least twice a day. She loves reading and writing. She plans one day to become an author.

Sharon Pearson received a diary for Christmas at the age of eleven and soon discovered the joys of writing her personal experiences. She has been published in several periodicals and is now a Special Education instructor. She lives in California with her husband, two boys and a friendly Pit Bull.

Sneha Pillai is studying for her Bachelors in Mass Media from Wilson College, University of Mumbai. She enjoys blogging, reading, traveling and music. She aspires to be a journalist and a writer. E-mail her at aries_sneha26@yahoo.com.

Marsha Porter, co-author of a movie review guide, has written numerous short stories and articles. She credits her writing skills development to her grade school nuns who frequently punished her with five hundred-word essays. Currently, she teaches high school English.

Denise Reich is an amateur trapeze artist, compulsive traveler and rock music fan. She'd like to learn to surf this year. Denise has written for many publications in the USA and elsewhere, including several *Chicken Soup for the Soul* titles, the anthology *She's Shameless, Bunker Hill*, and *Pology*.

Rachael Robitaille is a high school student who enjoys reading, writing, soccer, hockey, curling and dramatic arts. She hopes to someday publish a novel. E-mail her at rrobitaille3579@gmail.com.

Colette Sasina is celebrating her fiftieth wedding anniversary with

John, five children and ten grandchildren. She's a past contributor to the *Chicken Soup for the Soul* series. Her poems are published in *The Villages Daily Sun*, SeniorTimesMagazine.com and *Essays: On Living with Alzheimer's Disease, The First Twelve Months*, by Lois Wilmoth-Bennett, Ph.D.

Sarah Sawicki is a freelance author and a student at Taylor University. She has been published by Guidepost Books, *Church Libraries*, and the *Christian Communicator*. When she is not writing, Sarah enjoys horseback riding, theatre, playing guitar, and singing. She plans on pursuing memoir writing. E-mail her at sksawicki@gmail.com.

John Scanlan is a 1983 graduate of the United States Naval Academy, and retired from the Marine Corps as a Lieutenant Colonel aviator. He currently resides on Hilton Head Island, SC, and is pursuing a second career as a writer. E-mail John at ping1@hargray.com.

Lindy Schneider loves throwing big parties with extensive invitation lists! She is an award-winning freelance writer and illustrator with her work appearing in books and magazines and even on Red Vines candy packages! E-mail her at lindy_schn@yahoo.com or learn more at www.lindysbooks.com.

Award-winning author **Jacqueline Seewald** has taught writing at the university as well as high school English. She also worked as an academic librarian and educational media specialist. Ten of her books of fiction have been published. Her short stories, poems, essays, reviews and articles have appeared in hundreds of publications. Her latest teen novel is *Stacy's Song*.

Tracie Skarbo was motivated to write as a young girl by her father. Tracie's book, *Harmonious Flight*, is available at sbpra.com/tracieskarbo and she is working on her next two books. She was raised on Vancouver Island, Canada, and lives there with her family.

Alaina Smith's true tales appear in anthologies including *Chicken Soup for the Soul: Count Your Blessings*, *The Mystery of Fate: Common Coincidence or Divine Intervention?*, six *Chocolate for Women* books, and five *A Cup of Comfort* books. She enjoys writing, working for a musical theater company, and moviegoing with her husband.

Mary Z. Smith is a regular contributor to the *Chicken Soup for the Soul* series, as well as to the inspirational magazines *Angels on Earth* and *Guideposts*. She has just published a book entitled *Life's A Symphony*. Mary and her husband Barry reside in Richmond, VA, enjoying frequent visits from their children and grandchildren.

Erin Solej graduated as the valedictorian from Felician College in 1997. She is a middle school Language Arts teacher in New Jersey. This is her second *Chicken Soup for the Soul* story, and she is currently writing her first book. E-mail her at esolej@optonline.net.

Tanya Sousa has written for newspapers and magazines for over twenty years and has begun writing children's books. One of her first published children's picture books, *Life is a Bowl of Cherry Pits*, won a Moonbeam Children's Book Award. Find out more about Tanya at www.RadiantHen.com.

Christine Stapp is the retired Operations Manager for a professional training organization. She has written a number of feature stories and focus articles for various newspapers and company newsletters. Among her duties as wife, mother and grandmother, she is currently working on her first novel, a senior sleuth spoof.

Rae Starr loves Jesus, animals, kids, the outdoors, writing and working/making things with her hands. She enjoys horseback riding, swimming, biking, hiking and camping. She plans to work with children in need, rescue animals and continue inspirational writing.

Marla H. Thurman lives in Signal Mountain, TN, with her baby dogs

Sophie and Jasper. Marla has been published in many venues and is now working on a book of short stories to publish on Kindle by the end of 2011. E-mail her at sizoda1@gmail.com.

Andrea Q. Verde received her B.A. in Graphic Communication at San Diego State University. She is married and currently at home raising her three children. Andrea is involved in community and church activities and enjoys writing, art, and dance. She's writing short stories and screenplays.

Stephanie Warner, a Professional Writing major at Taylor University, was born and raised in the Midwest. She excels at finding the epic in the ordinary. She loves Tae Kwon Do, exploring new cultures, and writing adventure stories that touch the heart.

Kimberly Winget is a student working on her Bachelors of Fine Arts degree. She loves to write poetry and compose music. Kim believes strongly in the impact the written or musical word has on a person. Kim enjoys singing, arts and crafts, teaching, swimming, and working with children. She hopes to become a professional musician someday and help others express themselves in a creative way.

Sandy Wright lives in Texas where the West began. She teaches gifted and talented children, and hikes and snowshoes with her Lab, Jake. She is a member of Royalty Writers and Joy Writers, both with NTCW. Recently, she completed her first novel and is working on another. E-mail her at wrightonsandy@yahoo.com.

D. B. Zane went to camp without a friend a few summers later and had a fabulous time. She's never been homesick since. E-mail her at dbzanewriter@gmail.com.

Meet Our Authors

Jack Canfield is the co-creator of the *Chicken Soup for the Soul* series, which *Time* magazine has called "the publishing phenomenon of the decade." Jack is also the co-author of many other bestselling books.

Jack is the CEO of the Canfield Training Group in Santa Barbara, California, and founder of the Foundation for Self-Esteem in Culver City, California. He has conducted intensive personal and professional development seminars on the principles of success for more than a million people in twenty-three countries, has spoken to hundreds of thousands of people at more than 1,000 corporations, universities, professional conferences and conventions, and has been seen by millions more on national television shows.

Jack has received many awards and honors, including three honorary doctorates and a Guinness World Records Certificate for having seven books from the *Chicken Soup for the Soul* series appearing on the New York Times bestseller list on May 24, 1998.

You can reach Jack at www.jackcanfield.com.

Mark Victor Hansen is the co-founder of Chicken Soup for the Soul, along with Jack Canfield. He is a sought-after keynote speaker, bestselling author, and marketing maven. Mark's powerful messages of possibility, opportunity, and action have created powerful change in thousands of organizations and millions of individuals worldwide.

Mark is a prolific writer with many bestselling books in addition to the *Chicken Soup for the Soul* series. Mark has had a profound influence in the field of human potential through his library of audios, videos, and articles in the areas of big thinking, sales achievement, wealth building, publishing success, and personal and professional development. He is also the founder of the MEGA Seminar Series.

Mark has received numerous awards that honor his entrepreneurial spirit, philanthropic heart, and business acumen. He is a lifetime member of the Horatio Alger Association of Distinguished Americans.

You can reach Mark at www.markvictorhansen.com.

Amy Newmark is Chicken Soup for the Soul's publisher and editor-in-chief, after a thirty-year career as a writer, speaker, financial analyst, and business executive in the worlds of finance and telecommunications. Amy is a *magna cum laude* graduate of Harvard College, where she majored in Portuguese, minored in French, and traveled extensively. She and her husband have four grown children.

After a long career writing books on telecommunications, voluminous financial reports, business plans, and corporate press releases, Chicken Soup for the Soul is a breath of fresh air for Amy. She has fallen in love with Chicken Soup for the Soul and its life-changing books, and really enjoys putting these books together for Chicken Soup's wonderful readers. She has co-authored more than three dozen *Chicken Soup for the Soul* books and has edited another three dozen.

You can reach Amy through the webmaster@chickensoupforthesoul.com.

Thank You

We owe huge thanks to all of our contributors. We know that you poured your hearts and souls into the thousands of stories and poems that you shared with us, and ultimately with each other. We appreciate your willingness to open up your lives to other Chicken Soup for the Soul readers and share your own experiences as preteens, which we know was both an exciting and a challenging time in your life. We loved your stories and they brought back our own memories of those years.

We could only publish a small percentage of the stories that were submitted, but we read every single one and even the ones that do not appear in the book had an influence on us and on the final manuscript. Our editor Madeline Clapps, who was a preteen herself just a decade ago, read every submission to this book and put together the manuscript with great care and a real understanding of the kinds of stories that would be most helpful, and also entertaining, for our young readers. Our assistant publisher, D'ette Corona, worked with all the contributors as kindly and competently as always, obtaining their approvals for our edits and the quotations we carefully chose to begin each story. Senior editor Barbara LoMonaco and editor Kristiana Glavin performed their normal masterful proofreading and made sure the book went to the printer on time.

We also owe a very special thanks to our creative director and book producer, Brian Taylor at Pneuma Books, for his brilliant vision for our covers and interiors. Finally, none of this would be possible without the business and creative leadership of our CEO, Bill Rouhana, and our president, Bob Jacobs.

Improving Your Life Every Day

Real people sharing real stories—for seventeen years. Now, Chicken Soup for the Soul has gone beyond the bookstore to become a world leader in life improvement. Through books, movies, DVDs, online resources and other partnerships, we bring hope, courage, inspiration and love to hundreds of millions of people around the world. Chicken Soup for the Soul's writers and readers belong to a one-of-a-kind global community, sharing advice, support, guidance, comfort, and knowledge.

Chicken Soup for the Soul stories have been translated into more than forty languages and can be found in more than one hundred countries. Every day, millions of people experience a Chicken Soup for the Soul story in a book, magazine, newspaper or online. As we share our life experiences through these stories, we offer hope, comfort and inspiration to one another. The stories travel from person to person, and from country to country, helping to improve lives everywhere.

Chicken Soup for the Soul

Share with Us

We all have had Chicken Soup for the Soul moments in our lives. If you would like to share your story or poem with millions of people around the world, go to chickensoup.com and click on "Submit Your Story." You may be able to help another reader, and become a published author at the same time. Some of our past contributors have launched writing and speaking careers from the publication of their stories in our books!

Our submission volume has been increasing steadily—the quality and quantity of your submissions has been fabulous. We only accept story submissions via our website. They are no longer accepted via mail or fax.

To contact us regarding other matters, please send us an e-mail through webmaster@chickensoupforthesoul.com, or fax or write us at:

Chicken Soup for the Soul
P.O. Box 700
Cos Cob, CT 06807-0700
Fax: 203-861-7194

One more note from your friends at Chicken Soup for the Soul: Occasionally, we receive an unsolicited book manuscript from one of our readers, and we would like to respectfully inform you that we do not accept unsolicited manuscripts and we must discard the ones that appear.

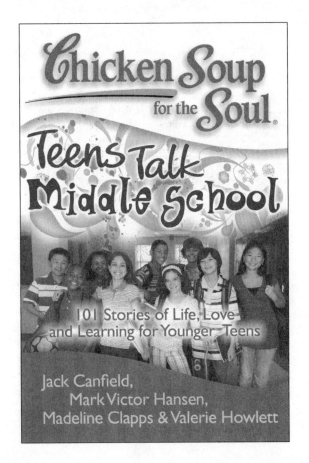

Middle school is a tough time. And this "support group in a book" is specifically geared to those younger teens—the ones still worrying about puberty, cliques, discovering the opposite sex, and figuring out who they are. For ages eleven to fourteen, stories cover regrets, lessons learned, love and "like," popularity, friendship, divorce, illness and death, embarrassing moments, bullying, and finding a passion. Great support and inspiration for middle schoolers.

978-1-935096-26-9

Teens Talk
Middle School

Teenage years are tough, but this book will help teens as they journey through the ups and downs of adolescence. *Chicken Soup for the Soul: Just for Teenagers* provides support and inspiration for teenagers as they grow up, reminding them they are not alone, as they read stories from teens just like themselves about the problems and issues they face every day. The stories in this book serve as a guide on topics from the daily pressures of life and school to love, friendships, parents, and much more. This collection will encourage, inspire, and amuse teens, showing that, as tough as things can get, they are not alone!

978-1-935096-72-6

Just for Teenagers

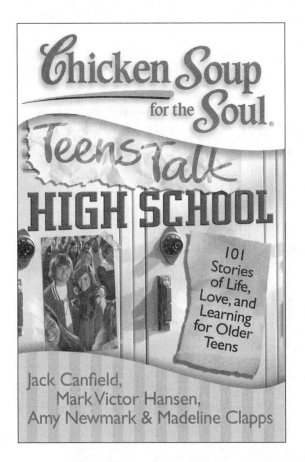

Teens in high school have mainly moved past worrying about puberty and cliques, so this book covers topics of interest to older teens—sports and clubs, driving, curfews, self-image and self-acceptance, dating and sex, family, friends, divorce, illness, death, pregnancy, drinking, failure, and preparing for life after graduation. High school students will find comfort and inspiration in this book, referring to it through all four years of high school, like a portable support group.

978-1-935096-25-2

Teens Talk
High School

This book is a morale boost for teachers! There is a lot of buzz about it in the teaching industry—more than half the stories are from "celebrity" teachers, including all of the 2009 State Teachers of the Year and the 2009 National Teacher of the Year. Those teachers who don't receive this book as a gift are sure to buy it for themselves, to read the 101 true stories by great teachers and appreciative students, with lots of laughs, poignant moments, and some tears.

978-1-935096-47-4

Tales for Teachers

Christmas is a magical time of year—a time of family, friends, and traditions. And all the joys, blessings, and excitement of the season are captured in this book of 101 new holiday stories. With stories about finding the perfect Christmas tree, being with family, and seeing the wonder in a child's eyes, this book will delight every reader, from the young to the young at heart, and bring back the magic of the holiday season. "Santa-safe" for kids!

978-1-935096-54-2

Christmas!

www.chickensoup.com